The Emergent Approach to Strategy

Description

Despite how much is written about strategy, and money spent on it, reports of chronic failures persist. Two causes dominate. Strategy is still not fully defined, and strategy practice is still largely based on a planned view of the world. Change and innovation, however, are not wholly planned but emerge from the myriad interactions of the players involved—some by design, many not. This science of complex adaptive systems must be the bedrock on which strategy is built.

The Emergent Approach to Strategy derives strategy definition, theory, and practice from adaptive systems. Aimed at corporate business and functional leaders, but broadly applicable, the approach includes an agile method for strategy framework design that replaces stepwise "chevron" methods and presents a new set of tests of strategy called the five disqualifiers.

This book offers no promise of easy "transformations." Change and innovation are hard, sometimes ugly, with no guarantees. But with sound principles and discipline, organizations can efficiently raise the probability of success.

Keywords

Emergent strategy; business innovation; strategic management; adaptive strategy design and execution; leadership; strategy tests; agile design; scenarios; strategy theory; strategy matrix; strategy framework; metrics

Contents

Online Content
{www.emergentapproach.com}
Chapter Supplements
Added example of the five disqualifiers
The Five Task Sets—guidebook for implementation of the approach
Templates for use in documents

Acknowledgments

I thank: Joseph Steed and Zach Gajewski, my developmental editors and advisors, for putting up with me for several years each, helping me with language, organization, and critical thinking, and teaching me much. Joanne Smith, Mark Blackwell, and Iain Crerar for their detailed and critical readings of the manuscript and their many important corrections and suggestions. (Special thanks to Iain for his website advice as well.) Sherly Xie for critically reviewing much of the manuscript and assisting with references and graphics. Jim Spohrer, Miray Pereira, Steven G. Taylor, Annie Tang Gutsche, Oliver Gutsche, Daminder Johar, David Lahti, Steven Freilich, Robert Hanlon, Mark Anderson, Shaun Coffey, Alicia Juarrero, Sam Severance, John Elliott, Elise Kidd, Angus Grundy, Paul Howley, Andy Fisher, Charles Compo, Julie Trelstad, Nell Cote, and Tim Fisher for giving valuable feedback on chapter and manuscript drafts at various stages. Brendan Filipovski, Erin Keebough, and Dioli Payo for helpful editing. Rebecca Bing for graphics direction and website design. Rana Mohammed and Alper Firati for graphics. Dan Cristo for website advice and Volodymyr Hlazun for website development. Colleagues at DuPont, and especially the product management group. My agent, John Willig, and Scott Isenberg and Charlene Kronstedt at Business Expert Press for their guidance. Gunabala Saladi and the rest of the team at Exeter Premedia Services. Dominick Mazzone for encouragement. And Carol and Oscar for living through it.

I truly appreciate you all.

Introduction

The Chronic Strategy Problem

If you want to get somewhere, you need to know where you're going. Sounds unassailable. Every organization aims to know where it is going. It may be in the hope of discovering new places or reaching old ones using new routes. Either aim requires change and innovation—taking a system from one state to another, from one degree of capability to a better one. And this is true broadly, whether the system is a business or a person, a machine or a computer application, or an organization's culture or skills. Even holding performance steady requires innovation because conditions change.

Strategy, along with the other components of a framework—including goals, plans, projections, diagnosis, tactics, and metrics—is meant to guide decisions and actions toward reaching a (believed-to-be) desired state. The strategy and the rest of the framework should bring order to endeavors, reducing paralyzing anxiety (or blissful ignorance), and enable creative tension that drives change and innovation. The impulse for strategy has probably been around since humans could muster abstract thought and the possibility of multiple futures.

Yet, despite how much is written about strategy and how much money is spent on it, academics and consultants continue to report strategy practice failures as shown in Figure I.1, including observations like "No one understands your strategy—not even your top leaders." Richard Rumelt in his book, *Good Strategy, Bad Strategy*,[1] deplores the substitution of often incoherent objectives for strategy: the "high-sounding" language that hides strategy design failings and slogans and "fluff" that pervades companies' planning. Henry Mintzberg, in his 1994 *Rise and Fall of Strategic Planning*, said, "Ultimately, the term 'strategic planning' has proved to be an oxymoron."[2] The strategy problem hasn't seemed to be solved since then.

The term strategy has a range of related meanings and authors have generally felt quite free to use it quite idiosyncratically. **Rumelt, 1979**

The reason corporations have such trouble with innovation is that most planning systems fail to take into account the unpredictability of innovation. **Pinchot III, 1985**

Why do so many companies fail to have a strategy? **Porter, 1996**

Strategic planning is not strategic: rather, it is a calendar-driven ritual, involving plans and sub-plans, instead of something challenging and innovative that might lead to discovery. **Hamel, 1996**

A picture emerges of strategies existing primarily to satisfy the psychological needs of the managers, in particular the need to feel in control. **Van der Heijden, 1996**

Strategy has become a catchall term used to mean whatever one wants it to mean. Executives now talk about their "service strategy," their "branding strategy," their "acquisition strategy," or whatever kind of strategy that is on their mind at a particular moment.
Hambrick & Fredrickson, 2001

Most people can't summarize their company's strategy in 35 words or less, and even if they could, their colleagues wouldn't put it the same way...it is a dirty little secret that most executives don't actually know what all the elements of a strategy statement are, which makes it impossible for them to develop one....In an astonishing number of organizations, executives, frontline employees, and all those in between are frustrated because no clear strategy for the company or its lines of business. **Collis & Rukstad, 2008**

Bad strategy is gaining ground.
Rumelt, 2011

Only 14% of employees understand their company's strategy and direction.
Witt, 2012

A list of goals is not a strategy.
Kenny, 2014

Two-thirds of the 1,000 organizations in over 50 countries interviewed struggle to implement their strategy, and half of the 7,577 managers from 249 companies surveyed state their company's top three to five objectives differently from their colleagues. **Sull & Eisenhardt, 2015**

In another [PwC] survey of more than 500 senior executives around the world, 9 out of 10 conceded that they were missing major opportunities...about 80% said that their overall strategy was not well understood, even within their own company. **Leinwand & Mainardi, 2016**

Many strategies fail because they're not actually strategies. **Vermeulen, 2017**

More than 70% of executives surveyed said they don't like their strategy process, and 70% of board members stated that they don't trust the results.
Bradley, Hirt, & Smit, 2018

Survey of 124 corporations concludes no one knows your strategy—not even your top leaders. **Sull, Sull, & Yoder, 2018**

Only 37% of six thousand corporate executives said that their companies had well-defined strategies [PwC survey released 2019]...35% felt that the strategies would lead their firms to success...20% felt there was agreement in their companies about which capabilities were key to their firms' success.
Carroll & Sørensen, 2021

Figure I.1 Chronic Reports of Strategy Problems (for references and additional quotes, see emergentapproach.com/supplement)

What drives these students of strategy to say such things about a concept that has been studied since antiquity and that people believe they are using all the time? After all, strategy is a cornerstone for accomplishment in business, military, and government, to name just a few endeavors that might be considered important. Why the ongoing struggle? This book presents a theory and practice of strategy that address two significant reasons. First, despite the many definitions offered in the literature—including plans, master plans, patterns, making choices, or simply what is long-term and important—there is still no common understanding of what strategy is and what is its function. The few authors who focus on strategy as a special kind of rule point us towards what is needed for a rigorous strategy definition, but work remains to complete it.

A common understanding of strategy is not helped by buzz speak. The noise level of the *consulting-corporate-academia* strategy complex keeps rising—disruption, breakthrough, excellence, accelerate, value-adding, advancing capability, speed and velocity and agility, pivoting, adaptability, resilience, sustainability, and the most abused of all, transformation, add to the confusion created by multiple strategy definitions. How often are these terms used as marketing as opposed to offering specific insight? Clayton Christensen himself, along with Michael Raynor and Rory McDonald, were compelled to instruct people to stop using his concept of *disruption* as a general-purpose buzzword that describes any product or business that upends an existing one.[3] There is no governing body to drive the alignment of business concepts and language.

The word *strategic* has pretty much lost its meaning too. Is there a difference between your direction and your strategic direction? Will you pay attention to your strategic dashboard and ignore your dashboard? What would a nonstrategic initiative be, one where you ignore your strategy or an unimportant initiative? Sometimes books will have 30 or 40 different words preceded by *strategic*.[4] In practice, however, "strategic" often stands for little more than some notion of what is believed to be important, long-term, or smart. We could improve strategy methods just by eradicating the word strategic and instead insist on jargon-free descriptions of customers, markets, competitors, offering, and approaches.

It is convenient to blame poor execution for strategy's confusing condition, as in the story of the CEO who said, "Execution eats strategy for lunch … if my competitors found my strategy on an airline seat, I wouldn't care." But it is hard to execute on a PowerPoint filled with forecasts, long lists of strategy themes, strategic initiatives, and subgoals, and directives like deliver each quarter and optimize capital allocation. Poor execution may be a problem, but it's not the first problem to attack. How can people execute on or be inspired by strategy when strategy seems so misunderstood? How can people execute on PowerPoints sitting on the electronic shelf collecting electronic dust? What execution is ain't so clear either.

The second, and deeper, reason for chronic strategy problems, and one reason why strategy has proven so hard to define, is that the whole idea of strategizing is still largely based on a planned and deterministic view of the world. This includes using variations on stepwise approaches like *goal*→*analyze*→*plan*→*scenarios*→*implement*→*control* or *plan it in detail*→*execute it*. Alternatively, an adaptive view of the world says this is not a good model of change and innovation, and that the unassailable logic, that if you want to get somewhere you must know where you are going, kind of misses the point.

Though we do need aims, the adaptive view says the discovery of future states can never be truly planned or orchestrated. The place we reach is so often not the one envisioned, and that's if we reach one at all. Getting from A to B in a nice continuous path is rare, as in the riff on a Gifford Pinchot III graphic in Figure I.2.[5] He pointed out 35 years ago that we only imagine the direct line has been accomplished. And maybe, we were aiming at C all along. With such a view, strategy cannot consist of planning the future and then "executing." We need a way of being guided by deeper principles.

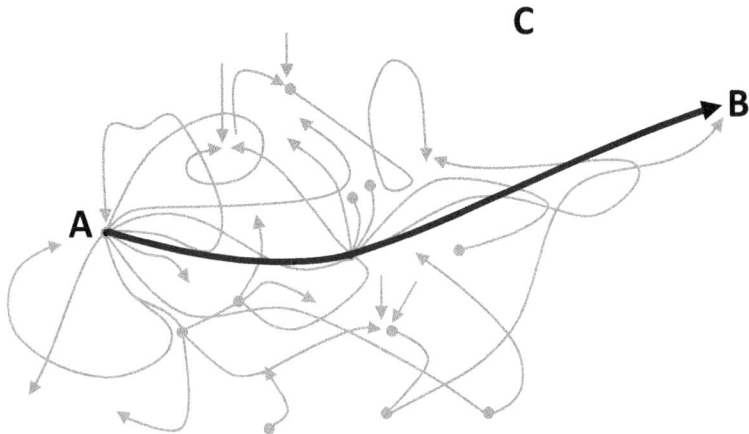

Figure I.2 Getting from A to B in a nice continuous path doesn't really happen

Still early in development, the emergent adaptive view of innovation has many threads in a growing literature, including writers who identify the link between complex adaptive systems and strategy.[6] At its core, the adaptive view must be the evolutionary mechanism of Darwinian variation-selection-retention. Biology is replacing Newton's mechanics as the model of change and innovation and evolutionary terms pervade our language. We speak of an organization's DNA and lifecycles and generations of technologies. There are taxonomies of music and art, family trees of languages, and genealogies of scientific theory. There are technical hybrids; there is competition. The "immune system" of an organization can be triggered. People describe market niches and ecosystems of suppliers, manufacturers, distributors, and consumers. Often, ideas are co-opted from one domain and used in another. There is the decline of old economies as new ones emerge. Undisciplined and ungrounded organizations tend to drift. Those who don't change with the times are soon-to-be extinct dinosaurs and neanderthals. And just as in nature where 98 percent of all species that ever existed are now extinct, most businesses fail.

In complex adaptive systems (or just *adaptive systems*), instead of aiming at changes and innovations with a clear vision and pushing them to the fore with Newton's direct forces, they *emerge* from generations of relentless interactions where unfit variants of ideas, structures, and technologies are destroyed by less-direct forces—the *stressors* of the environment. The survivors of the stressors get the lion's share of resources so they can evolve further. There are many environments, for example, the mind, where variations of ideas are stressed by thought and information transmitted from others; markets, where consumer stressors expose the fitness of products; or teams, where ideas or models are stressed by disciplined evaluation. The process over generations is nonlinear, outcomes are always uncertain, and surprising behavior can emerge. The interactions and disciplines are at low levels. It is difficult to impose high-level outcomes on the system. The terms self-organization and emergence highlight that there is no central executive fully orchestrating these interactions, though leaders still play a vital role.

Adaptive systems are the basis for the concepts of not only self-organization and emergence, but also agile design, resiliency, creative tension, and obviously adaptability (and antifragility, which is another term for adaptability). Adaptive systems reveal why managing by results leads to unremarkable results.

Existing strategy practice and methods reflect the adaptive view to varying extents, perhaps unintentionally at times, which should be no surprise because complex adaptive systems describe the dynamics of change and innovation. Anything involving humans and innovating is in the domain of complex adaptive systems because the mind is the quintessential complex adaptive system. In contrast with practice, however, strategy theory does not yet substantially incorporate the adaptive mechanism.

The Emergent Approach

This book aims to lessen the chronic problems of strategy by further advancing adaptive strategy theory (Part I) and practice (Part II). It builds the theory and definition of strategy on a more rigorous foundation as opposed to generalizing from case studies. The examples throughout the book, real and made up, are for illustration only of the derived functionality and mechanics of frameworks and their strategies. No advice is given on what your aspirations or strategies should be; only an approach with design principles for finding them and harnessing good advice from others is provided.

An influence diagram model of complex adaptive system dynamics lays bare that a strategy is the *central rule of a framework, designed to bust the bottleneck to achieving aspirations*, whatever the aspiration might be. The term bottleneck is used generically to represent choke points, obstructions, or other impediments, whatever limits the rate of progress. Busting means reducing, lessening, or getting around what is in the way. The strategy rule (Rumelt refers to a central policy) channels action toward the bottleneck. The model also reveals intrinsic obstacles to change and innovation (called the killer problems) and how a central rule best overcomes these intrinsic obstacles. The adaptive view of strategy also leads to a new set of strategy tests called the five *disqualifiers* that help eliminate the bad, the unfit, instead of predicting the good.

The theory addresses language confusion that plagues strategy and adaptation. It also rejects the belief that disciplined processes cannot lead to creativity and innovation or that analysis leads to paralysis. Bad analysis leads to paralysis. Good analysis will reveal when it's time to do something.

The emergent approach practice in Part II is like solving a puzzle instead of stepwise methods. In an agile adaptive process like that used in software development, a rough "minimum viable" strategy alternative matrix is drafted early. Then you evolve it, you *work it*, by repeatedly stressing the matrix with tools and techniques and internal and external critique until a compelling framework alternative emerges, one with a compelling strategy that energizes the organization. The winning alternative is not picked, but rather—as in all adaptive systems—it is the *last standing* variant that emerges after generations because it is the most fit to the stressors. The output of the process is an implementation package containing the final framework with its strategy, but it is fully assumed that you will return to the design phase often to adapt to what is learned in implementation.

The process is a messy, loose, and fluid one controlled by the low-level discipline of adhering to the design principles. The primary objective is not just to get "the answer" and certainly not a prescriptive plan. It is to internalize the dynamics of your internal and external ecosystems and what is possible. From internalization comes the emergence of new ideas and new variations. Adherence to low-level design principles versus following sequential steps makes the approach nonlinear.

When finalizing this manuscript, an email popped up advertising a $115 book from a major business school claiming, "Lead a powerful half-day session to design and launch your transformation." No such promise of easy success appears here; no simple formula for quick transformation, as if there ever will be one. In fact, you will find no promise of success at all. True change and innovation can be ugly, sometimes frightening, take significant time for discovery, and come with painful trade-offs and no guarantees. The emergent approach embraces the difficulty with practical techniques and principles to ensure that the frustration is worth it. As other good methods do, it eliminates collecting the usual suspects of strategy development approaches—financial reviews, technology reviews, growth rates, environmental scans, market forces, and market share—until, and only if, there is a need for them. Early on, effort is directed toward articulating aspirations, diagnosing the bottlenecks to achieving them, and even prospective strategies to busting the bottlenecks. The focus on bottleneck enables the team to keep its energy throughout the work and spend time only on what is crucial to forward progress. At any time, if sufficient clarity is developed, the team can declare "this is good enough, we need to move from designing to testing or implementation." Denying easy transformations does not mean aim low; it means aim high while recognizing the fight to come.

The emergent approach eradicates the phrase "planning under uncertainty" because there is no such thing as its opposite—planning under certainty.[7] There are *always* multiple futures and there *ain't no data from the future*, only models that make predictions. The environment and the actions of customers and competitors can never be known with certainty. Talking about "planning under uncertainty" gives leaders a loophole to imagine that deterministic and planned approaches apply to them just fine (and perhaps that people not executing is the problem). Yes, some futures are more certain than others, but usually the more certain, the less potential it holds for advantage. Strategist Michael Raynor says, "Traditional strategic planning is not blind to uncertainty, but it treats it as an afterthought."[8] A group from McKinsey says that we only "pretend to deal with uncertainty."[9] We need to face uncertainty head on, not just for special futuristic studies, but for all strategy work.

The emergent approach aligns with Mintzberg's teaching that you cannot plan the future, but it is not an alternative to what he called a "deliberate" approach.[10] All strategy is deliberate because strategy is guidance that must be established *before* taking decisions and actions. That in some cases outcomes are dramatically different than expected, or that the organization continually modifies the strategy as they learn from experience, does not change this requirement. What can be varied in designs is the degree of constraint imposed by the framework. If the future seems particularly uncertain, the strategy rule can be to make few hard plans and to react, or to test. But this doesn't mean everyone does whatever they want to do—the strategy still needs to provide guidance on what constitutes useful reacting and testing. On the other hand, if there is a strong belief that an aspiration and the strategy, tactics and plans for achieving it are right, that there is lower uncertainty, then a team can choose to limit the degree of optionality included, but there is still no guarantee of the outcome. The concept of emergence is that results are guided by the dynamics of adaptive systems, not that it is impossible to shape the future. In the emergent approach it is expected that designs will change as the system evolves.

One other point. Stating that emergence results from low-level disciplines does not mean "bottom up" as opposed to "top down" in the organizational sense. Adaptive development for emergence of innovations means bottom up, top down, sideways, and every direction, and the leader is a crucial part of the system. In adaptive work, the fitness of ideas is determined by logic and evidence.

This book is targeted at the leaders and facilitators responsible for the strategy process. Those who have the burden of bringing people together to coherently aim at a common aspiration by shaping, cajoling, inspiring, and struggling. The approach is completely general because your aspiration determines the scope. It is well-targeted to larger, multifaceted, and spread-out organizations where alignment around a common framework is so difficult yet particularly essential, but applies to small endeavors too. It applies not only to business units, but also to overall corporate strategy and any function within a business corporation, including supply chain, manufacturing, HR, R&D, marketing, and product management. It applies to nonbusiness endeavors too.

Developing the Approach

I created the theory and practice of the emergent approach over the years, including during the 25 years I spent at E.I. DuPont, the venerable chemical, materials, and later biotechnology, company. Starting as a chemical engineering scientist in 1988, my career took me into a diverse set of leadership positions in marketing, supply chain, business planning, and business and product management. I worked in 60-year-old commodity businesses as well as tech ventures and was the corporate leader for integrated business planning development. This book, however, is as much about what I learned from my failures as my successes.

I had long been interested in creativity and innovation and had an inkling that the mechanism for them was Darwinian, a mechanism where there is no clear view of the future and innovations emerge from generation after generation of testing variations and possibilities; "groping toward a vision," as Gifford Pinchot III called it,[11] or just happening upon one. I was attracted to the indirect way of thinking that adaptive evolution requires—forces repeatedly destroying the unfit entities—instead of directly picking the winner. Whether the entities were animals in nature, or cultural ideas, or physical objects, it didn't matter.

I was suspicious of explanations of creativity that focused mainly on free-thinking. I came from a multigenerational musical background, and I knew in my heart that the secret to creativity was a certain kind of discipline, even if the composer or artist couldn't tell you what the discipline was or what constraints they were imposing on themselves. The discipline of adaptation jived with my experience not only of studying composition, but also the music often held up as the epitome of creativity—jazz improvisation (my father was a New York jazz violin and bass player). Yes, there is freedom in improvisation, but without an underlying discipline the result is random nonsense or musical clichés. Business clichés and randomness are no better.

The importance of adaptive emergence crystallized during chemical engineering grad school at City College, New York, when I read the biography of Marie Curie written by her daughter, pianist and journalist Eve Curie. Eve described her mother's discovery of the radioactive element radium in turn-of-the-20th-century Paris saying, "She had used up all the evident possibilities. Now she turned towards the unplumbed and the unknown." There was no great eureka vision that led Curie to her discovery; it was the discipline of systematic destruction of all of the evident, the logical, explanations. The answer that there must be a new element, the least intuitive then, was the hypothesis that survived Curie's exacting analytical work. The Parisian scientific establishment assumed she made a mistake, but without doing the work, they couldn't have her insight and intuition. I had much to learn, but the core idea of innovations and creativity emerging from disciplined destructive processes, as counter intuitive as it sounds, never left me.

I was introduced to traditional business strategy when I joined DuPont, which often consisted of aspirational statements coupled with lists of initiatives, subgoals, plans, and metrics. Sometimes, the lists were supplemented with encouragement like "focus on rapid execution," or "increase customer intensity." I didn't yet know what a strategy was, but these lists troubled me. The whole vibe of them was the opposite of the adaptive emergent paradigm I had embraced.

The collective business-world confusion around strategy was particularly unfortunate for DuPont, as it was acknowledged within that there was enormous need for change. After its first century as a leading explosive manufacturer in Wilmington, Delaware, DuPont broadened its chemistry and applications platforms and emerged as one of the great materials companies of the 20th century, inventing a host of legendary products, including Nylon, Freon, Tyvek, Teflon, Stainmaster, Kevlar, Neoprene, and Lycra. By the '80s, however, several DuPont platforms had matured, and the company was bloated and sluggish. In my time there, DuPont set aggressive goals aiming to reinvent itself for a third time, including expansion into biology-based technologies.

There were multiple reasons why the goals weren't achieved and the transformation did not happen, but the lack of true strategy at the corporate and lower levels was a core contributor. There were pockets of brilliance and there were efforts to manage differentially and to strategize meaningfully, but it was never consistent or deep enough. Sometimes it was too late. When I left, DuPont was amid divestitures and a breakup into several companies, including an activist board-driven 2016 merger of what remained of DuPont with Dow, and a subsequent breakup of that entity into three. The shedding of business units in what is called the New DuPont (one of the three) continues as I write this in 2021.

As I struggled along with the company, I was inspired to make sense of strategy and the noise of terminology inside and outside DuPont and understand what it takes to innovate in small endeavors as well as when facing a colossal challenge like corporate reinvention. When I could grab time on weekends and vacations, I dug deep into strategy and the foundations of adaptive systems. I discovered that DuPont was hardly alone. I began testing my approach in receptive DuPont organizations and had excellent dialog especially with the product management group. Several business and manufacturing organizations valued and adopted it with success. It was interesting, however, that many leaders believed their position was due to strategy expertise and had little openness to a new approach. It probably didn't help that I was "building the airplane" on the fly and didn't always present unfinished work in a way that people wanted to hear it.

What I did do well was observe and think about what I was seeing. I took thousands of notes and had a good view of the company. My tendency to work and interact with people at both low and high levels helped, as did the diversity of my roles, working with consultants, and periodic interactions with the board. I had a different view than many academics and consultants because, like an anthropologist living with the tribe, I was struggling along with everyone else over the long haul. Repeatedly, I saw just how much heavy analytical and critical thinking and constancy of purpose are needed for real purposeful change and innovation. I saw how difficult it is to predict what will be winning products and technologies, and how many times in DuPont's history great developments were not planned but emerged over time. I saw how failure is part of success. After 25 years, I left to work full time developing my adaptive strategy theory and practice, and to write this book.

The Book's Content

Part I presents the theory of strategy, the five disqualifiers, and modified views of tactics and execution that arises from the theory. Part II presents a modified practice of traditional approaches that reflects the new theory. It includes the concrete techniques for working in an agile-adaptive versus stepwise linear mode. The focus is on detailed design principles for ensuring the proper functioning of strategy and other framework components. It includes techniques for making diagnosis of propositions, external constraints, scenarios, and most importantly, the bottlenecks to aspirations.

There are *Five Task Sets* that make up an online guidebook to framework design and implementation. You will also find additional chapter supplements online that include appendices and commentary, added examples, and templates for the strategy alternative matrix and other techniques. These are referenced in the text by {brackets}. For instance, "*Literature Strategy Tests* {web/supplement}" points to emergentapproach. com/supplement, the location where the document is found. The task sets, additional example of the disqualifiers, and templates are likewise found at {web/tasksets}, {web/disqualifiers}, and {web/templates}.

Note that while it is popular to distinguish inspiring, visionary, and courageous leaders from badly bureaucratic, micromanaging, status quo-loving, kowtowing-to-the-boss managers, I will not do so. Would anyone post a job description with these "manager" behaviors as the desired abilities of the candidate? It's not really leadership versus management; it's good leadership versus bad leadership; good management versus bad management. *Leaders* and *the people* will be distinguished. These can be supervisors and subordinates or bosses and employees or simply one team member taking the leadership mantle and gaining followers with no official authority. Everyone is a leader sometimes and everyone is part of the people all the time. The reason for this division between leaders and people is to focus on the people—the power of the people. My hope, beyond a theory of strategy, is that the emergent approach enables people to do more on their own, not be as dependent on experts for "the answer," to internalize their reality, so they can truly innovate. The Emergent Approach is the book I wish I had when starting my career.

PART I

A New Theory of Strategy

The introduction made strong claims that a rigorous adaptive foundation is needed for attacking the chronic problems of strategy. Part I provides the theory. It brings together an analysis of the good and problematic in the many definitions of strategy, a basic understanding of emergence of innovations in adaptive systems, and a model of complex adaptive systems that shows the power of strategy as a central rule. Along the way, we get a modified view of tactics, a clarified understanding of execution, and the *five disqualifiers,* the new set of strategy tests.

There's heavy lifting here. Adaptive thinking requires a different point of view with new and, in some cases, somewhat strange concepts. There's no shortcut to explaining the dynamics of strategies and the other framework components in complex adaptive systems. But it's worth the effort.

And awaaaay we go.[1]

---

[1] Gleason, J. H., 1952, CBS, New York

CHAPTER 1

One More Time

Defining Strategy

Before deriving from complex adaptive systems why strategy must be a central rule, it is helpful to understand what is valuable in other definitions of strategy and where they fall short. A collection of 75 definitions from authorities in multiple fields shows how widely opinions vary. (The list is shown online {web/supplement}). The definitions are found in dictionaries, strategy textbooks, and other literature; they come from business, military, and geopolitical strategists; scenario planners; economists; and complexity and game theorists. Analyzing the definitions also helps clarify language, which is important because divergent terminology itself is a bottleneck to developing a common understanding of strategy. Keep in mind this is a critical review of strategy definitions only, not a discussion of the 75 authors' strategy insights, advice, or design approaches.

Unscrambling the Many Concepts of Strategy

The majority of what is proposed in the literature can be captured in eight concepts, each of which is analyzed in this section.

- Aspirations
- Long term, big, and important
- Plans
- Frameworks (master plans; ends, ways, and means)
- Making choices
- Defined by requirements
- Patterns and actual outcomes
- Rules and policies

Strategy as Aspirations

Several in the list of 75 define strategy as aspirations, which would mean accepting any of the following as strategies:

- Grow revenue in frontier markets 15 percent per year while not losing share in existing markets
- Create a new application for our technology by 2028
- Improve use of artificial intelligence for supply-chain efficiency
- Improve our most impoverished inner-city schools
- Maintain the tax base in our city
- Lose 25 lbs. and keep it off this time

These may be useful desired outcomes, but they are not strategies. They give little guidance on what to do or not do. "Strategy themes" and subgoals such as Figure 1.1 are not strategies either. Strategy themes are

---

Our strategy for delivering superior returns to shareholders is to:

1. Increase revenue by 10% per year and profitability by 14% per year.
2. Increase customer-based innovation.
   a. Develop agile capability to deliver new product requests from customers 20% faster than the competition.
   b. Drive product innovation and aggressive expansion into white-space technology platforms.
3. Optimize our cost structure and CAPEX
   a. Improve cost position to rise to the top quintile of our industry benchmarks.
   b. Reduce asset footprint by $110 million through strategic partnerships.
   c. Right-size our legal and finance division with 20% cuts in 2 years.
   d. Optimize and integrate manufacturing operations through a lean IT backbone.
4. Drive Marketing Excellence
   a. Become the chosen partner for customers.
   b. Improve sales-team capability and add 18 new salespeople in Africa.
   c. Design an advertising campaign that captures the imagination of the 20 to 29-year-old male demographic.
   d. Launch customer-centered-awareness (CCA) training.
5. Inspire employees using the new People Mindset Module (PMM)

Figure 1.1 A list of goals, plans (and clichés) in the form of strategy themes posing as a strategy

essentially categories of aspirations, including items like *superior growth*, *optimize capital allocation*, *build the business*, and *increase customer value*. Granularization of aspirations by flowdown or cascading aspirations down the organization does not create a strategy.

When aspirations, including visions and missions, are used as strategies, it creates an enormous gulf between desired outcomes and what the organization needs to do day to day, one cause of leader's lamenting, "If only my people would execute." No one can achieve or execute on aspirations directly, and the larger and more complex the organization and endeavor, and the more spectacular the aspiration, the more this is true. If aspirations could be achieved directly, there would be no need for the concept of strategy.

Strategy as Long Term, Big, and Important

In many definitions, strategy is equated with *long term*, to which *big* or *important* may be added. But aspiration—not strategy—determines the time horizon, size, and importance of any endeavor. If your aspiration is to achieve something in three months, then your strategy horizon is three months, and if your aspiration is to make a big change, then your strategy will need big power. Strategy can only serve aspirations, just as do plans, tactics, metrics, and any other framework component (we will see that tactics are not just for the short term either). Defining strategy as what applies to an arbitrary long-term horizon can mislead people into believing that strategy is not relevant in turbulent periods. Yet turbulent periods are exactly when a guiding strategy light is needed. A true strategy is big and important in one sense: nothing should violate it.

Strategy as Plans

Probably, the most common concept of strategy is plans. A plan is an intended set of actions; do something by a certain date, as in "strategy is an integrated set of actions designed to create a sustainable advantage over competitors." Simulating the future with plans is important for coordination and synchronization, road-mapping, and reality testing of a framework, but they cannot be strategies because, as we will see, they give insufficient real-time guidance and unification of what to do. Strategy as plans also implies that you know in advance how to get from your current to your future state. But the adaptive view of innovation says it is folly to specify all future actions at the start of an endeavor. Military wisdom says that a plan never lasts longer than the first engagement with the enemy—a strategy should last longer than the first engagement. It is plans that are not useful in turbulent periods.

Strategy as Frameworks (Master Plans; Ends, Ways, and Means)

Often, there is a larger sense of "plan" that means the collection of not only plans as future actions, but also tactics, scenarios, value propositions, organization and budgets, metrics, and even the aspirations—collectively describing the organization's aspiration and everything about how to get there. In this case, the strategy is in the sense of a *master plan* or a *strategic plan*, which are frameworks. In some cases, the word strategy will be used twice: the framework itself will be called the strategy or strategic plan, and there will also be a strategy component (but not usually a central rule) to go along with the other components like aspiration, tactics, and metrics. But in many cases, the one component missing in the "strategic plan" is the strategy.

Military writers especially define strategy as the *ways* and the *means* to achieving *ends* (i.e., aspirations). Ways and means may be further described as the *how* to achieve as opposed to *what* to achieve. *Means* may be considered resources. Although it may be helpful to distinguish ways, means, and hows for achieving ends, these concepts essentially describe the framework—the master plan—just using less-specific concepts for the components.

Strategy Defined by Its Requirements

In his widely read and groundbreaking paper, *What is Strategy?*, Michael Porter never actually defines strategy. There is no statement such as a strategy is a_____, or strategy functions as a_____. Instead, he states that strategy is what gives a "unique competitive position for the company." Porter and others go on to say that strategy must create fit between the various functions of an organization; and also promote coherence, be integrative, feasible, unifying, externally oriented, people-focused, and holistic; have trade-offs and serve stakeholders; and include an understanding of risk.

While these requirements may be wonderful, some essential, they cannot define strategy. An automobile motor may need to be efficient, easy to manufacture, and robust to severe weather, but these don't define a motor. These could be requirements for the car's air conditioner. Strategy and other framework components, like automobile components, are defined by function, not qualities (a motor's function is to convert chemical or electric energy into mechanical work). Further, many of the characteristics suggested for strategy can refer only to the overall framework, not to the strategy component alone, and not necessarily for individual functions of a business such as IT, HR, manufacturing, and R&D.

Last, in his effort to teach that "operational excellence" is a poor over-all aspiration for a business—no doubt essential except perhaps for some true commodities—Porter says that operational excellence is the opposite of strategy.[1] But this is apples and oranges. Operational excellence requires a framework with a strategy for innovating just as any unique value proposition requires one. This misleading contrast between "operating" and "strategy" appears in several of the 75 concepts.[2] Chapter 9 will show a similar misleading contrast between "executing" and "innovating."

Strategy as Making Choices

Strategy is often defined as making choices. Yes, deciding on a strategy is a choice, a hard choice with tough trade-offs aimed at achieving many requirements such as just described. But every component of a framework—goals, missions, metrics, tactics, budgets, plans, and organization—are important choices too; so, there must be something more than making a choice to define the strategy component. Defining components as choices does not explain their different functions.

Every author of a strategy approach provides principles for making strategy and framework design choices. These principles are meant to enable the framework and its strategy to achieve the desired requirements.

During implementation, the organization then faces countless additional choices, and for these choices to be coherent and integrated, there must also be a guiding light for making them. The guiding light is the framework with its multiple components, including the strategy rule (note the rule may leave plenty of freedom for the organization to discover new ideas, it could even stipulate "run experiments only"). The choices aren't the strategy, the guiding rule is the strategy. Design principles must be in place before the act of choosing a strategy, and the strategy must be in place before the act of making choices during implementation; otherwise, strategy would have no meaning.

Despite the detailed principles authors provide, defining a strategy as making choices can encourage a less sophisticated filling out forms habit to answer the questions, "Where should you compete?," "How should you compete?," and "Which channels, capabilities, products, and processes should be used?" Or a question like, "Do you prioritize cost control, people development, or new products?" The answers obviously matter, but the results can be predictable, repetitive, and backward-looking unless the organization faithfully follows principles that promote creative tension and unity between framework components. Who will say that they don't need cost control or good people? Political scientist Jeffrey Meiser decries military strategists filling out forms in his article *Ends + Ways + Means = (Bad) Strategy*.[3] Note also that a definition of strategy must hold for any function in a business, including IT, HR, R&D, manufacturing, finance, and so on (and nonbusiness as well), which excludes definitions based on specific product, market, and channel choices.

Strategy as Patterns and Outcomes

Driven by frustration with disconnects between what people say their strategy is and what actually happens, Henry Mintzberg and others define strategy as a pattern, or actions taken. Mintzberg differentiates a plan for the future (intended strategy) from patterns from the past (realized strategy). J. Boone Bartholomees, Jr., of the U.S. Army War College, makes similar distinctions in the military realm.

Mintzberg is a leading voice criticizing the planned view of the future, but a pattern is an outcome, a series of events known only in hindsight. A future pattern is a projection. As just discussed, strategies are for guiding decisions and actions to achieve aspirations; they are not the future patterns or the choices themselves. For a strategy to have any meaning, it must be articulated *before* results, even if the strategy is changed frequently.

If, for example, a product manager's strategy restricts new product development to only a narrow range of applications, but then because of pressure from the sales team, R&D violates the rule, it doesn't mean that the rule was not a strategy. It means R&D didn't *adhere* to the strategy. And this is true whether the violations led to the expected negative patterns of profit loss, or to surprising emergence of new patterns of success. Intel's Andy Grove purportedly said, to understand a company's strategy, look at what they actually do rather than what they say they do. Yet would Grove have agreed that if Intel employees ignored his strategies, it invalidated them as strategies?

Others

Other definitions in the list of 75 include strategy as a hypothesis or theory, which, of course, it is, but so is everything else about the future; some as doing things differently in contrast with tactics which are for doing things better, but tactics are needed for new ventures too; some as the marshaling, determining, or deploying of needed resources, which can begin to sound like budgeting. One author calls it a "concept," another a "commitment;" both are good points, not definitions. Another equates strategy with execution, but as with patterns, you can't know execution until after strategy is designed. Some say strategy is a process; it is true that strategy design and implementation require a process of some kind, but a strategy itself is not one. One says strategy is an interlinked chain of problems that must be solved. A few add that a strategy must be a prudent or sustainable approach, one that results in above average returns, or useful for creating value, which is like saying that for an electromechanical device to be an automobile engine, it must be a good automobile engine. The authors provide insights, but none of these can be used as a definition of strategy.

What Strategy Is: The Central Rule of a Framework

The last concept of the 75—strategy as a rule—retains the beneficial ideas presented in the list yet does not suffer from the problems identified. Policies are also rules. Bhidé and Malik, among others, identify the importance of policy and Watkins argues for a set of guiding principles. Igor Ansoff, in one of the first systematic approaches to business strategy in 1965, proposed "decision rules." Sull and Eisenhardt and Rumelt (*guiding policy*) apply rules to bottlenecks.

Rumelt incorporated his guiding central policy rule along with goals and plans as the "kernel" of the strategy (Sull and Eisenhardt don't focus on a central rule). But the arguments made throughout Part I lead to the conclusion that Rumelt's goals, plans, and single guiding policy rule are three of the components of the larger framework. His guiding policy, the *central rule,* is the strategy:

A strategy is the central rule of a framework, designed to unify all decisions and actions around busting the bottleneck to achieving aspirations.

If the strategy rule is adhered to, that is, if the organization exerts stressors to destroy decisions and actions that are inconsistent with the rule, the probability of achieving aspirations increases. That there is only a probability of achieving aspirations is due to the uncertainty of all futures.

A strategy rule is a self-imposed constraint. It specifies, in some cases, what must be done and, in other cases (much better for making change and innovating), what must not be done. The strategy rule is central because no decision or action can conflict with it in that system.

The central rule captures what is beneficial in any other of the 75 definitions: Designing a strategy rule is a tough choice with tough trade-offs. The rule can and must address the most important issues, it can touch everything. Rules can address the long- and the short-term because they have no specific time horizon associated with them, that is, they remain in play until there's reason to change them. Rules lead to patterns if followed. The strategy rule works in an integrated way with the other components of the framework to drive change and innovation.

Rules may sound like the opposite of what would lead to creativity and innovation. They may conjure bureaucracy. How could rules—rigid, closed-minded, constraining rules—lead to innovations, diversity, growth, and newness? Impossible! Quite to the contrary, rules are the most powerful enabler of adaptation and freedom, because of their ability to provide real-time guidance for decision making and action without overconstraining. Plans and subgoals say what must occur; rules can specify boundaries of what cannot or should not occur. Plans are prescriptive, rigid, requiring prediction and detail. Rules leave people free to discover the future. Rumelt says, "Like the guardrails on a highway, the guiding policy, directs and constrains action without fully defining its content." The simplest and most elegant laws and regulations in society are those that specify what cannot be done, allowing freedom for anything else. Can you imagine the laws of a country specifying everything you can do? Likewise, can you imagine a strategy that lists everything you can or should do in the future?

The Specific Framework Used in the Emergent Approach

So, a strategy is not the framework; it is not the collection of visions, goals, plans, metrics, tactics, and other components. A strategy rule is one—the most important—component of the framework.

The impulse to create some kind of framework comes naturally. When faced with a problem or an opportunity or any need for change and innovation, people begin *framing* their approach as if building on a scaffolding. They start cataloging beliefs and thinking about ways to achieve goals, with or without clear language. They imagine constraints and ways to deal with them and what the operating environment looks like. They consider the tools and capabilities they have and what new ones to get. Some people and organizations do this a lot better than others, but everyone does it to some extent.

All strategy approaches have frameworks, but their specific components and terminology vary widely. Multiple terms result from redundancy, double senses or meanings, and different traditions in different fields of endeavor. As described earlier, the frameworks may be called the strategy, or the strategic- or master-plan (remember, many frameworks will not have a strategy component). And just to add to the fun, some call their approach for designing and implementing frameworks and their strategies, *a framework.*[4]

Figure 1.2 shows the framework used in the emergent approach. It applies to any business unit in a corporation, the overall corporation itself, or functional organization including IT, HR, R&D, or operations (and nonbusiness as well). Each component has a distinct function; there is no overlap among them and effort has been made to use the most intuitive term for each. This set is sufficient to approach—or frame—most endeavors because every aspect of making change and innovating can be put into one of these components. Your framework is *your* hypothesis of how to achieve your aspiration, including the articulation of the aspiration. If each component is in place and functioning properly, you will have a coherent way to improve your chances of success.

You will not always need every component; it depends on the scope of your endeavor. Further, the framework should not (and could not) hold everything about your corporation, business unit, or function. It is not an overview and need only include information relevant to the aspiration you are trying to achieve.

It is convenient to divide the framework components into those that must be designed, including aspirations, rules, plans and metrics,

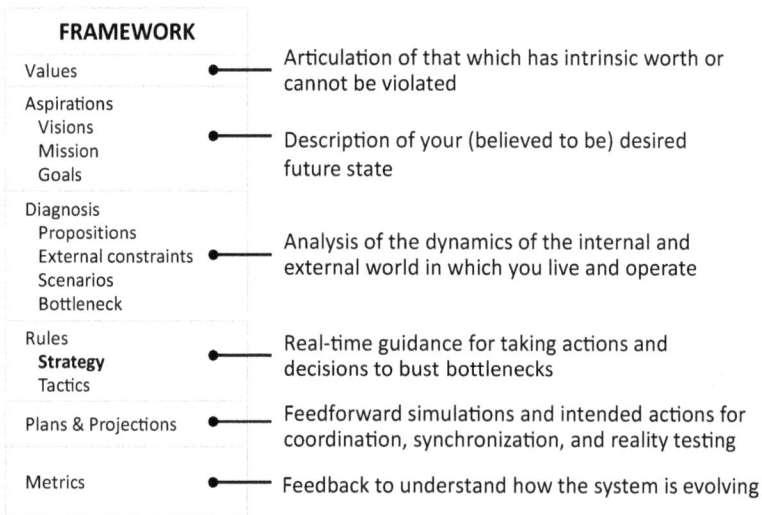

FRAMEWORK	
Values	Articulation of that which has intrinsic worth or cannot be violated

Aspirations
  Visions
  Mission
  Goals
	Description of your (believed to be) desired future state

Diagnosis
  Propositions
  External constraints
  Scenarios
  Bottleneck
	Analysis of the dynamics of the internal and external world in which you live and operate

Rules
  Strategy
  Tactics
	Real-time guidance for taking actions and decisions to bust bottlenecks

Plans & Projections	Feedforward simulations and intended actions for coordination, synchronization, and reality testing
Metrics	Feedback to understand how the system is evolving

Figure 1.2 The framework used in the emergent approach

and those that are discovered or just articulated, including values and the diagnosis.

Starting with those that are designed:

Aspirations articulate desired future states (or at least what you think you desire). *Visions*, as traditional, are high-level broad concepts that do not necessarily require specific measurable outcomes. The *mission* establishes boundaries and purpose. Missions are classified as aspirations because they are usually statements at such a high level that, although it is a free choice to be constrained by them, it is not always a free choice to achieve them. Additionally, whereas strategy must change as bottlenecks change, missions do not often change. (Because missions are often rule-like and central, they are sometimes confused with strategy). *Goals* are the specific, often measurable, and usually smaller-scale aspirations. Once again, you may not need all three types of aspirations— vision, mission, goals.

Metrics are measurements for gaining feedback on how your system is evolving during implementation. Every number, however, is not a metric. Metrics indicate the difference between what is and what is believed to be desired, a reference state. In the emergent approach, metrics will include milestone achievements and audits that are less numerical.

Plans, as discussed earlier, are articulations of future actions used for coordination, synchronization, evaluation, and even inspiration. Plans are a type of simulation of the future, which means they give feed-forward insight as opposed to the feed-back insight that metrics do. All simulations are models of a sort because they are of the future, and there is no data of the future. A *roadmap* is a type of plan. *Projections* and *forecasts* are numerical simulations.

Rules provide real-time guidance for taking decisions and actions. The strategy is the special central rule that that applies to the entire scope of the system. *Tactics* are rules also; what makes them different from strategy is that they apply to a partial scope of a system, and are often called policies, or *tactical policies* (Chapter 6). Each framework has one strategy only (bolded in Figure 1.2 to stress its essential role). Larger and multifaceted organizations require multiple nested frameworks, each with its own strategy (Chapter 7).

Next, are the components that are discovered or articulated:

Values are statements of what deeply matters and cannot be violated, such as core values. If you find yourself designing or often changing them, then what you have are probably not values.

Diagnosis is a term used by Rumelt and others. Its four components cover a wide range of analysis about the internal and external world in which the framework will be used. While Rumelt does not define diagnosis exactly as here, in spirit, the definitions are close, especially the focus on bottlenecks. *Propositions* state the capabilities you bring to the world such that you should be able to achieve your aspirations and serve customers. *External Constraints* are imposed from outside your system. *Scenarios* are different possible external environments in which you will operate and live but that you have little or no control over. And, *bottlenecks* of different types, as described in the Introduction, are that which is in the way of achieving aspirations, an unwanted type of constraint.

Notice that components that are sometimes associated with implementation are in the framework, including plans (includes budgets, personnel), tactics, and metrics. It is known that the key aspects of implementation must be in the framework because capability to implement influences aspiration and strategy design.

A framework may also be called a *system*, as in a system for making change and innovating. For instances, the 3M system for product development or the St. Louis Cardinals System for developing baseball players. Urban Meyer, the successful American college football coach, says, "Now I understand. Average leaders have quotes. Good leaders have a plan. Exceptional leaders have a system."[5] Meyer's system is a framework with aspirations, rules of various types, plans, techniques, feedback methods, and a discipline of adherence to these components (he lost his job as coach of the Jacksonville Jaguars in 2021, due in part to not following his own rules, and perhaps because he applied a college framework to a professional team, a misdiagnosis). In the Emergent Approach, however, the term *system* is reserved to describe the holistic view of an organization or entity covered by a framework. The common concept of an IT system, for example, is consistent with the emergent approach use. An IT system is a subset of a larger business system.

We could call the framework a *change and innovation framework* to stress its raison d'être. This would also differentiate it from other types of frameworks, such as an analytical framework or, say, the framework of a constitution. Or, we could call it the *strategy framework* to stress how crucial the single strategy component is. But we will just call it the *framework*, and it will be understood that the strategy is one component of the framework.

Why Can't the Framework Be the Strategy?

Wouldn't it be easier to call the whole framework the strategy, as is most often done? And just call the central rule the *central rule*, or *central policy*? After all, we call the act of designing or formulating frameworks strategizing, not framework-izing. There are several reasons not to do so. Most people would agree with Collis and Rukstad that a strategy should be describable in something like 35 words or less, else the organization won't internalize it.[6] But describing an entire framework in 35 words is impossible.

Second, the framework includes relevant aspects of what many approaches consider to be implementation, including metrics, detailed plans, tactical policies, staffing, and roll-out plans. It would be confusing to subsume all these features under the term "strategy."

A third and growing reason not to call the framework the strategy is the need to align with computational methods. The practitioners of game theory, artificial intelligence, and genetic algorithms must define strategy as rules: the "tit for tat" solution to the prisoner's dilemma, the rules for the algorithmic trading strategies that now dominate financial markets, or recombination rules in genetic algorithms, for examples. It would be shortsighted to use a different conception of strategy in management practice than used in a domain as important as computation, especially as computational and human decision making evolve to become more and more intertwined.

Example of a Framework with its Strategy—Maintain the Tax Base

As discussed earlier in the chapter, the statement *our strategy is to maintain the tax base in our city* is an aspiration not a strategy. So, what might a strategy rule and its framework for achieving this aspiration look like?

Imagine you are a city council president. The tax base is declining due to employers abandoning the city. You are convinced the reason for this exodus is that complicated regulations of all kinds have simply become too onerous for companies. You also believe the city's economy is your foremost issue, because as the tax base falls, schools are the first to suffer budget cuts, which is unacceptable to you.

Should the strategy be to "reduce regulation?" The answer is no, because it is not your free choice to simply reduce regulation. The council members who legislated the onerous regulations believe in them, and they still have a majority say. Reducing regulation therefore is just a more specific aspiration. To find a strategy, you need to diagnose the bottleneck to reducing regulation. Your diagnosis is supporters of the regulation are irrational and do not understand the economic implications, nor do they listen to business owners. What could be a strategy to bust this bottleneck? Here are some possibilities:

1. Risk burning political capital (and your personal values) by focusing all resources into a brutal and on-the-edge-of-truth negative campaign to unseat the regulation supporters.
2. Become more willing to compromise on other issues that the regulators value, in exchange for eliminating the regulations that are particularly onerous to businesses.
3. Stop resisting and focus on the next election; let the opposition put in even more complicated regulation, hoping that voters will finally see the absurdity of it before it's too late.

4. Give business owners more influence in your political party to gain favor (and risk losing control in other areas besides regulation).

5. Sacrifice other needs and dedicate all time to dialog with the regulators until either you can change their minds, they change yours, or it is clear no one will budge.

Each of these possibilities could, in principle, be a valid strategy. Each is a central rule, contains a trade-off, and gives real-time guidance for decisions and actions as opposed to repeating the goal. Only a better diagnosis of the situation or some trial and error will allow you to figure out which of the five is best.

Now, say you chose the second strategy alternative. Figure 1.3 shows how the rest of the framework might look in that case.

Goal	Reduce regulation to maintain tax base
Diagnosis	**Proposition:** You grasp the problem and have the energy to drive change
	External constraints: Your party has several policy areas where they are not willing to compromise
	Scenario: "Reduce regulation" supporters dominate in the next national election, lending support to your effort
	Bottleneck: Irrationality of regulation supporters
Strategy	**Compromise on other issues in exchange for business regulation reduction**
Plans	• Meet with your party and draw up list of areas that would be acceptable for compromise; identify off-limits topics. (by June 1; led by first deputy)
	• Create an office of small business opportunity to buy time (Assign staffer to design and launch by August 1)
	• Engage consulting firm to generate data showing negative impact of regulation (first deputy to lead; study due October 31)
	• Convince party to hire an additional staffer to work full time on regulation (By April 1, leaving time to prepare for the June 1st meeting)
Tactics	• Early on, show good will by compromising on several issues, but never appear willing to compromise on the off-limits areas
	• To calm emotions on both sides, (1) reduce the number of press conferences and other public appearances by two thirds to limit opportunities for negotiating in public (responsible: press secretary); (2) instruct staff to act non-confrontational (a change from current habits); (3) adopt a policy of saying nothing rather than engaging in arguments
Metrics	• Your approval rating within your party measured monthly (you can't afford to lose your base)
	• Audit staff adherence to the tactical policy by periodic sampling of their social media accounts and through casual discussions with the opposition
	• Quarterly shutdowns and startups of businesses
	• Monthly polls to determine if scenario is becoming more probable

Figure 1.3 City council president's framework

A key takeaway is that strategies must be found from the bottleneck to aspirations, not the aspirations themselves. Hence, the focus throughout the emergent approach on the triad of aspiration, bottleneck, and strategy written as **strategy←bottleneck←aspiration.** These three components and the connections between them are the core of what makes a framework unique for a particular endeavor. Everything else—plans, metrics, tactics, and so on—must align with this triad. In a modest endeavor with a light framework development effort, this triad might be one of the few things needed. (Note that the triad is different from Rumelt's *kernel*, which he defines as *goal [aspiration], central policy [rule], plans*.)

This example also illustrates that other people's strategy rules may not sound as momentous or deep as the aspirations they are designed to achieve. Without understanding an individual's or a group's reality, without walking in their shoes and knowing their bottleneck, their strategy may sound downright trivial.

The chapters of Part I that follow show how the central-rule definition of strategy is confirmed by and arises out of a model of the dynamics of complex adaptive systems. The first step is to describe how change and innovation emerge in more detail.

CHAPTER 2

A Primer on Adaptation and Emergence

Change and innovation in human endeavors follow adaptive evolutionary mechanisms akin to change and innovations in biological nature. Change and innovation in business, government, military, technology, or the arts are not fully planned or envisioned but *emerge* from countless interactions as part of *complex adaptive systems*. Even artificial intelligence and other computational methods are evolutionary mechanisms that follow the laws of complex adaptive systems, which is why they can pick up faint signals.

But this is not your grandparents' evolution. Perish the myths and misunderstandings: evolution is not slow, it is not random (though it has chance elements), it does not require DNA, it does not always involve competition and selfishness, it doesn't always result in improvements, and the mechanism of evolution isn't even different than the mechanism of revolution. Evolutionary mechanisms describe the brutal reality of how hard it is to change and innovate or even survive in nature and culture, not in the narrow sense of the culture of an organization, but human endeavor broadly. Evolution demonstrates why predicting and planning the future cannot be the basis for strategy.

This chapter describes the fundamentals of innovation in complex adaptive systems on which the emergent approach is built. Evolution is a big topic, and its related terminology—including adaptation, agile, anti-fragile, resilience, self-organization, creativity, innovation, swarm intelligence, creative tension, and selection pressure—is nearly as confusing as the terminology of strategy. But we can pare down to the essential concepts. We will start with the *variation-selection-heredity* cycle, the mechanism of evolution in both biological and cultural systems. The wide range of references for an adaptive view cited in the Introduction is shown online {web/supplement}. It includes the work of psychologist and social scientist Donald Campbell (1916–1996) who recognized the essential parallel between biological and cultural creativity in the 1960s.

What Is Adaptive Evolution in Biology and Culture?

In any population—whether a biological species of animals, plants, or bacteria, or cultural species of ideas, technologies, or physical entities— there exists variations in traits and characteristics of individuals that make up the population. The individuals go through generations, including individual ideas. In each generation, new variation can arise. In biology, variation occurs by DNA mutations and recombination during reproduction. In culture, variations of ideas and physical entities that lead to new traits and characteristics occur too, mostly in people's minds.

Variations are inherited by the next generation. In biology, heredity is achieved by the genetic system and DNA. In culture, heredity, called *retention*, is achieved by learning and other evolved capabilities, including those specifically aimed at retention, such as pen and paper and 1s and 0s on silicon chips.

All biological and cultural populations exist in an environment, and every environment produces *stressors* on the individuals. A stressor is a force. Environmental stressors are driving forces in evolution. In biological nature, stressors can be competitive forces where other individuals block access to resources and mates, or noncompetitive forces like agents of disease and habitat disappearance. In culture, stressors can be market forces where, for instance, consumers no longer buy a given product; physical forces where, for example, a poorly designed automobile cannot withstand aggressive driving on bad roads; or informational forces, like data or other evidence that shows a belief or a theory to be untrue. The culture of an organization—culture in the narrower sense of an organization's style and habits—very much determines which positive or negative stressors are put on employees. The stressors exerted in the past in large part determined how the culture got that way.

The impact of stressors is that some individuals of the biological or cultural population don't survive—they are destroyed or die away due to lack of resources. This is where the idea of *fitness* comes in. Certain individuals have a higher probability of surviving because their traits and overall design makes them more *fit* to the stressors of the environment. Some animals are more capable of resisting disease, drought, or the aggression of other animals. Some people are more resistant to stressors like criticism, fear, or the pain of hard work. Some people are less susceptible to seduction by luck or wishful thinking. Certain theories, because they are correct, are more resistant to challenges. Certain ideas are more resistant to the logic of our thinking, especially ideas that have emotion attached to them. And in the tangible realm, some products and technologies are better able to resist the rigors of market and physical stressors because of their design and manufacture.

Therefore, fitness is an entity's ability to resist environmental stressors. Fitness is *not* defined as "what survives" or "reproductive success," which is circular reasoning; these are outcomes of fitness, not characteristics of the evolving entities. Fitness also doesn't automatically mean the most aggressively competitive. Darwin described a seedling on the edge of a desert whose fitness is the ability to resist the drought. A kind and altruistic person may be the fittest in a community. Competition is only one of many sources of stressors.

In biological populations, the difference between individuals' fitness to environmental stressors creates *selection pressure*, a stress in the population (stressors cause stress, and pressure is a kind of stress). The greater the stressor acting on a population, the greater the selection pressure, and the greater the potential for change. In the environment of the mind, we call the selection pressures that result from fitness differences between ideas *creative tension*, a desired stress.

So, when some individuals of the population are destroyed or die away in a generation, the survivors can then evolve further in subsequent generations. They can evolve new variations of traits and characteristic that modify their fitness (and if they don't change, they may find new niches and environments where their fitness is good enough). When this cycle of variation-selection-heredity/retention is repeated over and over across generations, variations can accumulate (because of heredity/retention) and result in *lineages* of new species. Familiar lineages (technically genealogies or phylogenies) include the modern horse evolving from the dog-sized *Eohippus*, and the iPhone evolving from the iPod and early iPad prototypes (Figure 2.1).[1]

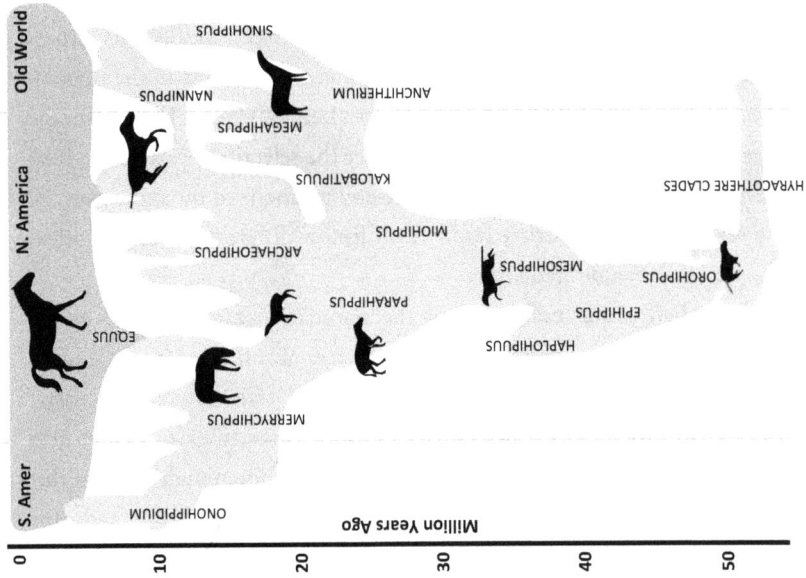

Figure 2.1 The evolution of the horse (adapted from MacFadden, 2005) and the iPhone

Darwin called variation-selection-heredity *natural selection*, and the variation-selection-retention analog in culture is *cultural selection*. New surviving variants and species are *innovations* whether in biology or culture. An innovation in business systems is some new capability or entity, including one that solves a problem or busts a bottleneck to achievement of aspirations.

Biologists define species in various ways. Like all classifications, however, there's no perfect way to do so; classification just helps with understanding. Schemes for classifying cultural species don't yet exist, but we classify them all the time informally. We call them generations, but different iPhones are species; the *iPhone 12* is a species of iPhone, which is part of a family of iPhones, which are part of a family of all smartphones, which is part of the mobile branch of all digital mobile electromechanical devices, and so on. Countless generations of variation-selection-retention occurred to create the iPhone 12, its subsystems, and its ecosystem. These generations occurred in experiments and computational and physical models and especially in the minds of people inside and outside of Apple. (iPhone and iPad software engineer Ken Kocienda describes variation-selection-retention at Apple in his book *Creative Selection*.)[2] Most ideas, for example, the nonpredictive touch keyboard, were destroyed by evidence from research and experiment and by the logic in individual and collective brains. Each idea that survived was then built upon, developed further, and put through the mill again until the next model emerged. Strategist Adrian Slywotzky describes Apple's grind-it-out iterative process in "Steve Jobs and the Eureka Myth."[3]

Adaptable, Antifragile, Agile, Robust, and Resilient

Darwinian evolution is *adaptive evolution* because the probable survivors of each generation—the more-fit variants to the stressors of a given environment—are said to be more *adapted*, more suited, to that environment. Adaptive evolution is a *real-time concept*, which is crucial because a strategy must give real-time guidance for taking decisions and actions. Change and innovation are driven by stressors acting on biological or cultural entities in real time, not looking ahead (of course, people can look ahead, and we will address this later in the chapter).

"Adapt" is used in other ways as well: a species is more *adaptable* if it can easily evolve for the better over generations when stressed, or if its characteristics can be widely varied. This *adaptability* may be called evolvability. *Antifragile* is a term for the concept of adaptable to stressors coined by Nassim Taleb, who argued there is no existing term for such a concept.[4] He also describes stressors using terms like volatility, randomness, turbulence, stresses, disorder, or even variations. Antifragile has helped people see the importance of the evolutionary process, but the emergent approach uses *adaptable*, the established term for expressing an entity's ability to evolve for the better (or worse). Such capability is the objective of frameworks and their strategies.

A species that can survive in many different environments is also called *adaptable*. Rats and roaches are adaptable because, as generalists, they can survive nearly every environment on earth; specialists like pandas and bluebirds cannot. Likewise, companies that depend on just a few customers or products are often more negatively impacted market changes. *Resilient* or *robust* are other terms related to adaptability to many different and stressful environments. The Fed's stress test (a pressure test), which is a set of simulations of possible difficult economic scenarios, is designed to assess a bank's resilience.

The increasingly used term *Agile* has also taken on multiple evolutionary meanings in business writing. It is used generically to mean adaptability—an agile business is nimble and can quickly change (or pivot) for the better. The other use of agile means to innovate in short generations. In agile software design, for instance, instead of developing the fully envisioned program, a *minimum viable product* is designed and then evolved with customers. The strategy practice in Part II of The Emergent Approach uses this agile-evolution model to design frameworks. Instead of creating strategy and the other framework components in sequence, a minimum viable strategy alternative matrix is drafted early in the process. The matrix contains alternative frameworks and fitness criteria for assessing them and is evolved through team debate, external input, and research and experimentation. It is near impossible to create software, or a framework and its strategy, in a one-pass procedure. Unfortunately, like "disruption" and "transformation," agile has become a buzzword often used to describe "everything good": quick to mobilize, nimble, collaborative, easy to get things done, responsive, free information flow, quick decision making, empowered to act, resilient, and speed to failure.

The Cultural Selection of Early Automobiles

In 1886, Karl Benz and Gottlieb Daimler filed patents for a new species of transportation formed by placing a gasoline engine on a horse carriage—Benz's was three-wheeled, whereas Daimler's was four-wheeled. Horseless carriage species attracted investment dollars and were therefore fit to the market because of the potential to free transportation from the limitations of the horse.

Over the next three decades, engineers around the world tried countless automobile design variations, forming an explosion of species. Variations ranged from the overall vehicle architecture to the smallest fasteners used, to the methods for designing and manufacturing. But market stressors, and the logic and experiences of countless people in the ecosystem, destroyed the less-fit configurations. Engines, for example, varied from gasoline internal combustion (air- and water-cooled), steam, electric, to even a hybrid system, and countless subvariants among these. But the water-cooled internal combustion engine emerged as the winner: Air-cool engines survived only in various niches (the VW beetle was the largest) until the last of the air-cooled Porsche 911s in 1998; steam engines became extinct because of explosions and heat-up time even though they were the most powerful for a period; and electric, though initially the most popular, effectively disappeared for 100 years.

Unfortunately, the word "selection" is confusing. Eventual winners are not really selected. No one orchestrated the selection of the gasoline engine over steam and electric. It was countless market forces leading to countless events that eliminated the flow of money to steam and electric auto companies. The lack of money was the environmental stressor that killed them. Money is the sustenance of any product just as food is the sustenance of animals. Starved of money, product lines atrophy and eventually become extinct. Darwin might have been better off calling his mechanism *natural destruction*.

The resurgence of electrics and hybrids in the 21st century is because new technology variations have evolved under new market stressors.

Though gasoline engines are powerful, reliable, and give a long range, a sizable group of consumers are no longer paying for them in part because of their harm to the earth. Electrics and hybrids with computer control and powerful batteries (co-opted from other industries), coupled with the emergence of ecosystems for battery production and charging stations, can now resist consumers' stressors for convenience, safety, performance, and affordability. In reverse, the reduced flow of money is stressing the fossil fuel ecosystem. And let's remember that gas automobiles solved an earlier massive pollutant—horse manure.

Not the Opposite of Revolution

Believe it or not, the evolutionary mechanism is not different from or the opposite of revolution. To understand this, we need to clarify the two different ways in which the term revolution is used. The first way is in the sense of forcing fast dramatic change, such as overthrowing a government in a political revolution or a business "blowing up" a technical approach to a product platform and starting with a clean sheet. The second way is in the sense of the creation of a dramatically new capability or ecosystem such as the industrial revolution or the iPhone revolution. These are revolutionary outcomes.

In the first sense, revolution can be planned. You can destroy *anything* by exerting extreme-enough stressors (the force). The mechanism is Darwinian because all you are doing is increasing the level of the stressors. While you are free to destroy, however, you are not free to demand a given desired outcome. Overthrowing a government does not guarantee a better one will emerge. If the system isn't changed, likely all that is done is to change the names of the dictators. Blowing up a technical approach may be prudent because it looks like a dead end, but no success is guaranteed with a different approach.

The second sense, that of a revolutionary outcome, can never be planned. No one planned the industrial revolution, or the way the world wide web looks today, or true corporate transformations. We label these as revolutions after the fact.

Steve Jobs and many others at Apple and elsewhere had a huge influence, but there was no omnipotent designer that saw the iPhone revolution. A great deal of the iPhone existed before the iPhone was conceived, and there were dead ends. Jobs was inspired by the iPad which was put on hold once it was seen that the technology could be used for a phone. And one of the key innovations to making the iPhone work, the predictive touch keyboard entry, wasn't even thought of at the start. The leaders upheld the discipline of not accepting anything that did not meet Apple's standards in functional and aesthetic design, but they did not give the organization every task to implement. Few people saw that in less than five years, the $499 iPhone with a predictive touch keyboard would obliterate Blackberry and the other physical keyboard smartphones that were the dominant species.

Henry Ford and Co. were a huge part of the automotive revolution.[5] In fact, they revolutionized all industry, not to mention society itself, by creating a car that working people and small businesses could afford, not fancy vehicles for the rich. Fifteen million Model Ts were sold at a price that bottomed out at 260 dollars in 1925, also stimulating the emergence of an ecosystem of roads, services stations, aftermarket parts and modification, and regulations. But when he began, Henry Ford did not envision the final Model T manufacturing process that would make Ford the number-one car company in the world. His famed moving assembly line, co-opting ideas from meat processing and Oldsmobile, and suggested to him by employees, debuted in 1913, well after the launch of the Model T in 1908. He did not orchestrate the Model T in the sense that he would tell everyone exactly what to do. He didn't know exactly what to do— leaders are part of the system. He learned along with everyone else.

Ford was, however, fiercely driven by a strategy rule. To reduce the Model T selling price and increase volume, he would never allow incorporating style and features to get in the way of cost and production speed. He destroyed the countless variations of ideas and techniques that were counter to this rule, always focusing on the ideas that were fit to it, until the extreme mass production of the Model T emerged. His ruthless application of the strategy rule was a powerful environmental stressor for the organization.

Austrian economist Joseph Schumpeter identified "gales of destruction" when a new industry takes over an existing one. He was describing the unplanned case of a revolutionary outcome, such as the near destruction of the horse and carriage industry as the automobile industry swelled. Schumpeter's destructions are large-scale unplanned outcomes, not causes of outcomes. The causes are countless acts and interactions by the players in the ecosystem, sometimes called agents, reacting to market stressors, including many small acts of destruction. (By the way, many horse and carriage and bike manufacturers adapted by converting to the automotive ecosystem.)

So then, if evolution is not the opposite of revolution, what is? The answer is atrophy and directionless drift (in geek speak, a random walk). Drift is the case where environmental stressors are so weak that there are no longer differences in fitness between individuals in the population. In the 1960s and early '70s, Ford, GM, and Chrysler drifted because they could make money so easily and U.S. gasoline was dirt cheap. Then when oil producers raised prices starting in 1972, and emission standards were imposed, their bloated gas-guzzling behemoths were revealed to be woefully unfit compared to Asian and European automobiles. There was no instant "transformation" possible for the U.S. makers. It took years for them to reverse the atrophy in skills and technology.

Note that drift is not necessarily bad in design or discovery processes. If it's unclear what the stressors or direction should be, it is a viable approach to allow thinking and actions to drift for a while; the system could end up somewhere interesting.

Levels and the Paradox of Freedom and Discipline

The lack of goals and omnipotent designers were radical features of Darwin's *Origin of Species* in 1859, and still radical today in biology and culture. The winners in any population are not picked by an orchestrator and brought to the fore. They *emerge* over generations from the carnage caused by the discipline of repeated cycles of variation-selection-heredity/retention, the continual destruction of the unfit, allowing the fit to be built upon in each new generation.

But to truly understand emergence as it relates to making change and innovating, we need one more detail. A concept that is perhaps the most important for designing frameworks and their strategy—the concept of levels. Though there is a continuum between them, we can simplify and talk about two different levels. Low, local levels and high, global levels. You may see levels referred to as micro and macro.

To see the importance of levels, consider a paradox about the people in innovative organizations like Apple and Ford as described so far. They are extraordinarily disciplined about following principles, but at the same time, enormously intuitive and freethinking. Yet disciplined thought and freedom of thought are seemingly at odds with each other; so much so that business and military strategists offer a solution to the paradox.[6] They propose that creative people and organizations alternate between disciplined and free modes: between skill and art, between freethinking and rigorous thinking, and between intuitive and analytical. In essence, two different kinds of thinking. Some proposals go as far as to describe the solution as alternating between creative innovation and discipline itself, equating creativity with freedom. You may see simple illustrations of this alternating explanation like Figure 2.2, along with the guidance that success requires effort on both sides.

While solving the paradox, alternating doesn't explain how innovations occur or how people alternate between disciplined and free modes. The levels concept of adaptive systems gives a different solution: The

Figure 2.2 Alternating solution to the paradox of freedom and discipline

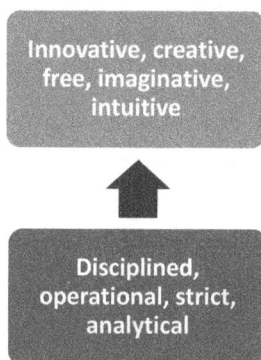

Figure 2.3 Levels solution to the paradox of freedom and discipline

discipline is at the low, local level, as with Henry Ford constraining the organization to adhere to the "cost and speed versus style and features" rule in everything they did. The freedom is at the high, emergent level, as in Ford accepting the way the Model T and its manufacture came out. The discipline at low levels is the adaptive interactions, the repeated destructions of variants that can be shown to be false. These are the variants that are unfit to logic, evidence, and argument. The high-level result of the low-level discipline is the emergence of innovations as variations accumulate. The freedom at high levels is the ability of creators to accept and promote emergent innovations, no matter how unexpected, confusing, or disconcerting they are. Henry Ford saying that customers could have the Model T in any color they want, "so long as it's black," was not because he disliked other colors; it was because black was the color that best survived the logic of the cost and speed rule. Black was an emergent result of adhering to the rule. Figure 2.3 shows the levels-based solution to the paradox.

Discipline at high levels, that is, imposing high-level constraints—demanding a given result, tampering, demanding that results meet plans and predictions—is outcome thinking that leads to paralysis and poor results (planned economies are an extreme example). Freedom at low levels leads to slipshod thoughtless results. Innovative people and organizations are free because of their confidence (conscious or not) in their low-level discipline, not despite it. Deep creativity and intuition are an emergent result of low-level discipline and analytical thinking that leads to internalization, not direct eureka creative acts. Creativity is a harsh process.

Henry Ford's discipline was at low levels at first, not specifying the exact outcome, only the guiding rule. But as time went on, his discipline moved to high-levels, constraining his company to maintain the focus on high-volume, low-cost, and low-feature cars. He was seduced by his Model T paradigm way past its prime. He imposed on his people how the industry should be, and by doing so, paralyzed the company's ability to innovate and change as the market environment changed. This was unfortunate, because as the roaring '20s progressed, consumers wanted more style, more features, and more choices, options that GM and Chrysler provided in the U.S. Also, automobile manufacturing became more standardized and commoditized, narrowing Ford's cost and output advantage. Paralyzed by success and his rigid personality, Henry Ford's ability to innovate declined as he lost his low-level analytical reasoning and ability to internalize market information. By the end of the 1920s, GM took market leadership. The cost and speed strategy turned out to be an evolutionary dead end.

When Austrian philosopher Paul Feyerabend said, "The only principle that does not inhibit progress is: anything goes," he was only right at high levels. If anything goes at low levels—where most of the work is done and the rigor of adherence to the constraint of strategy must exist—you get garbage. True creativity and innovation are the farthest things from *anything goes*. True creativity and innovation are *anything can emerge*.

The levels explanation of emergence is a core tenet of the science of complex adaptive systems. New patterns, structures, and learnings—innovations—arise at high, global levels from the myriad disciplined interactions at low, local levels, *without an orchestrator*. This mechanism is why emergence is sometimes called *self-organization*, where the agents, the participants in the system, react only to their local environment when making choices. (Note that this is a *dynamic* view of emergence that describes how innovations arise. Classic illustrations of dynamic emergence include how birds create flocks and how social insects develop their sophisticated colonies without orchestrators, hence the term *swarm intelligence*. You will also find discussion of what might be called *static* emergence, which is more focused on somewhat philosophical questions about static reductionism and the properties of the whole and its parts at a point in time.)

The dynamic theory of emergence gives a more subtle description of issues with top-down leadership. Top-down is damaging when specific high-level outcomes are demanded—management by results. No one can choose to get results or innovate, and leaders can't demand them top-down, which is why management by results leads to unremarkable results. Innovation is an outcome, not an action or a choice. You don't "do" innovation any more than you "do" strategy. You follow strategy in the hopes of innovating. What's more, actions at the low, local levels that lead to innovation need not look anything like the high-level innovations that emerge (ants responding to pheromones looks nothing like the sophisticated colonies they create). In fact, the best actions will look nothing like the high-level result. On the other hand, leaders demanding and encouraging that the organization maintain discipline at low levels and adhere to the framework and its strategy, especially during tough times (or fix it if it needs correction)—without fully specifying the outcome—is beautiful top-down leadership. Such leadership is even more beautiful if the organization was part of creating the framework.

You may notice that little space has been allotted to how variations come about in the first place. This is in part because variations will come naturally if a person or team is deeply engaged in their endeavor. Not only are we overwhelmed by information in media and access to research, but the mind is constantly recombining memories to create new ideas. We don't store full memories; we construct them from fragments, which supplies endless opportunities for new combinations and "mutations."[7] Yes, energy is needed to reach out and find or create new information, and there are good discussions in the literature around how to encourage variations,[8] but more difficult is having the sensitivity to know what is interesting and the insight on what to do with new information. If people truly internalize their endeavor and focus on the low-level disciplines and not the high-level outcomes, the resulting creative tension will drive them to generate variations and will enable them to be sensitive to information transmitted to them.

Intel's CPUs

Levels is illustrated by the well-known story of Intel's transition in the 1970s from memory chips to central processing units (CPUs).[9] Intel had a simple rule—each month, add up all the product orders from customers and then create a factory schedule that puts the most profitable orders at the top (establishing such tactic is easy; following it, i.e., executing, and determining what is profitable, is much harder.) At some point, however, CPUs, then a specialty item, were starting to go to the top of the list. Only after this trend persisted did the company's leadership—including Gordon Moore (of Moore's law), Andrew Grove, and Robert Noyce— wrestle with the difficult question of whether to switch the company's mission from memory to CPUs. They took considerable time in the boardroom to analyze, debate, and struggle, all the while fearing the wrong choice. Eventually, they took the plunge, switching the company's focus to CPUs. They were so good at it that Intel became one of the premier companies of the personal computer revolution.

Intel's CPU business was not ushered in with a vision. There was no aim of a CPU-dominant business. There was no eureka act. The potential for CPUs entered the company's consciousness only *after* the discipline of adhering to a boring, low-level operational factory rule to maximize output value—a tactical rule that had nothing to do with creating a CPU business—revealed it to them. Visions came later.

The simple profit rule was sensitive enough to pick up the faint marketplace signals of a growing personal computer ecosystem and the faint signal that memory was commoditizing. Andrew Grove titled his book "*Navigating Strategic Inflection Points*," yet he admits all great storms start as gentle gusts of wind. If Grove and his colleagues knew the CPU inflection point from the start, then why did they need extended painful debate and anxiety? They needed painful debate because they were unsure; they were scared to let go of past success and scared to accept the emergent result from the manufacturing rule.

Somehow, they had the ability to "feel" the new data, to have a vibe about it. How many business leaders, when seeing the data showing CPUs going to the top of the profit list, would have let the opportunity pass them by with top-down directives like, "this is noise, we are a memory company, we will not be distracted by niche opportunities, we will stick to our core products that our most important customers want"? Grove and the others had the ability to accept an innovative high-level emergent result because of the low-level analysis and debate.

That people can clearly see profound change coming is fantasy, but the discipline of a rules-based, low-level adaptive system can reveal potentials. Once the storm strengthens, then everyone sees it. If people cannot feel or interpret the weak early signals, or if they are not free to accept them, it may then become too late to do anything about it. A better title for Grove's book might have been, *How to Feel Coming Inflection Points*.

By the way, was Intel's evolution slow? Hardly.

The Positivity of Low-Level Destruction—The Safety Triangle

Worker safety was a great achievement of 20th century society, and greater improvements are demanded as standards rise and new hazards appear.

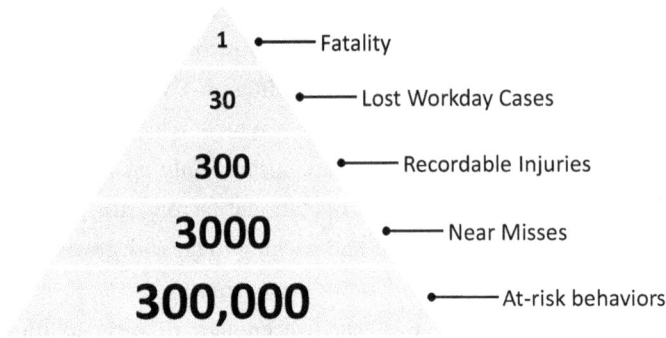

Figure 2.4 The safety triangle

(From the beginning, Dupont was an innovator in safety frameworks.) For every workplace fatality or severe injury, there are many thousands of *at-risk behaviors*. When someone forgets their hard hat, the probability of getting knocked out increases. A relationship between behavior and injuries is captured in the *safety triangle*, Figure 2.4.[10]

Safety theory demands leading at the low-level base of the triangle as opposed to managing by high-level results. It demands destroying at-risk behaviors using a framework that includes low-level local policies for workers to follow in real time, with absolute discipline—no exceptions. An example is the OSHA lifesaving rule of *Lock, Tag, and Try*, which applies to working on equipment driven by the likes of electricity, steam, or hydraulics.[11] Before starting, workers must (1) lock down the energy source (e.g., a circuit breaker in the off position), (2) identify themselves as the key holder with a tag, and (3) try the equipment to verify that the source is indeed locked. What CEO would dare say, "As long as no one is injured, I don't care whether you lock, tag, and try. All we care about are results—safe people!"?

Focusing on high-level goals and slogans and exhortation for results in monthly meetings may sound like positive leadership, but it doesn't make people safe. What value is the high-level constraint "you must not get injured when working on machinery"? This statement can't even be fixed with the clause, "or off with your head." Safety excellence is an emergent result of harsh, repetitive low-level, local destructions of at-risk behavior by situational analysis, training, audits, encouragement and rewards, and disciplinary action when rules are ignored. These actions look nothing like the desired emergent outcome. Management by results—set goals, measure, and take action if injuries occur—does not lead to safety excellence, it leads to mediocre performance.

Freedom and Discipline Everywhere

The levels explanation is not limited to science and technology. Freedom and discipline are embodied in common-sense wisdom when faced with a difficult challenge such as "get to the root of the problem" or "stick to the fundamentals." In baseball or cricket, great players don't aim at home runs or sixes, they focus on executing, the discipline of adhering to their mechanics and their mental approach. They don't think about the score or their record; they focus on the next pitch or bowl. Their performance is the high-level emergent result of constant destructions of deviations from the disciplines honed and developed through countless hours of practice.

The story is no different in the arts. The music held up as the epitome of freedom, jazz, and especially jazz improvisation, is disciplined if it's any good. The freedom is accepting, reveling in, and building on what comes out. Pianist, composer, and educator, Dr. Billy Taylor, talked about the saxophonist considered by some to be the greatest jazz improviser who ever lived:

> ... one of the major clichés [about jazz improvisation] is that the muse strikes, bam, lightning comes down and all of a sudden, ideas flow. They come if you, as Charlie Parker and other great artists have done, if you've prepared yourself.[12]

Artistic endeavors may seem un-analytical and nontechnical because the disciplines and constraints are difficult for most folks to identify with or because it's hard to describe them in common language and experience—even for the artist. Yet lack of shared understanding and experience hardly stops people from believing that, for one example, quantum mechanics is analytical, even though it is perhaps the weirdest and least intuitive discovery of all time. We simply trust that quantum particle physics is analytical and technical.

Probability Explains Levels

Innovation from great eureka acts is unlikely because too many factors must be right. Triangulation through trial and error at low levels is much more probable: making connections, seeing patterns, testing against external reality, and constantly destroying the weak, unfit solutions until fit solutions, *innovations,* emerge. The likelihood of the Intel leaders waking up one day and envisioning and planning the detailed features of a new multihundred-billion-dollar CPU business was low. The probability of Intel solving lower-level issues like factory expansion costs or how to convince investors was much higher, and these issues required many generations of still lower-level and local thought and trial and error. The likelihood of Henry Ford envisioning and planning his mature Model T manufacturing process in a short time was low. The likelihood of Ford making one small innovation after another over time, driven by his strategy rule, was high.

Probability also explains why so many new developments are built upon foundations that are co-opted from structures and technologies that already exist, sometimes called *exaptation.* Ford co-opted parts of the assembly line and then evolved it further. The iPhone co-opted much of the architecture of the iPad. Everything in evolutionary systems has predecessors.

Darwinian evolution and creativity and innovation in any domain are rooted in probability and speed. Destruction is the crux of creativity because the probability of judging correctly that something is wrong at low levels is far greater than the probability of judging that it is right. Probability also explains why more is learned from failure than success. Success requires many factors to be right and it's hard to discern which is key; failure requires only one factor to be wrong. (Because the probability of seeing what is unfit grows as we dig deeper into lower levels and internalize, does it suggest that the most creative work occurs unconsciously?)

Don't Humans Have Goals and Orchestrators?

Now, it is obvious that humans have goals and intentionality, that we to varying degrees can see and predict some aspects of the future and orchestrate achievement of aspirations. Humans have evolved the ability to use the adaptive mechanism unconsciously and consciously. People can think abstractly and ponder different futures and options for shaping ideas, behaviors, and physical entities. Because the mind is a complex adaptive system, we can exert stressors on variations in our minds. We can imagine the implications of actions, imagine possible cause and effect, eventually leading to the ability to synthesize and generalize information from trial and error and systematic experimentation. Humans have evolved purpose.

It is the next idea, behavior, or physical entity that is uncertain. Any claim to foresee the next innovation and how to achieve it is only a belief, especially since it is difficult to predict an environment we don't control. Only in hindsight does one imagine that the innovation was grasped instantly. The next improvement in Intel's understanding of the potential for a CPU business, or a better way to improvise in jazz, depended on capturing variations whose fitness was not yet understood until tested repeatedly by environmental stressors.

Therefore, we create plans, visions, and ways to orchestrate to help us navigate and test the future, but they are always provisional. There is a huge difference between planning the future and exploring the future with plans, as embodied in the adage, "plans are useless, but planning is essential." What's more, the more predictable and plannable a future is, the less potential it holds. Death and taxes? Sure, we will all die, but this is not useful information for creating an advantage because (most) people know it. Life expectancy, however, is less predictable, yet more valuable information. The sales rate of a commodity product is more predictable than the rate of a new product that has new functionality, and therefore more growth potential.

Implications—Framework design for Emergence

The emergent approach aims to align the theory and practice of frameworks and their strategies with the dynamics of adaptive systems. This does not mean starting from scratch. Existing practice reflects adaptive mechanisms to varying degrees, perhaps more by intuition at times than formal methods. As Nassim Taleb said, "We have been unconsciously exploiting antifragility [i.e., adaptability] in practical life and, consciously, rejecting it—particularly in intellectual life."[13] The aim is to go further, make adaptation deeper and habitual, and eliminate those practices that stifle the emergence of purposeful change and innovation.

A key to making the transition to an adaptive view is recognizing that innovation is not something you "do," it is an emergent outcome of disciplined low-level work. Innovation is not a technique or a target to be contrasted with just improving or being operational. You can target new products and services versus improve the design and manufacture of those you have, but both require innovation—creating new capability.

Despite not starting from scratch, it's a daunting change to make. We are used to direct forces: smack the $%#& out of a golf ball with a given initial velocity, launch angle, and atmospheric conditions, and the ball flies in a known way—as given by Isaac Newton's equation of motion: $a = F/m$. More force, *more steam!* leads to more acceleration. But we have seen that adaptive systems are different. Instead of direct forces pushing change and innovation to the fore, the less fit are destroyed by the forces, the stressors of the environment, leaving the more fit as the last standing. This mechanism feels passive because we don't get more acceleration by simply swinging harder. It's difficult to let go of the leadership paradigm of planning the future and then swinging harder and harder to meet or beat the projections.

One last point, just because an outcome is bad doesn't mean the dynamics of the change were not governed by the workings of adaptive systems. Similarly, there is no alternative to Newton's laws of motion in the (nonrelativistic) mechanical world. If a golfer hits the ball into the water, it doesn't mean Newton's law was not governing the flight of the ball. There is no alternative to Newton's law for bad golfers or good golfers who lose their discipline.

CHAPTER 3

The Killer Problems of Change and Innovation

Chapter 2 concluded that change and innovation emerge at high levels from disciplined work and constraint at low levels. Aspirations—the high-level desired outcomes—cannot be managed or achieved directly, and the actions at low levels don't need to look anything like the high-level results they cause. So, how do we work at low levels to achieve high-level aspirations? How exactly does strategy work? And how are plans, metrics, and tactics used? We need answers to these questions so we can design frameworks.

The answers come from a model of complex adaptive systems using a particular type of *influence diagram*. The model reveals a set of observations that describe four intrinsic impediments to purposeful change and innovation, which we will call the *killer problems of change and innovation*. These limitations are inherent to all adaptive systems, and each of the designed framework components (aspiration, plans, strategy, tactics, and metrics) plays a role in overcoming them; in other words, a role to *solve* the killer problems. What is discovered is that strategy as a central rule is the most important framework component because it is the fullest solution.

The Influence Diagram

Influence diagrams visualize the possible decisions and actions connected to a given aspiration. Ours is a simplified version of diagrams used in *Decision Analysis*, sometimes called *Decision and Risk Analysis*,[1] and is loosely related to Six Sigma trees, cause-and-effect fishbones (Ishikawa diagrams), game theory trees (though they work oppositely), structural equation models, and the grids used in the neural networks of artificial intelligence. In all cases, the diagrams reveal influences on outcomes. We aim to also reveal which decisions and actions we are free to take.

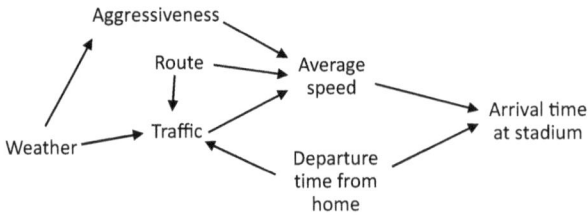

Figure 3.1 A simple influence diagram for arriving at Barabati stadium

Figure 3.1 is a simple example showing the actions needed to achieve the aspiration of arriving at Barabati stadium by car at 10:00 for a cricket match. The diagram shows the influences on when you will arrive. Each element in the diagram can both influence and be influenced by others. Your arrival time is determined by your average speed and when you leave home. Of these two influences, you are probably free to choose when you leave, but you are not free to choose your average speed. You can *influence* your average speed by choosing the route and how aggressively to drive, but the weather and traffic also influence your average speed and are completely outside your control. You can reduce the probability of experiencing traffic by taking certain routes and leaving at different times, but no matter what you do, your arrival time is *always* uncertain.

Technical geeks would say that an influence diagram determines the *independent variables* needed to achieve a *dependent variable*—the Xs needed to achieve a Y. The dependent variable is often called the *objective function*. In the Barabati example, the objective function is when you will arrive. Your aspiration to arrive at the stadium at 10:00 is a specific value of the objective function. Influence diagrams don't say which independent variables to choose; you need a framework with a strategy for that. Influence diagrams identify the independent variables and tell you how those variables interact and constrain your decisions and actions. Without this knowledge, it is difficult to make choices.

To illustrate the killer problems of adaptive systems, we will use a more detailed example of a bike shop. The idea is that you will open a bike shop and create frameworks for evolving it. Though a shop may not seem sophisticated enough to illustrate the impediments facing leaders; it provides enough realism without unnecessary complication. Also, the conclusions drawn will apply to any system. But be clear, the shop is a simplified illustration only—not advice nor a study of the biking industry.

Launching Your Bike Shop

Let's start with some information about your aspiration to be a bike shop owner: You simply love biking and everything associated with it. When people bike instead of drive, it is good for their health and the environment, they save money, and biking is fun for young and old. Your friends in the enthusiast biking community already rely on you for advice on repairs and equipment set up techniques and admire your knowledge of biking innovations. Money is not what drives you; the cash to live decently and drama free is good enough. What you value is having a profession in the biking world. Discovering new biking technologies invigorates you, as does gaining respect from the biking community for your commitment.

Why is launching a bike shop realistic? You believe new demographic groups, including commuters, are becoming more aware of the benefits of biking. You hope these folks will supplement the loyal enthusiast community and will pay for quality, performance, innovative designs, and an ongoing service relationship. The two existing bike retailers in your town, the mega discount variety store and the mom-and-pop shop that serves family buyers, don't satisfy all these values, leaving a niche. Framework 3.1 is how your beliefs are depicted in the framework language presented in Chapter 1.

🚲 Bike Shop Framework 3.1 *At the beginning*	
Values	Love every aspect of biking and believe it is good for society
Aspirations	Vision: Happiness by working in the biking world Goals: (1) respect from peers; (2) sufficient cash flow Mission: Launch a bike shop
Diagnosis	Proposition: Can provide the innovations and quality that existing stores cannot External constraints: TBD (to be determined) Scenarios: Increasing awareness of health and environmental benefits will drive new demographics to biking who will pay for innovations. Bottlenecks: TBD
Strategy	
Key tactics, plans, & metrics	

What must be done to turn this shop into reality? You need financing and accounting. There are decisions to make regarding what and how to sell, the shop location, and which suppliers to use. Advertising, pricing, look and feel and name of the shop, appearance and behavior of the employees, after-sales service, and return policies are all important to success. You need a sense of the income to expect and how much money can be invested. You are new to business, so you use an influence diagram to make sense of these decisions.

✍ Constructing the Bike Shop Influence Diagram

To construct an influence diagram, work backwards from any aspiration—vision, mission, or goal—always asking, "What information would I need to know to calculate the element?" (We won't calculate anything; it is just a heuristic.) Then, keep working backwards until reaching actionable elements, always aiming to capture the complete set of influences. Even when starting in the wrong place or making mistakes, if you stick with this simple technique, you will find yourself correcting as you go. Not only is this an excellent influence diagram quality, but a fine example of emergence from discipline at low levels too.

So, let's create a diagram to determine the actions for achieving your bike shop aspirations (for a slightly more detailed version, see *Bike Shop Diagram* {web/supplement}). Because it is simpler, we will begin with cash flow. What would you need to know to calculate your cash flow in any period? You'd need to know that cash flow is *influenced* by costs, revenue, and tax rate as in Figure 3.2 (A). (Note, we are orienting the diagram from right to left, but any direction will work. Also, for our purposes, there's no need to capture the time-value of money nor distinguish between CAPEX and cost.)

To determine your costs and revenue, you would continue working backward as in Figure 3.2 (B). Your total cost is equal to the sum of the various elements of cost (you could break these down differently) and the revenue is influenced by volume, which is equal to the number of bikes and accessories you sell, the hours of billable service you perform, and the prices obtained for each of these offerings.

OK, progress. We have converted cash flow, the aspiration on the right-hand side (RHS) of the diagram, to elements that are closer to

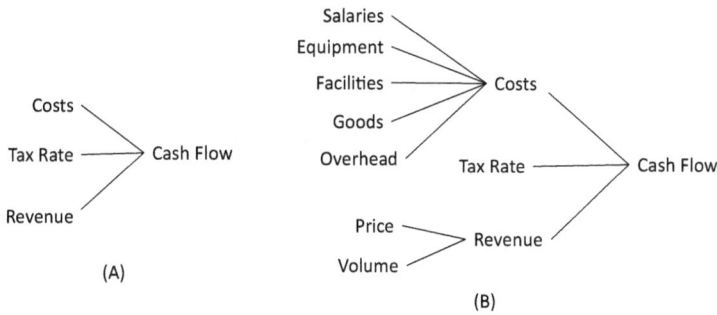

Figure 3.2 Starting the influence diagram

actions you can take. You can't choose how much cash flow to have, but you can choose to some extent what prices you will set for products and what facilities to rent. But before moving further to the left to get to more actionable influences, notice a few things about the diagram:

As we work to the left-hand side (LHS), the number of elements grows geometrically, and it would be easy to expand the diagram with another level of granularity. For example, Figure 3.3 is how the diagram would look for the price element alone. If taken out several levels to the left, influence diagrams take on the characteristic shape shown in Figure 3.4. The tip of the influence diagram icon can be thought of as the aspiration side, or the emergent side, and the open side can be thought of as the action and decision side.

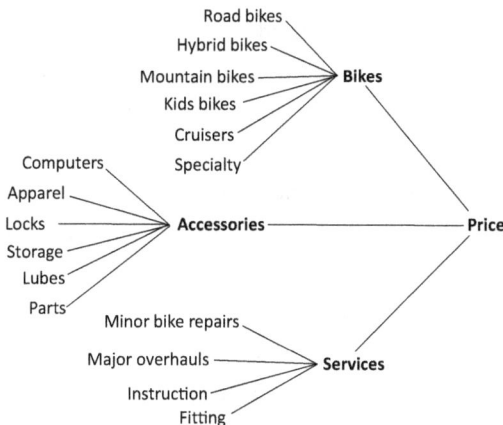

Figure 3.3 The categories of products and services for which prices need to be set

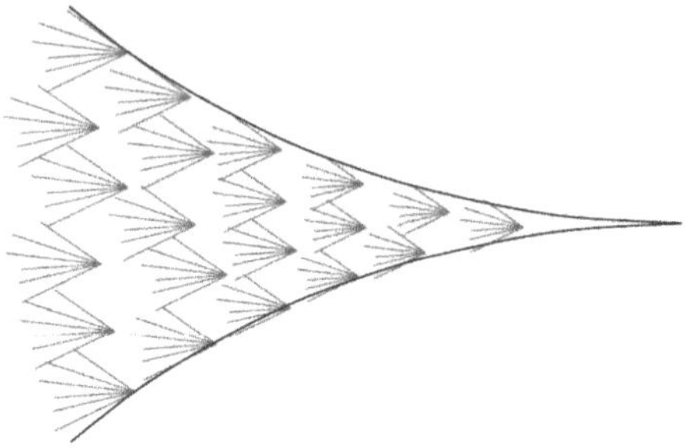

Figure 3.4 The characteristic shape of the influence diagram

In practice, influences are aggregated; this keeps the diagram from expanding ridiculously. The price diagram in Figure 3.3, for example, could have listed every individual bike that the shop sells (i.e., *red mountain bike model no. 1833-97* would be just one item). This level of detail would require hundreds of branches.

Next, note that the diagram is still simple and orderly. Each element is a sum or product of other elements (e.g., revenue is a function only of price and volume), and no element influences more than one other element (e.g., price and volume influence only revenue). Life, however, is not simple and orderly. First, the items to add next, as in Figure 3.5, influence more than one higher-level element; your choice of offerings, including which bikes, parts, accessories, and services to sell, influences both the cost and the revenue branches. (From here on, the diagram is simplified by not drawing connecting lines between every item in a grouping.)

The products and services offered are not the only influences on price, volume, and costs. The look and feel of the shop, the location and hours of the shop, and communications like advertising, promotions, and website design all play a role as shown in Figure 3.6. Just adding these influences increases complexity and uncertainty in several new ways.

Lines cross. Most elements influence more than one value. Advertising and promotion influence both revenue and cost. In fact, almost every choice from this point on will influence both revenue and cost.

Influences flow backward. Lines are now directional. If you sell a wide variety of bikes, you will need a larger shop with greater floor space to show them. Even the tax rate gets a reverse arrow because higher cash flow might put you in a higher tax bracket.

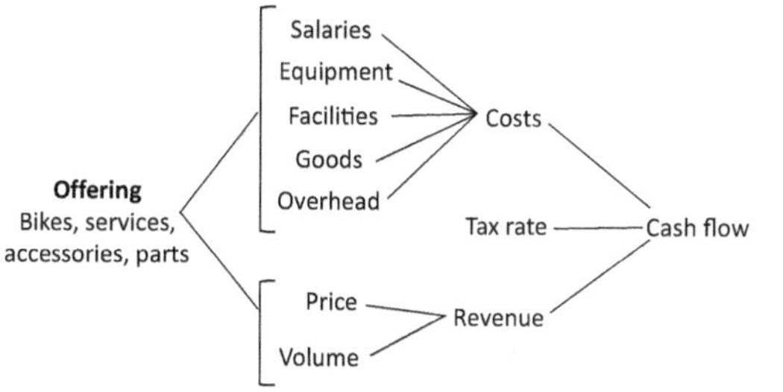

Figure 3.5 *The offering you choose influences both costs and revenue*

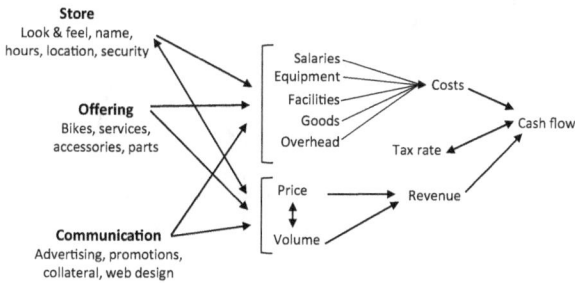

Figure 3.6 *Store characteristics, the offering, and communication methods all influence both costs and revenue*

Lines point up and down. That you cannot set prices and volume independently is illustrated using a double arrow line that shows that price and volume are linked. You cannot change price without some expectation of a change in volume.

Next, consider the other aspect of your aspiration, respect from the biking community. Because respect is subjective, it is trickier to represent than cash flow, but it is no less important. Respect might be influenced by elements you've already captured, like offering variety and cash flow success. Respect will also depend on your service levels, so add that element too (Figure 3.7).

Finally, you need one other crucial class of influences, *the outside world*, including the actions of competitors, which, of course, greatly influence your ability to achieve prices and volumes. Outside influences also include factors like local and national economies. So, add the multiple outside influences as a single element showing they can influence broadly

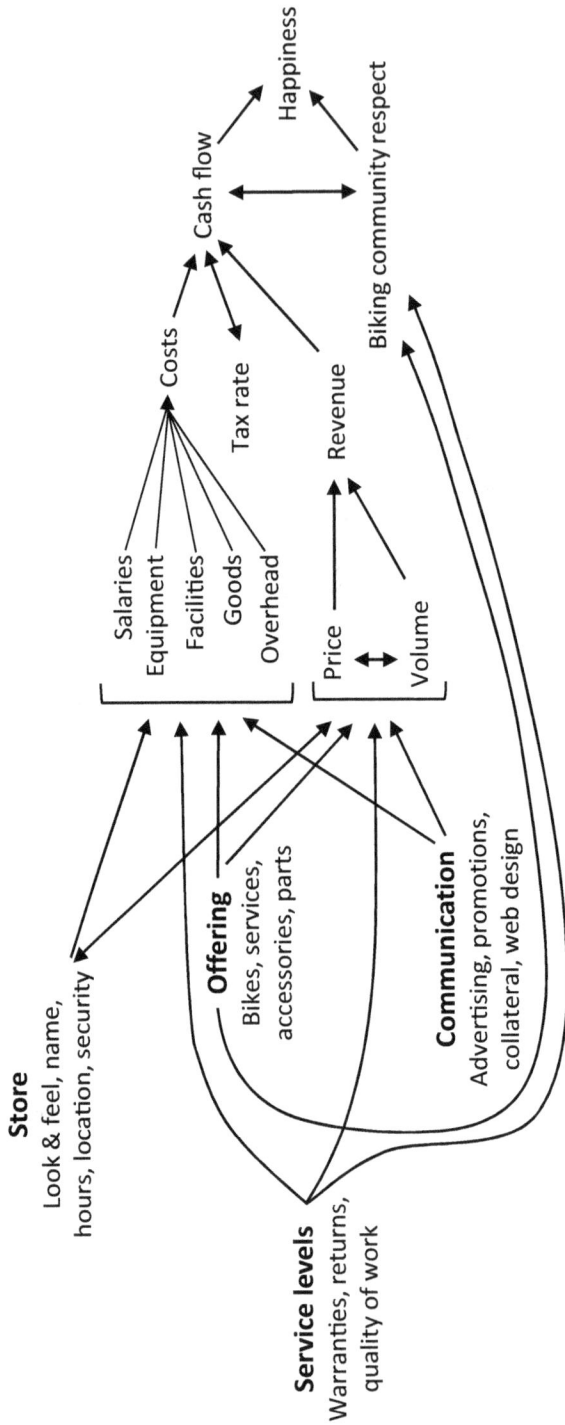

Figure 3.7 Adding the influences on gaining respect from the biking community

(you may also influence competitors), and add a few other missing influences, such as employee policies, inventory levels, borrowing, and the provider choices of banking and computer systems—without even bothering to show in detail how they connect, and when you are done, you get Figure 3.8, something that begins to look as messy as real life.

Influence diagrams can apply to any field of endeavor, even the arts. For instance, see Figure 3.9 for the aspiration of composing a successful piece of music. This diagram applies to what people commonly call classical music. You know, Mozart, Beethoven, and Brahms—those cats. For simplicity, the music diagram omits the connections between elements, but it illustrates the three main features seen for the bike shop diagram nonetheless: the number of choices grows quickly, they are hierarchical in nature, and there are complicated associations between elements.

The Killer Problems and Why You Can't Always Get What You Want

The final Bike Shop diagram, Figure 3.8, has enough detail to reveal the killer problems of change and innovation, the limitations that make taking the right decisions and actions difficult.

Killer 1: The Sheer Number of Decisions and Actions. Your bike shop aspiration on the RHS includes only respect and sufficient cash (or one goal if you want to take it all as happiness). To achieve these, you must make decisions on at least the 40 elements in the influence diagram on the LHS, and this is after minimizing the number of elements by aggregation. Further, the connections between the choices on the LHS and the aspirations on the RHS are complicated with many pathways, and new decisions will appear over time as well. Imagine the number of choices in large companies, governments, the military, or a deep endeavor like scientific discovery or creating art. You can't possibly spend the time to have a unique thought process for each. Further, whatever method is used to reduce the number of decisions must make them all consistent and congruent, other-

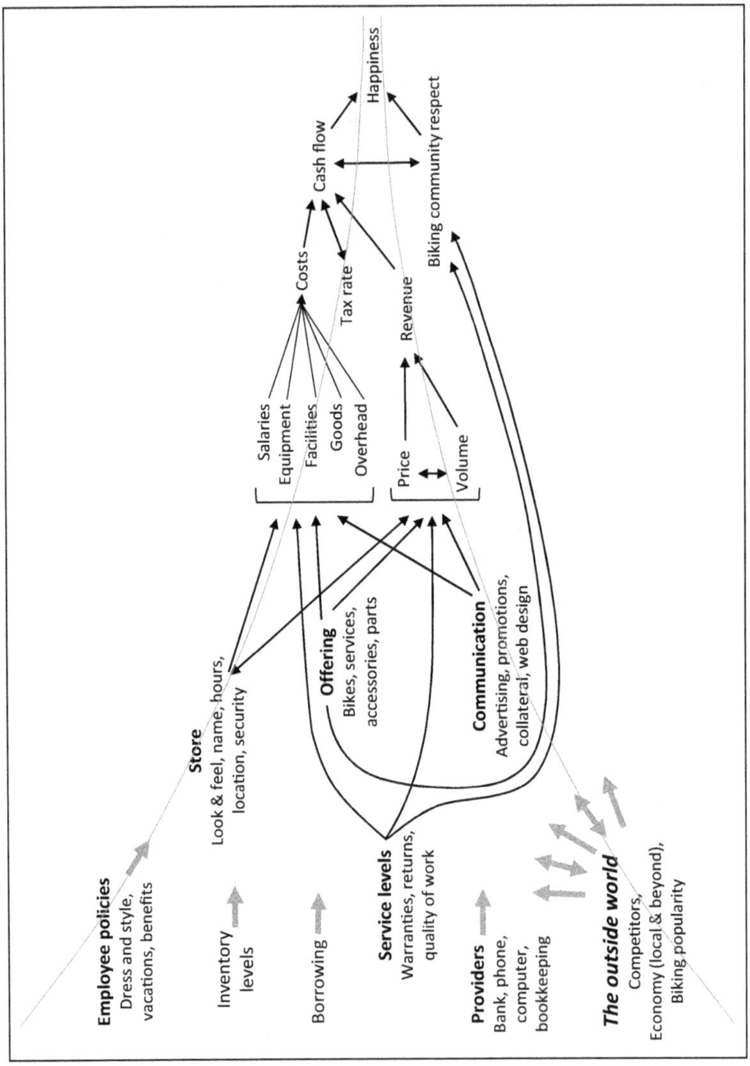

Figure 3.8 Final Influence diagram for actions and decisions needed to launch a bike shop

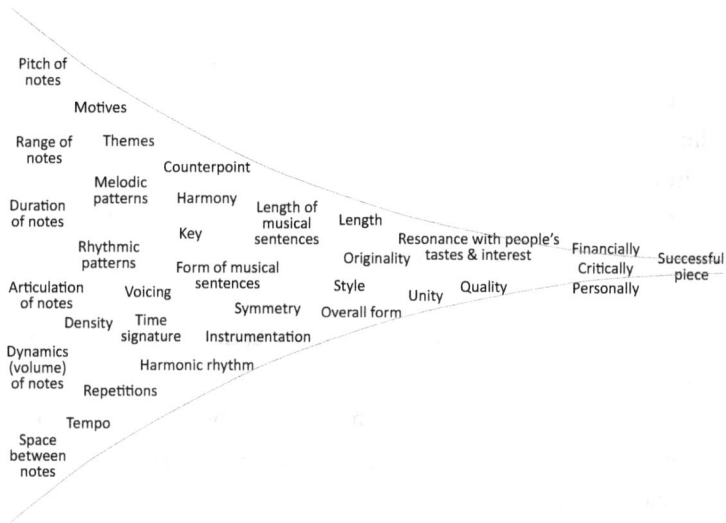

Pitch of
notes

Motives

Range of   Themes
notes
                 Counterpoint
        Melodic
Duration patterns   Harmony
of notes   Length of
            Key   musical   Length
    Rhythmic   sentences   Resonance with people's   Financially
    patterns   Originality tastes & interest   Critically   Successful
         Form of musical   piece
Articulation   Voicing sentences   Style   Quality   Personally
of notes   Symmetry Overall form Unity
     Density   Time
            signature Instrumentation
Dynamics
(volume)   Harmonic rhythm
of notes   Repetitions

     Tempo
Space
between
notes

Figure 3.9 Influence diagram for composing successful music

wise, they may work against each other. For instance, it would be of little use to stock high-end, specialty bikes and accessories if your bike shop approach is to sell high volumes. You would not choose 9:00 to 5:00 shop hours if working professionals are your targeted customer base. You cannot lower or raise prices and not expect a change in the number of units sold.

Killer 2: Time Delay. There is a time delay between taking actions on the LHS and the impact on the RHS. How long it takes for actions to lead to results may be days, months, or years. For your bike shop, good service and quality products require time for word of mouth to have impact. Leaders may think they can avoid this time delay—but this is wishful thinking. The waiting period may be reduced, but never avoided. The severe implication of the delay is the difficulty of judging decisions and actions when impact can't be known until the sometimes-distant future. During the time delay, conditions will almost always change to some extent, and the diagnosis may become invalid.

Killer 3: Unknown, Uncontrollable, and Changing Influences. The influence diagram shows how achieving aspirations is influenced by the actions of entities outside your control and by forces outside everyone's control—this alone makes change a nightmare. That you cannot know all influences, and that they change with time makes it worse. If a superior shop opens down the street, if cultural forces render biking less popular, if the quality of inexpensive bikes that mega variety stores sell improves dramatically, or any number of other scenarios occur, you may fail.

Killer 4: What Matters Most is the Least Actionable. Achieving the aspirations on the RHS of the diagram is your definition of success—what matters. But the RHS is not actionable. You cannot simply choose to have respect from the biking community, sufficient cash flow, and ultimately, happiness. (In Six Sigma parlance, "You cannot manage the Ys.") The RHS is not actionable because each influence diagram element depends on every influence that precede it, and the further to the right, the more this is true. To choose bike shop revenue, for instance, you would need to correctly choose every influence encircled in Figure 3.10. The probability of doing so is low. As you move to the LHS

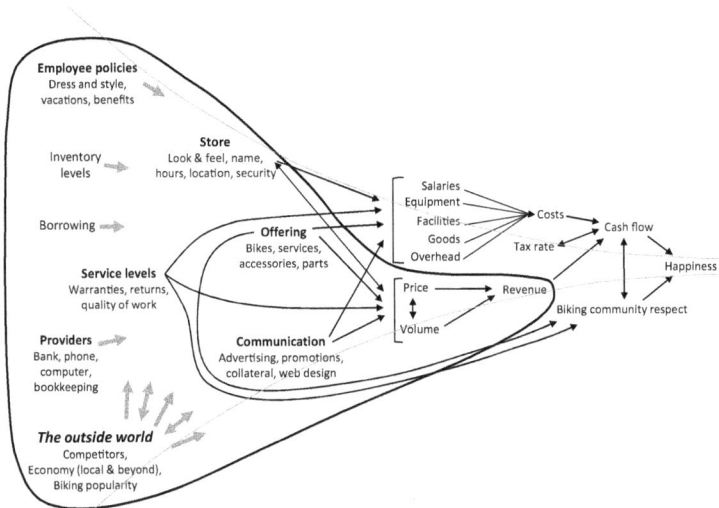

Figure 3.10 To know the revenue element, all its influences must be known; therefore, revenue is not a free choice

side, however, each element is influenced by fewer and fewer elements, so you become freer to make choices. What vacation plan to offer employees, or what accessories to stock are much more independent choices than choosing revenue. But there is a dilemma on the LHS too. The three previous killer problems showed just how difficult it is to make these decisions on the LHS to achieve the aspirations.

Taken as a group, the killer problems help explain why the world does not conform to wishes, why it is hard to lead, manage, govern, command, and why it is so hard to purposefully change and innovate to get what you want (or what you think you want). And remember that even maintaining what you have requires change because the world around you is changing. Though derived from your modest bike shop venture, the limitations apply generally because the influence diagram of any endeavor will show elements growing dramatically in number when working backward from aspirations, and those elements will have complex interactions.

The killer problems can be summarized as in Figure 3.11 showing that what you are free to do and what matters are at odds with each other. Richard Rumelt, 40 years ago, intuited this result when analyzing strategy methods. He likened the dilemma to a "pernicious

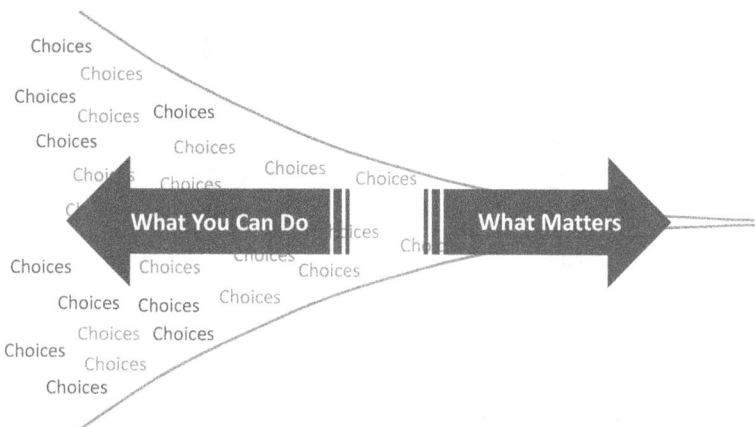

Figure 3.11 The conflict between what matters and what you can actually do; Rumelt's "pernicious variation of Heisenberg's principle"

variation of Heisenberg's principle,"[2] where "one can apparently gain concreteness only through a narrowing of scope, and breadth of vision is purchased at the price of essential detail." In other words, when we look at the aspiration on the RHS of the influence diagram—the full breadth of what matters—the decisions and actions on the LHS are a blur. When we look at the concrete decisions and actions we can take on the LHS, then the aspirations become a blur. Maybe these are the killer problems of life.

The Connection with Emergence and Levels

Now we can see how the conclusion drawn from the influence diagram align with the theory of adaptive emergence. Figure 3.12 shows that if we orient the influence diagram upward and compare it with Figure 2.3, the disciplined low-level work described in Chapter 2 is, in fact, "what we can do" on the LHS of the influence diagram. Likewise, the creativity and innovation—the emergent result—is what matters on the RHS of the influence diagram.

Achieving your aspirations requires innovating—creating new capability. But you can't directly innovate. Henry Ford's revolution of the auto

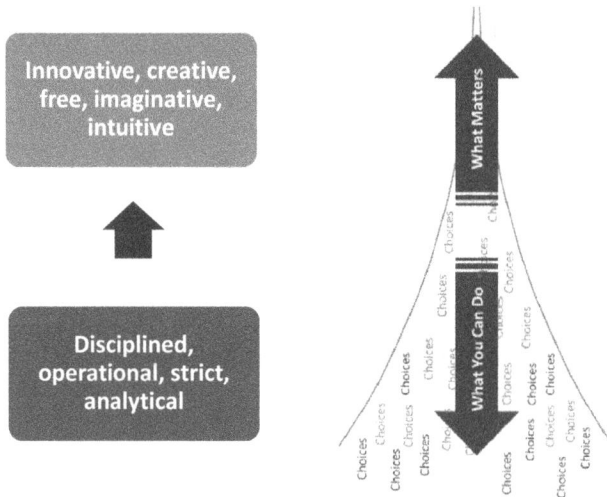

Figure 3.12 Comparison of emergence of innovation from low-level disciplines (Chapter 2) and the emergence of achieving aspirations from what you are free to do

industry and Apple's iPhone resulted from countless disciplined decisions and actions on the LHS. Excellent safety performance emerges from countless decisions and actions to stomp out at-risk behaviors on the LHS. A composer cannot just choose to write successful piece of music, all they can do is decide where sounds should occur on the LHS. The only way for innovations to emerge is to have a guiding light for making the myriad low-level choices on the LHS plus the discipline to follow the light. This is where the framework and its strategy comes in.

Solving the Killer Problems

The purpose of a framework is to solve the killer problems and provide a way to make the choices on the LHS to achieve the aspirations on the RHS (Figure 3.13). While the killer problems in complex adaptive systems can never be completely overcome, the *best possible solution* is attained if framework components meet three requirements:

1. **Free choice:** The solution to the killer problems must be a free choice. Any solution needs to operate on the LHS of the influence diagram because only there are you free to take decisions and actions as given in killer problem 4. And to be clear, you are free to choose what aspirations appear on the RHS: happiness, $12,000 per month

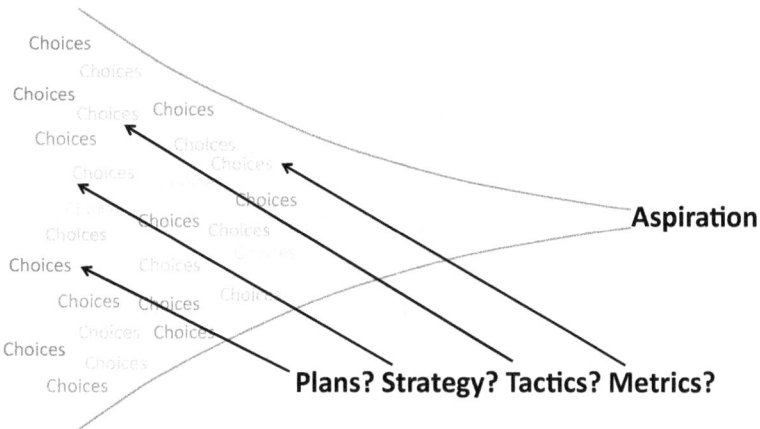

Figure 3.13 How does each designed component of the framework enable making choices on the left-hand side of the influence diagram?

free cash flow, respect from peers, invent a new bike, become a bike shop goddess, or anything else you want or can imagine. What you are not free to choose is the achievement of these aspirations.

2. **Real-time Guidance:** There must be some way to judge whether you are adhering to your solution *before* the "results are in"; *a priori*. Adaptation requires real-time stressors. Killer problem 2, the time delay between action and results, is one reason. Would you wait for bike shop results before choosing the actions you will take to get the results? Sounds crazy, yet this is essentially what managing by results suggests doing. Without guidance at the time the actions are taken, everyone must guess or intuit the right thing to do. Killer problem 3 also demands real-time guidance. If, after implementation begins, unanticipated events caused by outside agents necessitate a framework change, you need guidance while there is still time to make a change. This crucial requirement of real-time guidance puts an enormous burden on any prospective solution.

3. **Unify:** Any of the countless actions or decisions on the LHS can be taken freely. Killer problem 1, however, says there are simply too many decisions to allow an individualized thought process and a method that aggregates choices is needed to make them consistent and coherent. Therefore, the solution must focus and *unify* the myriad low-level choices of decisions and actions on the LHS, making them consistent with each other in the service of achieving aspirations.

The next three chapters show how the design components of the framework—aspirations, plans, strategy and tactical rules, and metrics—fare against these three requirements. In other words, what each component offers to solve them for change and innovation. While each component has an important role (else, you wouldn't have 'em), here's where we will see why strategy as the central rule has the greatest power. And that without this strategy rule, it is impossible to properly choose plans, tactics, and metrics.

And again, the killer problems will never be completely solved because uncertainties will always exist. Diagnoses will always be flawed. There will always be limits to the perception of reality in the internal and external worlds in which you operate and live. Perception is limited by skill and bias, and there is never unlimited time. Even the ability to know one's own values is limited. All that can be done is make the best possible design, then remain sensitive to anything new (including new insight), and modify the design as needed. With discipline, skills can be improved. The more capable the organization becomes, the more it can overcome the killer problems of change and innovation, and the more creative it can be.

CHAPTER 4

The Limitations of Aspirations, Plans, and Metrics

While three of the designed framework components—aspirations, plans and projections (simulations), and metrics—contribute to the solution to the killer problems of change and innovation, each has limitations. None fully meet the free choice, real-time guidance, and unification requirements, which explains why managing only by aspirations, plans, and metrics leads to limited success. We will also see that neither granularizing aspirations nor shrinking the time horizon can overcome these limitations. Understanding the limitations sets up the need for a central rule.

Aspirations Against the Killer Problems

Evaluating aspirations against the first two requirements of solving killer problems is easy. As said in Chapter 3, you can choose any vision, mission, or goal but it can never be a free choice for them to come true, nor can they provide real-time guidance. Achieving aspirations is a future event, and it is impossible to adhere to a future event.

What of unification, the third requirement? The bike-shop influence diagram was created by working backward from the aspirations of "cash flow" and "respect from peers." This means every potential action and decision in the diagram was already unified by these aspirations. But using the information that aspirations provide again to unify decisions and actions adds nothing new. It's kind of like saying that the method for being successful is to be successful. Who would ever suggest such an idea? Yet, when systems get complicated, and outside events batter the organization, and backs are against the wall, leaders can fall into "just get results." They flee to the safety of managing by aspirations. This and the lack of free choice and real-time guidance of aspirations is why aspirations are easily abused as a leadership tool.

Plans Against the Killer Problems

Plans and any other feed-forward simulation like projections represent achieving something in the future, and therefore, like aspirations, cannot be a free choice (the arguments about plans apply to subgoals as well). However, there is a range. The smaller the plan, the closer to the left-hand side (LHS) of the influence diagram, the fewer decisions and actions required to achieve it, the less of the influence diagram needs to be specified, and the more of a free choice the plan becomes. So, for example, a plan to achieve a given amount of revenue by some date means specifying every circled influence in Figure 3.10 and is hardly more of a free choice than cash flow or happiness and therefore just as uncertain an outcome. A plan to put a given number of bikes into inventory by some date takes in little of the influence diagram and is therefore much more of a free choice. The outcome of an army commander's plan to capture an air-strip is much less certain than the plan to refuel Charlie Company's vehicles at Rendezvous Point 3. Neither is a given but refueling needs less specification. Refueling is much further to the left of the influence diagram, along with all the other decisions needed to capture the airstrip.

The ability of plans to offer real-time guidance is judged using the same logic used to judge free choice. The further a plan is to the left-hand side (LHS) of the influence diagram, generally the shorter the time required to achieve it. It is more feasible for the Battalion commander to know in real time whether she is achieving the plan to refuel Charlie Company's vehicles at Rendezvous Point 3, than it is to know in real time whether she is taking the airstrip. She can audit the location of vehicles and fuel tankers in near real time, but auditing whether she is taking the airstrip is dependent on so many more events, many out of her control.

What of the ability of plans to unify? The further plans are to the LHS of the influence diagram, the fewer decisions and actions they unify. By setting a rendezvous time and place, the actions of both the fuel tanker platoon and Charlie Company are unified into a single design; they are *coordinated*, at least for the time it takes to complete that task. But this is just a small part of the "plan" to take the airstrip that contains many more choices and is further to the RHS of the influence diagram and is essentially an aspiration.

We have again run into killer problem 4 and Rumelt's pernicious version of Heisenberg. The bigger a plan is the more it is like an aspiration and therefore the less of a free choice it is to achieve and the less real-time guidance it provides. Smaller plans toward the LHS of the influence diagram are more useful in frameworks because they are more free choice and give more real-time guidance. It is the specificity of smaller plans and goals that makes them wonderfully useful for coordination and, assessment. The price paid for moving to the LHS, however, is less unification, because small plans encompass less and less of the influence diagram. This describes the inherent limitation of plans (and subgoals) to solve the killer problems.

The limitation of plans as free choice is embedded in collective knowledge: Everyone has a plan until they get punched in the mouth (Mike Tyson, from Joe Louis). Life is what happens to you while you're busy making other plans (John Lennon). If you want to amuse God, tell her your plans (Proverb). The United States Army Operations Manual (FM-100-5) says, "No plan of operations can be projected with confidence much beyond the first encounter with the enemy's main force." It goes on to propose the use of "contingency plans" to correct this problem, including "branches … built into the basic plan [i.e., framework]—for changing the disposition, orientation, or direction of movement and also for accepting or declining battle." Yet how is the commander to know when to invoke these contingencies? Only a rule in the spirit of an if-then concept can tell her when.

The limitations of plans are true for projections. Strategists want projections about the high-level outcomes of the RHS of the influence diagram (e.g., profit or victories), yet these are the least certain. Because numerical projections are extremely specific about the future, they are even less able to unify.

Metrics Against the Killer Problems

The question of free choice is not applicable to metrics because you are free to measure anything you want. The question about metrics is whether they can provide real-time guidance and unification for solving the killer problems. The answer is that like plans, metrics have limited capability to do so. Metrics give feedback, at any point in time, about results of actions (within measurement error). But measurements of progress against the RHS of the diagram, that is, against aspirations, gives no information until the end of the endeavor. Only measurements of success against items toward the LHS give feedback closer to real time. And like plans, the closer the measurement is to the LHS, the less feedback you get about the unified set of actions. You can get quick feedback on whether you have stocked certain bikes in your shop, but you must wait to measure the strength of overall bike shop sales which is influence by most of the elements of the diagram.

There are, however, two metrics that can provide real-time guidance. One is measurement of adherence to a rule. You can know in real time if you are following the rule "double orders of *mountain bike model LVB-1770-1827* when forecast demand reaches 12 bikes per month." The other is measurement of deviations from your diagnosis. If you assume a scenario that competitors will not build new bike shops in your town, and they do, you can know this as soon as they start. We can label this added real-time capability as "limited+." (These two measurements are the adherence and foundation metrics in the Four-Station Dashboard in Chapter 18). Adhering to rules is part of execution (Chapter 9). Table 4.1 summarizes the limitations of aspirations, simulations, and metrics to meet the three requirements of a solution to the killer problems of change and innovation.

Table 4.1 The ability of designed framework components to meet the requirements of a solution to the killer problems

	Free choice?	Real-Time Guidance?	Unifying?
Aspirations	No	No	N/A
Plans and Projections	Limited	Limited	Limited
Metrics	N/A	Limited+	Limited

The Granularization Problem

Every attempt so far to get subgoals, plans, and metrics to be free choices and supply real-time guidance by moving to the LHS of the influence diagram came at the cost of unification—Rumelt's Heisenberg. A natural impulse for solving this loss of unification is to construct many subgoals (or plans and metrics) by flowdown, thereby making sure every facet of the business is covered, as in Figure 4.1. But the problem is that granularization does not solve unification, which is why strategy themes such as Figure 4.2 (and Figure 1.1 in Chapter 1), strategy maps derived from them, and OKRs (objectives and key results) generated by cascading goals down the organization are not strategy.

Granularization of the ultimate aspiration gives no information on the cross relationships between the themes and subthemes. Without guidance for doing otherwise, each functional silo in the organization is forced to think of their own framework independently. And the larger and more independent the functions, the more this can happen.

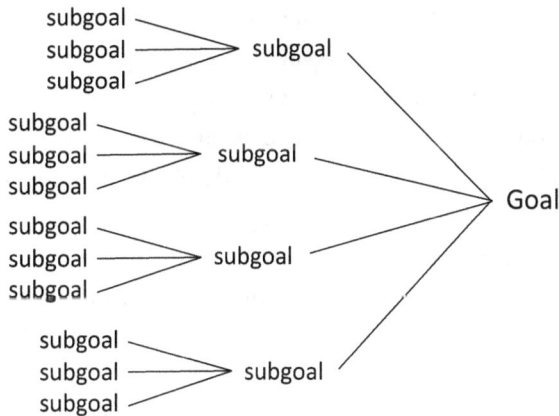

Figure 4.1 *Granularization of goals by flowdown and cascading down the organization*

Figure 4.2 *"Strategy" themes*

The influence diagram does not tell you what to do; it shows the influences on your aspiration and therefore the areas where you must take decisions and actions. Killer problem 1 stated that the many decisions and actions must be made in a coordinated way. In your bike shop, you could advertise expensive fancy bikes and at the same time stock cheap low-quality bikes. Each action might look great on its own yet fail together. Success requires the consistency of either advertising and stocking fancy bikes, or advertising and stocking inexpensive bikes. Such a requirement is a rule.

It's easy to see the ridiculousness of this bike shop action, but conflicts may not be as discernible in a large business. If manufacturing has a cost reduction mission, the best ways to meet it might be to limit resources for new product trials or to maximize rates of easy-to-produce products even though these products may not be crucial for marketing's growth mission. To enable functional organizations to support the aspiration of the overall company, leadership must supply guidance to each on how to make trade-offs. Likewise, a software company needs rules for managing the trade-off between marketing and the development team. Marketing may desire to announce upgrades early to keep customers from looking elsewhere. Development may want to delay announcing until those upgrades are sufficiently functional. Other company functions may also, totally unknowingly, choose goals that are good for their numbers if there is no guidance to do otherwise.

To achieve Michael Porter's and other strategists' demand that strategy create integration and "fit among company activities" (Chapter 1), there must be a rule. Granularization of the overall aspiration of the company cannot provide this information.

Granularization can lead to overconstraint too. If a business aspires to grow in Northern Africa, creating subgoals for each of ten countries makes perfect sense. Or even more granular: create ten different customer segments based on their buying patterns, then break them into small customer groups managed by individual salespeople, and so on. The list can contain supporting plans: set up a sales office in Tunisia by April 2025, design the sales brochures for Algeria, and hire two more salespeople in Mali. However, the more specific the description of each little goal and plan, the greater the constraint on the organization. Asking the Northern

African sales organization to sell a million units overall is less constraining than forcing them to sell 230 K units in Tunisia, 420 K in Mali, and 350 K in Algeria. An aggregate goal creates the freedom to sell wherever people want to buy. If there's good reason for forcing specific sales numbers in each country, fine, but the more granular the goals, the greater the potential to paralyze the organization with overspecification. There's also the potential for unwanted self-competition within the region.

The Shrinking the Time Problem

A second attempt to short-circuit the killer problems is the following thought process: if aspirations can't be made manageable by granulizing them into a zillion parts, instead shrink the period between setting and achieving them so that the time delay becomes inconsequentially small. If the diagnosis is that you need to sell 200 bikes per year, but the goal seems daunting, then shrink this to the seemingly more manageable 17 bikes a month, or four bikes a week (or, hey, 0.7 bikes a day). Unfortunately, shrinking the size of the aspiration, proportionately shrinks the time to achieve it, which means that these new shrunken goals give no new information.

Perhaps breaking a 10,000 meter race mentally into twenty 500 meter segments helps somewhat, but you still have to run 10,000 meters. Certainly, there is value to translating yearly sales goals into monthly or weekly goals for planning and coordination. In some cases, there can be hundreds of thousands or even millions of disparate items to produce, sell, and ship, which requires supply chain or operations science. But prorating sales goals over shorter periods supplies little guidance on how to get customers to buy.

A more damning fallacy with shrinking the task to shrink the needed time is that change requires a minimum time to emerge. It is impossible to eliminate the time it takes for word of mouth of the durability of expensive bikes to spread about town. It takes time for expected breakdowns *not* to occur. It takes time to train employees, for advertising to take hold, for customers to recognize and spread the word of superior service.

Every system has a characteristic time of change. People and organizations can shorten the time required for change by improving their capability through practice and adoption of techniques and tools. Leaders may coax more speed out of people by force of personality or by making tough demands, but they cannot eradicate the time of change. The greater the aspiration, the more systemic the change needs to be, the more time that is needed. In truly new endeavors—think of launching new technologies or creating new governmental policies—the time is unknown. How long should be expected for these changers to occur:

- Upgrade the capability of your workforce
- Develop a new product or a new product platform
- Reduce the cost structure of manufacturing by 20 percent
- Change the culture of a company
- Change people's minds about something of emotional importance to them
- See the success of investing in a stock
- Improve your golf handicap by two strokes
- Reduce the failure rate of a government agency
- Change the economy (imagine a president taking credit, or blame, after three months ...)

How long does a "transformation" take, if it's systemic, and a real one? Sure, you can have milestones and checkpoints, but there must be a guiding direction for the entire change.

It gets worse. The pace of change is rarely constant. One reason is the time needed for incubation. A slow change at first may be followed by a more rapid change later. The system may be changing as new connections are made through trial-and-error and teaching and learning, but results may not be visible at first. In fact, performance usually degrades at the start of a change program.

Think of personal experiences in sports, playing a musical instrument, dancing, shooting a gun, or any skill. Say your golf swing needs improvement. You get a coach who finds flaws and develops with you an alternative swing to correct these flaws. What will be the initial result? You will stink because you destabilize parts of the system (you, the club, and the ball.) Depending on your abilities, effort, and how big a change was made, it will take some time before your game gets back to its original level and then additional time for it to improve beyond that. Now imagine the time delay required for a huge organizational or systemic change in business, military, or government, not to mention the time needed for individuals to change a life habit. To make true systemic change, there's no way around buying the time needed to make it happen.

The investment curve, Figure 4.3 illustrates the concept of getting worse before getting better. Though it is based on the idea of spending money to make money, it can be used to illustrate the "debit" incurred when changing a system to improve or create something new.

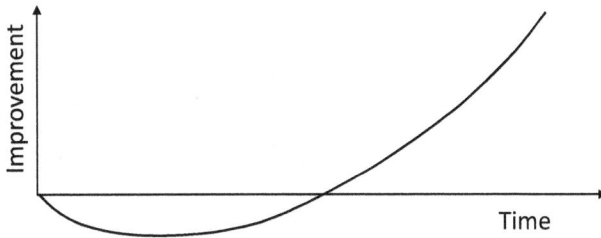

Figure 4.3 The investment curve

CHAPTER 5

The Creative Power of Strategy as a Central Rule

Chapter 4 demonstrates that goals, plans, and metrics have a limited capacity to meet the three requirements of a solution to the killer problems of change and innovation in complex adaptive systems—free choice, real-time guidance, and unification. This chapter shows that strategy, the central rule, can meet all three. This ability makes the strategy the most powerful component of a framework for bridging the gap between what ultimately matters and what you can actually do and why adherence to the strategy rule is the key to adaptation. Let's start by clarifying how strategy works, that is, how it functions to solve the killer problems.

How Strategy Functions

As stated in Chapter 1, a strategy rule is a self-imposed constraint. Some would call it a type of *enabling* constraint. How strategy functions is revealed by seeing its interaction with two other constraints: external constraints, and most crucially, the bottleneck constraint. All constraints limit the range of allowed actions, what differentiates them is their source and impact. The external and bottleneck constraints must be discovered and articulated as part of your diagnosis. Self-imposed constraints obviously must be designed.

The Bottleneck Constraint

Every hero needs a villain. If the strategy rule is the hero of our story, then the villain is the bottleneck. For an aspiration to be achieved, the strategy must win against the bottleneck—the strategy must *bust* it. Bottlenecks are constraints in the way of achieving aspirations; they are *rate-limiting* to making progress, as the diameter of the neck that limits the flow of a liquid. As said in the introduction, "bottleneck" is used generically to represent not only choke points, but barriers, obstacles, or impediments. Bottlenecks are inherent to all dynamic systems, whether mechanical or human, because there is always a limit to the speed and quality of change and innovation. They are core to Rumelt's and Sull and Eisenhardt's methods (Chapter 1; note the latter do not necessarily focus on the dominant bottleneck), and they are the "constraints" of Goldratt's *Theory of Constraints*[1]. While there are many bottlenecks in a system, there is a dominant bottleneck to achieving the aspiration, as Goldratt argued. Unless the dominant bottleneck is addressed, the system does not improve.

Bottlenecks vary widely. The easiest to diagnosis is lack of tangible assets like money, technology, and geographic presence. Diagnosing intangibles like poor brand association or what's wrong with a value proposition is harder. There are people bottlenecks too, including skill level and ability to diagnose as well as emotional barriers like fear, over-aggressiveness, complacency, and lack of motivation. Even a bad framework with conflicting or complicated policies or bad reward systems can be the bottleneck as can uncertainty about scenarios.

External Constraints

External constraints are imposed by agents outside your system, such as a boss, the law, or even tradition. In a corporation, external constraints can come from the outside world or from inside the company. The boss can define your span of authority, limits on spending, markets or technologies to avoid, or core values never to be violated. Whether external constraints can be changed should be questioned, but recognize you cannot change them unilaterally; it takes negotiation (or revolution), and perhaps a framework.

External constraints can be conceived as "rules of the game." Without rules, there are no games. Chess is specified by the 8 × 8 grid, the six different pieces, and the rules for placing, moving, and capturing pieces, and for winning and drawing. Like 'em or not, if you don't follow the rules, you are not playing chess. And the rules are hardly a negative. The centuries-long endurance of chess results from them (though the rules have evolved). Governmental laws are analogous to game rules in that they say what you can and, mostly, cannot do.

Self-Imposed Constraints

Self-imposed constraints, like a strategy, are for busting bottlenecks by minimizing, eliminating, or getting around them. Organizations, communities, and nations willingly impose constraints in the forms of laws, by-laws, and policies that limit individuals' and organizations' actions. While there will always be someone opposed to a given law, the constraint of law is not categorically undesired. The restrictions are believed to supply greater benefit than the "cost" of the restrictions themselves. Societies restrict certain personal freedoms to improve personal freedoms broadly. Likewise, a company that restricts the markets in which they will participate expects to lose some sales, losses they accept in return for, say, operational efficiencies or more-focused product designs that lead to greater sales in their target markets. The "cost" of imposing a constraint on your system is the *trade-off*. What makes trade-offs difficult is that the cost is usually clearer than the future benefit.

The Three Constraints: A Street Intersection

Managing a street intersection illustrates the three constraints. A traffic engineer has an aspiration of efficient and safe flow of vehicles at inter-sections. The bottleneck constraint is that vehicles approaching from different directions must use the same pavement. If two or more vehi-cles occupy the same pavement at the same time, it's a bad thing. In busy intersections, drivers are forced to slow down or creep when driving through creating backups, and yet accidents happen.

Engineers can bust the shared-pavement bottleneck by installing a traffic light with the self-imposed stop-on-red rule. As expected, this constraint has trade-offs. Drivers must stop for the duration of the traffic-light cycle whether vehicles are coming from other directions or not. Additionally, traffic lights require installation, operation, and maintenance—all regulations add overhead. Then there is the aesthetic cost of poles and objects hanging from wires. If traffic volume is always large, the shared pavement bottleneck can be busted with a bridge or a traffic circle, but at much greater financial trade-off. If a traffic light is stopping vehicles excessively, a less-aggressive stop sign solution has lesser trade-offs.

No solution guarantees success. Crashes still happen, and a power outage can render the intersection worse off than if there were no light all. A self-imposed rule can only increase the probability of busting the bottleneck and achieving aspirations, not guarantee it. Results are always uncertain.

What are the external constraints? The traffic engineer must adhere to Department of Transportation standards for installing lights and to local budgets and regulations around aesthetics and energy consumption. Motorists and pedestrians are constrained to have a properly functioning vehicle and follow the road laws: observing speed limits, not texting, not drinking or drugging, and of course, stopping at red lights.

The Central Rule

The street intersection shows that self-imposed constraint (stop on red) busts the bottleneck constraint (shared pavement) to help achieve the aspiration (fast and safe travel) operating within the bounds of externally imposed constraints (regulations for engineers and drivers). Communities accept the trade-off of *not moving* at specific times in return for moving faster and safer on average. Communities also accept costs for lights and ugly stuff hanging from wires.

The self-imposed constraint is the *strategy* when it is aimed at busting the dominant bottleneck to the foremost aspiration of an endeavor—the aspiration on the far right-hand side of the influence diagram. Strategy is the *central rule* because it channels and unifies decisions and actions toward busting the bottleneck constraint and raising the probability of achieving the aspiration. The focus on the bottleneck solves the granularization problem from Chapter 4 because every part of the organization, every function, every "silo," receives guidance on making trade-offs.

Say, for a simple example, the bottleneck to a business's aspiration to penetrate a new region is that their existing products don't have the suitable characteristics. Marketing, wanting to make costly process modifications to existing products to create the desired characteristics, comes against manufacturing's cost-reduction imperative. Leadership must devise a strategy rule for this endeavor that busts this bottleneck and gives marketing and manufacturing direction. One might be to accept marketing's approach and give manufacturing the OK to add the cost. An alternative strategy might be to stop modifying current products for penetrating the target region because it results in too many compromises and instead approve development funds for a new platform tailored to the target region. In this case, marketing gets their product and manufacturing can differentially manage existing products for cost reduction while participating in the new platform development as a separately managed program. Either strategy enables marketing and manufacturing to rally around busting the bottleneck to the aspiration, regardless of the impact on individual numbers. The aspiration cannot itself supply this guidance, and therefore flowdowns from aspirations and cascades of subgoals cannot supply it either.

Each time a bottleneck is busted, the system's capability—its fitness—increases, and another bottleneck becomes rate-limiting. If the business above succeeds in creating a suitable product platform for the target region, they can then attack whatever the next bottleneck is; for instance, it might be distribution or a brand image problem. Keep busting bottlenecks, and the system evolves in positive directions. (Note that traffic lights are so understood that adding one is not a strategy but rather a commodified technique. But techniques, like tactics, are also self-imposed constraints.[2])

That no action should conflict with the central rule explains why there can be only one strategy per system—one foremost aspiration, one dominant bottleneck in the way of that aspiration, and one strategy to bust the dominant bottleneck. Chapter 6 shows that tactical rules and techniques are for busting the lesser bottlenecks in the system, and Chapter 7 shows that multiple coordinated *nested* systems simplify large endeavors with multifaceted organizations.

⚷ Your Bike Shop Strategy

Framework 3.1 captured your values, aspirations, and value propositions for opening a bike shop in your town. You used the influence
diagram to work out the decisions and actions needed to launch a
shop (Figure 3.8). Now you need a strategy for unifying these decisions, so you start by diagnosing the bottleneck.

Three possible bottlenecks previously came to mind as you constructed your influence diagram: (1) finding money, (2) attracting
a bike technician, and (3) feeling overwhelmed by all the decisions
you need to make. Which of these is the dominant bottleneck that
requires busting? At first, getting money seemed the hardest of the
three, but it turns out that interest rates are low, and the bank, with
surprisingly few requests for detail, agrees with your shop's potential
and gives you a loan. Your favorite aunt and uncle step up and lend
you some money too.

For the second possible bottleneck, you were lucky to recruit your
friend Steve Trayler, who everyone calls "Wrenchy." He is a skillful
technician and up-to-date on the latest bike designs and fitting methods. He shares your values about biking, though he has never shown
much interest in making money.

The third possible bottleneck appears to be the tough one. You
feel overwhelmed by the seemingly countless decisions to make—
you're a bike nerd, not a business nerd. The global bike brands also
understand your bottleneck of so many decisions. Competition is
growing between the global brands, and they offer sweet deals to
set you up. Not only do they have their own branded shops, but
they also supply private shops with complete bike product lines
including accessories and clothing, and décor for the shop including posters, window displays, and print and web-based advertising
materials. They also provide inventory and accounting software
designed specifically for their products. The brands entice you further with a nine-month grace period on payments for the initial
delivery of bikes and accessories if you open by October to take
advantage of the holiday sales season. With these offerings, they

bust the decision-making bottleneck by unifying a whole bunch of your decisions, all wonderfully designed around their product lines. These offers are hard to resist.

Yet there is a rub. You want to be independent and do it your way with an individualistic, unique shop. Signing up with one of these powerhouses will severely limit your freedom, which is a hard external constraint to accept. So, despite the trade-off of forgoing the safety net that the brands provide, you decide to go it alone.

Your strategy for busting the bottleneck is to make no effort to reproduce the full global brands' offerings or style. Instead, you will reduce the number of decisions and actions needed by focusing only on either high-end or novel products that you believe will intrigue not only enthusiasts but also new customers who are willing to spend good money. You will not stock a full range of bikes and accessories and will accept the loss of sales to people looking for lower-end equipment. You add converting customers' bikes to hybrid e-Bikes, which some bike purists are reluctant to do. The strategy means devoting no effort to décor, leaving the space bare and as rough as you found it, no rugs, forgoing even painting the walls. For display racks, you buy lightweight bookshelves from Ikea, as well as some cheap plastic stools. The focus will be on service and helping customers figure out what they need, not on an attractive shop with vivid pictures of gorgeous models riding in Tuscany. You don't even pay for a music service and instead let Wrenchy fill the shop with the sound of his large vinyl collection of obscure electronica. For you, and especially Wrenchy, a functional shop is beautiful, but you realize this unusual design may turn off or scare away some prospective buyers. You call this simplified approach the *My Thing* strategy.

For the logistics and financial aspects of the shop, you cobble together advice from your bank, small business advisors, and friends. There's no cash register because you use a mobile credit card reader or online payments. There's no landline. In hopes of eventually attracting you, a few suppliers offer modest assistance with payment terms and some in-store displays. Still, you never let them dictate to you, limiting their interest.

To reflect your My Thing strategy, you modify the original framework (3.1), bolding the additions. Framework 5.1 is the way it looks on the day you open the shop (to modest fanfare):

🚴 Bike Shop Framework 5.1: After reflecting on bottlenecks	
Values	Love every aspect of biking and believe it is good for society
Aspirations	Vision: Happiness by working in the biking world Goals: (1) respect from peers; (2) sufficient cash flow Mission: Launch a bike shop
Diagnosis	Proposition: Can provide the innovations and quality that existing stores cannot External constraints: Scenario: Increasing awareness of health and environmental benefits will drive new demographics to biking who will pay for innovations **Bottleneck: The number of decisions and tasks for launching a shop is overwhelming.**
Strategy	**My Thing: Functional only for high-end and novel products as opposed to reproducing the global brands' shop approach. Trade-offs: riskier, more borrowing, more effort.**
Key tactics, plans, & metrics	

Strategy is the Fullest Solution to the Killer Problems

A central rule best meets all three requirements of a solution to the killer problems of change and innovation, making it the most powerful creative tool. Rules can be a free choice to impose because they require no future event to occur. The My Thing rule to offer only high-end and novel products is a free choice (assuming you pay suppliers), while a plan to sell so many of these bikes and accessories per month is not. This doesn't mean any rule is a free choice. You are not free to impose a rule in conflict with external constraints, and it is unwise to impose a strategy rule so difficult that the organization cannot adhere to it because then the rule is meaningless.

Rules provide real-time guidance for decisions and actions because unlike aspirations and plans where you must wait for a result to know if you have succeeded, you can know if you are following a rule in real time. At your bike shop, you can know in real time if the bikes and accessories you order are high-end and novel (by whatever definition you establish). A strategy never describes an outcome, a strategy describes what you can and cannot do when faced with decisions to raise the probability of achieving aspirations.

Any rule can meet the free choice and real-time requirements. What makes a strategy unique is it also unifies because no action or decision in the system may violate it. A strategy channels *all* decisions and actions toward busting the bottleneck. It is the central, overarching rule. Now we can update our table summarizing each framework components' ability to solve the killer problems (Table 5.1) showing that strategy gets three yesses.

Table 5.1 Strategy meets all three requirements of a solution to the killer problems of change and innovation

	Free choice?	Real-Time Guidance?	Unifying?
Aspirations	No	No	N/A
Plans and Projections	Limited	Limited	Limited
Metrics	N/A	Limited+	Limited
Rules Strategy	Yes	Yes	Yes

Meeting the three requirements will not, however, result in a good strategy. At this point, we are only establishing the requirements for something to be a strategy at all. Just because something qualifies as a street-legal automobile doesn't mean it is a good automobile. Yet unless street legal, it is not useful to most people no matter how well it performs. A good strategy can only be designed as part of the entire framework as is done in Part II.

Principles of Strategy and Implications for Design

In Chapter 2, we deduced principles about change and innovation via analyzing how adaptive systems work.

1. Change and innovation emerge over time at high levels by the myriad disciplined decisions and actions of the players (agents) in the ecosystem at low levels.
2. The discipline at low levels is the application of stressors to destroy unfit variants, leaving the more fit as the last standing to evolve further in subsequent generations.
3. The constraint of adhering to strategy is a stressor for achieving an aspiration.

We can now add three principles for a properly functioning strategy deduced from the influence diagram model of complex adaptive systems developed in Chapters 3 and 4,

1. Strategy must be a free choice.
2. Strategy must provide real-time guidance.
3. Strategy must unify lower-level choices and actions.

The unification is achieved by focusing decisions and actions on busting the bottleneck to the aspiration.

So, strategies are not derived directly from aspirations; they are derived from the bottlenecks to aspirations. If the bottleneck changes, the strategy must change, even if the aspiration has not changed. This flow is captured in the **strategy←bottleneck←aspiration** triad introduced in Chapter 1, which can now be shown in the context of the influence diagram Figure 5.1. Deriving strategy from bottlenecks keeps you from thinking everything matters. If everything matters, then nothing matters.

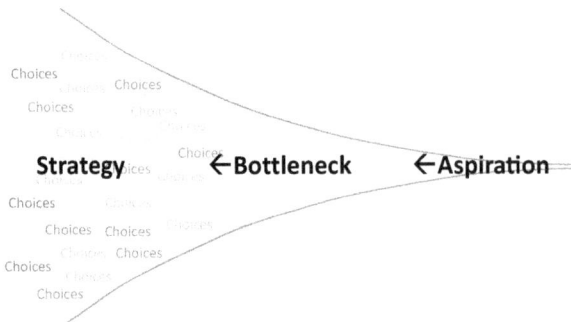

Figure 5.1 The triad in the context of the influence diagram

Focus on busting the bottleneck gives leverage to move the whole system because every "silo" must align with it. Focus on the bottleneck drives uniqueness because it is more likely that your bottlenecks are unique than your aspirations.

Additional design principles that follow from these conclusions include,

- The best strategies are somewhat abstract and expressed in terms of what *not* to do, leaving freedom for the people without stifling them—so they can adapt locally. Ed Catmull of Pixar said,[3] leaders of creative enterprises "must hold lightly to goals, and firmly to intentions." Intentions can be described best abstractly.
- The organization must be able to adhere or nearly adhere to the strategy, else the rule can have no impact; it becomes hypothetical.
- If there is no trade-off, the strategy is not doing anything.

And perhaps most important,

- Low-level rules drive freedom and creativity; high-level rules are just noise or lead to paralysis. The rule, "make a profitable bike shop," is an unenforceable and useless constraint. The rule, "only sell high-end and novel bicycles," has meaning and forces discussion about what "high-end and novel" means. Only low-level rules are a free choice.

🚲 Bike Shop 18 Months Later: One Bottleneck Busted

Fast-forward 18 months after launch. The shop runs smoothly because of its simplicity. In truth, you're surprised with how good you are at business management. Yet busting the so-many-decisions-to-make bottleneck wasn't enough. While the shop attracted a reasonable clientele of biking enthusiasts like you knew it would, you've attracted only limited new customers and the shop is just barely profitable. You are paying suppliers and Wrenchy, and your aunt and uncle extend your loan, but you take little money home, and you don't sense improvement coming. Something must change. Several possibilities enter your head as to what is the bottleneck to increasing sales:

1. *You're selling the wrong products.* In addition to performance bikes for your enthusiasts, you have put together a complete-enough line of high-end and novel bikes and accessories. These should have wide-enough appeal to commuters, health-conscious customers, and families. *Rejected.*

2. *The mom-and-pop store is innovating too.* You sent friends in to investigate; they report the mom-and-pop hasn't changed. Yet, you have not taken many customers from them, as they do a solid job of meeting traditional customer expectations. *Rejected.*

3. *You don't have the knack for selling.* While you have never thought of yourself as a salesperson, you have been surprised at your ability to connect with people. You've sold some expensive equipment and people respond well to your advice. You were even invited to talk at several events on environmental and health benefits of biking, and the talks were a big success. *Rejected.*

4. *Online shopping for accessories is cutting into sales.* You fear people buy from big online sites after you tell them what they need. Because bike shops make more money on accessories than on bikes themselves, it's a problem. However, bike sales and service demand at the shop aren't so good either. *Partially accepted* (you add this as a scenario).

5. *Nonenthusiasts don't understand your offering.* Pitching to customers and modest advertising aren't building enough buzz and intriguing customers. They're scared away by rumors of expensive bikes, not realizing that though they cost more, the bikes you sell will work like new for years. Cheapos assembled by kids at mega discount stores ride fine for a few months but then develop clicks

and clacks that can't be stopped, jump out of gear no matter how many times they're adjusted, or squeal like a pig when applying the brakes. They don't see the value of your fitting service that improves riding ergonomics. They don't see the potential of hybrid e-Bikes, commuter bikes with internal gearing, novel designs like chainless drives and new geometries, and new phone apps. They don't see the connection to health and environment. You could also do more to attract the growing number of women enthusiasts. *Accepted.*

Customers not understanding what the shop and biking can do for them appears to be a tougher bottleneck than your initial fear of running a business. Ideas to bust the new bottleneck don't seem promising either: A big fancy shop in a new, more-visible location, with all kinds of in-store décor and promotions. Sounds nice, but you can't afford it and it goes against your My Thing strategy that you love. You can't afford a big advertising campaign either, and you're not sure it will educate people enough anyway. Then you say, "Let's hire a bunch of svelte hotties to ride around town with your shop logo fake tattooed on their arms and legs!" Wrenchy says, "No."

So, like many people whose backs are up against the wall, you get inventive. You seemed to be able to connect with the few new customers in your shop and the people at the speaking engagements. You like inspiring people to combat obesity and diabetes and pollution by biking. Always a bit timid and shy, you never had such experiences before. Associating the shop with these benefits of biking might bring in a new clientele. You imagine getting on local talk shows, speaking at schools and health organizations, and setting up a blog and podcast. Moreover, you are thinking of contacting government officials to see if they will work with you to reach kids and adults on health benefits. The name *Evangelize* strategy pops into your head. Going forward, you will focus solely on evangelizing biking while minimizing your work at the shop. Unfortunately, this means hiring someone to run the shop and be the salesperson when you're unavailable. You modify your Framework 5.2.

🚲 Bike Shop Framework 5.2: 18 months after the launch	
Values	Love every aspect of biking and believe it is good for society; Independence
Aspirations	Vision: Happiness by working in the biking world Goals: (1) respect from peers; (2) sufficient cash flow Mission: ~~launch a bike shop without the global brands~~ **Make My Thing work**
Diagnosis	Proposition: Can provide the innovations and quality that existing stores cannot. External constraints: Pay the bills Scenario: Increasing awareness of health and environmental benefits will drive new demographics to biking who will pay for innovations; **online sales will kill shops** Bottleneck: ~~The number of decisions and tasks for launching a shop is overwhelming.~~ **People do not understand the value proposition.**
Strategy	~~My Thing: functional only for high-end and novel products as opposed to reproducing the global brands' shop approach.~~ ~~Trade-offs: riskier, more borrowing, more effort.~~ **Evangelize: Be only a full-time ambassador/marketer for the shop and for biking. No running the shop. (Trade-offs: Even more borrowing, risk associated with hiring a new shop manager, even more effort ... Possibly look like Don Quixote.)**
Key tactics, plans, & metrics	**P: Hire shop manager by August 1**

The moral of your story after 18 months (besides a hint of nothing ventured, nothing gained) is that the bottleneck changed so the strategy had to change, even though the aspiration remained the same. One other item to notice, My Thing is not gone. You now see it as your mission to remain independent and make the My Thing model a success.

Strategic

A grievance in the Introduction was that the word *strategic* had lost its meaning with misuse and overuse. This chapter confirms the meaning of strategic: *relating to the dominant bottleneck of a system.* Plans and other feed-forward simulations and metrics also attack bottlenecks, but they do so in a limited way. Only strategy can uniquely give unifying and real-time guidance for all decisions and actions.

Along with the superlatives about the power of a central rule, keep in mind what a strategy does not do:

- Supply the entire needed direction,
- Explain aspirations or lay out the entire long- or short-term approach to achieving them,
- Outline all the ways, means, and ends, or
- Make an organization unique all on its own.

These factors can be provided only by the framework with all its components. The strategy just happens to be the most important one.

CHAPTER 6

Both Strategy and Tactics are for "Winning Wars"

We haven't yet judged the capability of the remaining designed framework component to solve the killer problems of change and innovation—tactics. Often called policies, tactics function as rules; but they differ from strategy because, as introduced in Chapter 1, they apply to only a partial scope of the system. The strategy rule guides decisions and actions for busting the bottleneck to the overall aspiration; a tactical rule guides decisions and actions for busting the bottlenecks to smaller-scope aspirations (subgoals).[1] As all designed components, tactics are subservient to the strategy rule.

In your bike shop, the My Thing strategy gave the overall guidance: add nothing beyond the bare functional requirements for selling and servicing high-end and novel bikes and to not reproduce a full traditional shop product line. But other decisions remained. For instance, exactly which bikes to buy and from what suppliers? You need a way to decide these smaller-scope questions too. The bottleneck to this smaller scope might be that if you buy all the bikes you think will appeal to your target customers, you will end up buying from 20 suppliers, which is too complicated. A tactical rule set could solve this: (1) limit buying to five suppliers, (2) prioritize six customer segments (high-performance road, commuters, high-performance off road, women's, family, and special), and then (3) fill the priorities for each segment as best you can you with five suppliers. Another tactic might be around the advertising policy, with guidance on the copy and visuals and where to place online ads. Your My Thing tactic to add no shop décor, only functionality, is also in place. These tactics are added to your framework in Framework 6.1 (omitting sections for simplicity).

Because of their limited scope, like plans (you will add more plans later), and unlike strategy, there can be multiple tactics in a framework.

᠔Ō Bike Framework 6.1 Tactics added to the Bike Shop Framework	
Strategy	Evangelize: Be only a full-time ambassador/marketer for the shop and for biking. No running the shop. (Trade-offs: Even more borrowing, risk associated with hiring a new shop manager, even more effort … Possibly look like Don Quixote.)
Key tactics, plans, and metrics	P: Hire shop manager by August 1 **T: Five-supplier bike-buying rule** **T: Advertising policy** **T: No shop décor**

How do tactics fare against the requirements for solving the killer problems of change and innovation? Because tactics share all functionality with strategy except scope, they are free choices and supply real-time guidance; but like plans and metrics, tactics have limited unification capability (Table 6.1).

Table 6.1 The limited unification capability of tactics to solve the killer problems

	Free choice?	Real-Time Guidance?	Unifying?
Aspirations	No	No	N/A
Plans and Projections	Limited	Limited	Limited
Metrics	N/A	Limited+	Limited
Rules			
Strategy	Yes	Yes	Yes
Tactics	Yes	Yes	Limited

That tactics are rules, and that scope is the sole functional difference between strategy and tactics, may sound foreign considering traditional conceptions of tactics. This chapter explains the contrast with tradition. A strategist who described the scope-based view of tactics is General Mao Zedong* in his 1936 essay *Problems of Strategy in China's Revolutionary War* (which should be no surprise since the military is where the whole idea of strategy and tactics emerged in the first place):

> *The task of the science of strategy is to study those laws for directing a war that govern a war situation as a whole. The task of the science of campaigns and the science of tactics is to study those laws … that govern a partial situation.*

* Discussed here are Mao's principles written as a military leader, not his political thinking or actions before and after 1949. Whichever way the world judges Mao's total legacy, he was a brilliant military strategist.

The Challenge to Understanding Scope-Based Tactics

Traditional views of tactics are counter to the scope-based view of tactics and lead to traps. The most dangerous trap is *tacticization*, which occurs when leaders forget their strategy rule and define success by victories in smaller scopes of the endeavor. These traditional views, usually expressed as the difference between the function of tactics and strategy can be boiled down to four problematic definitions:[3]

1. Tactics are the actions or *hows* to implement strategy.
2. Tactics are short term; strategy is long term.
3. Tactics (as a function) are what commanders in the field do; strategy (as a function) is what staff generals and admirals do (and CEOs and Governors, etc.).
4. Tactics are for winning battles; strategy is for winning wars.

Problem Definition 1—Tactics Are the How

The idea that tactics are for strategy implementation is expressed in various ways:

- Strategy is the what; tactics are the how—the doing or deployment.
- Strategy is the ends; tactics are the means.
- Strategy proposes; tactics dispose.
- Strategy is planning; tactics is doing.
- One has strategy, which is done by tactics.

Chapter 1 showed that because ways, means, or hows are so general, they cannot define any single framework component. Further, saying that strategy is the "what" or the "ends" and tactics are the "how" implies that a strategy is an aspiration. It is also wrong to say that tactics means doing, implementing, or deploying, or that tactics dispose. You don't "do" strategy, tactics, plans, aspirations, or metrics during implementation, and you certainly don't do a rule—you take decisions and actions as guided by these framework components, the strategy and tactical rules especially, because you can follow them in real time. The closest thing to "doing" tactics, or any other framework component, is designing them.

Problem Definition 2—Tactics Are Short Term

Chapter 1 also stated that strategy is not just for the long term and tactics are not just for the short term. Rules do not contain time horizons. A rule stays in effect until changed or eliminated. You can plan to change a rule, as in, *follow rule A for nine months, and then follow rule B for nine months.* Such a plan is not, however, what people mean when they define tactics as short term and strategy as long term. They mean that strategy is for decisions and actions relating to long-term results, and tactics are decisions and actions for short-term results. The problem is you cannot put the long term on hold, or out of bounds, while addressing the short term. An action or decision taken with short-term intent can change the entire future of an organization. Sell your soul to the devil for a success and you may pay for eternity.

Once again, aspiration, not strategy, determines "planning" horizon. A goal of making a certain amount of money has no meaning without specifying when to make it, much to the chagrin of many a venture manager. Politicians may say it is impossible to put winning a war on a timeline, yet who would accept 50 years for victory? A proposal to launch a new bike shop is meaningless to your bankers without a launch date. The horizon of the strategy is given by the aspiration in each case.

Think of an organization in crisis where the aspiration is survival. Faced with raising $50 million cash in three months or lights out, a CEO's strategy rule should have a three- month horizon that unifies the entire organization around obtaining the cash (without violating core values). No action or decision can conflict with this strategy—there is no separate long-term rule. Heck, in these situations, three months may as well be called the long term. If the crisis passes, then the CEO can establish a strategy for a longer-horizon aspiration. (Note that a CEO saying, "We must meet Wall Street's expectations this quarter" is a goal, not a strategy, especially if it is unclear how much of the existing longer-horizon strategy should be violated.)

We are encouraged to believe that strategy is for the long term because it likely takes longer to change a larger scope of a system, and therefore time required may correlate with scope. If an aspiration is to revamp an entire marketing division, it will probably take longer than the time to hire a more capable website design firm. Now you might say, "This proves it, the changes that strategies govern take longer to materialize, therefore they are long term." But the long-term outcome is happenstance, an artifact of the larger scope, not a requirement. No one wants change to take a long time; it's not demanded. Sometimes blowing it up and starting all over again is faster than fixing parts of a system. It's possible that until, say, the marketing division in total is revamped, smaller activities like hiring a web design firm have no impact (but no system can be improved instantly, as discussed in Chapter 2).

Problem Definition 3—Tactics Are for Lower-Level Leaders

The concept that tactics are *functionally* what commanders in the field do, and strategy is *functionally* what staff generals and admirals do, is a misinterpretation of *levels of war* or perhaps better, *politico/military levels of war*. These levels, first associated with Prussian military theorist General Carl von Clausewitz (1780–1831), are actually names for the frameworks of the various leadership hierarchies of the government and the military (but do not confuse with the low and high levels of adaptive systems).

Levels of war in the language of the emergent approach are as follows: the government's framework is called *policy*, the military leaders' frameworks for determining how to utilize the armed forces in support of the government's framework is called *strategy*, and the field commanders' frameworks to determine how to use their capability in support of the military leaders' framework are called *tactics*.

Levels of war are nested frameworks needed in multifaceted organizations as shown in Chapter 7, but there are two problems. One is a nuisance factor: the confusion caused by using the terms policy, strategy, and tactics as names for frameworks of the hierarchical levels *and* as names for functional components (types of rules) in those frameworks. For example, tactics (a framework of a commander), can have tactics and strategy and tactical policy as components. The second problem is serious. It occurs when the levels of war concept are interpreted to mean—in military or business—that upper-level leaders supply the strategy and lower-level leaders implement the strategy. Nested frameworks show that all hierarchical levels must have a complete framework with strategy and tactics. In a corporation, this means the CEO, business unit leaders, and functional leaders such as HR, manufacturing, and R&D all need frameworks with strategy and tactics.

Problem Definition 4—Tactics Are for Winning Battles

Military levels of war encourage the notion that strategies are for winning wars, while tactics are for winning battles. No. Strategy and tactics, and every other component of the framework, are for winning wars only (however you define winning a war). Strategy is the rule for winning the war that governs the entire scope of the system, and tactics are rules for winning the war that govern partial scopes of the system. Winning battles must be for winning wars; why else would anyone sacrifice anything to win a battle?

The idea that winning battles is valuable on its own leads to the belief that the criteria for winning battles can be independent of the strategy. In other words, there are local criteria that are more important than the holistic criteria on which the strategy is based. When local criteria are considered in isolation, there's no choice but to use standard or "fixed" assessments—such as ground gained or lost, casualties, and matériel lost—to define what winning a battle, that is, tactical success, means. Mao could not accept this. Michael Handel, author of *Masters of War*, coined the term *tacticization* to describe the seduction of a fixed and local definition of winning that Mao described.[4] Mao's guerilla strategy, like that of many upstart forces facing large, well-supplied adversaries, was to avoid pitched battle with the opposing Kuomintang lead by Chang Kai-Shek. Influenced by Sun Tzu, Mao articulated this strategy as:[5]

The enemy advances, we retreat.
The enemy camps, we harass.
The enemy tires, we attack.
The enemy retreats, we pursue.

When Mao temporarily lost power in the early 1930s, the replacement commanders violated this strategy and successfully engaged the Kuomintang in direct battle, even though the Kuomintang was not retreating. To Mao, this strategy violation, *this tacticization*, is a seduction by local victories. He said, "Without a good plan [laws] for the whole campaign, it is absolutely impossible to fight a really good first battle ... even though victory is won in the first battle, if the battle harms rather than helps the campaign as a whole, such a victory can only be reckoned a defeat." (Chapter 9 shows that tacticization is a failure to execute.) If standard fixed "metrics of victory" determine whether a battle is won, the United States would not have failed in Vietnam, where it dominated in casualties and matériel lost.

A battle is "won" only if it helped win the war. And since battles are not designed after they are fought, the only judgment of whether a battle will help win the war is whether the battle is consistent with the hypothesis of what it takes to win the war—and that hypothesis is the framework and its strategy. If after a battle you see your framework is flawed, then adapt, and change the framework for the next battle. But this is hindsight.

The Seduction of Tacticization and Projectization

Wars and battles are, of course, metaphors for any endeavor. There's an old adage, "There is no such thing as a good investment in a bad business." Why? Why do leaders get seduced into such investments? Because it is easier to comprehend a financial analysis on a small scope of a business: a new product, an upgrade to a factory, or an improved IT system. Meaningless NPVs and ROIs go flying (highly valued because of supposed discipline of using numbers), with little connection to the big picture and with little regard for investments alternatives that might return so much more.

Treating smaller-scope decisions independently could be called *pro-jectization*. Like tacticization, each project is imagined as a victory when observed on its own, but, if considered as part of the whole, it may be a loss. It's difficult to financially analyze the whole of an endeavor. Investments must be analyzed relative to alternatives (Chapter 15). There is no such thing as an absolute return of any investment.

Arguing against projectization is not a condemnation of project management or the use of numbers and financial analyses. Battles do matter, and project management is crucial. The isolation of a project allows focus and lack of distraction. But if projects can be judged by an isolated financial analysis alone, then why is a framework and its strategy needed at all? Just go ahead and have a series of individual decisions with each project based on its isolated criteria. Decision making would be so much easier. Clearly, this is a false approach. A bad business is one that doesn't have the potential to make enough money *or* that must be managed in a way that is contrary to the corporation's overall framework and its strategy.

⚅ Bike Shop Tacticizations

How might you have tacticized your *My Thing* strategy? What if a supplier offers a new line of great-looking, inexpensive, but not-so-obviously lower-quality bikes. Their sales rep convinces you to use these bikes to compete with the mega discount stores, arguing that the resulting store traffic will drive traffic that will lead to greater high-margin products and service sales. At first you are quite happy with the sales numbers. Then repair costs start to come in. You can't turn down repair requests on these cheap bikes, even after the warranty has expired, because you have a reputation for taking care of your customers. The seduction of big sales from low-cost bikes is a breach of adherence to your framework and its strategy—a failure to execute—and can bring down the shop. You've won a battle but may lose the war.

CHAPTER 7

Nested Frameworks to Integrate Organizations

The discussion in Chapters 3 to 6 focused only on a single system, and therefore a single framework. Your bike shop has just one influence diagram, one framework with one set of aspirations and one strategy. Real situations, however, usually require multiple systems called *nested frameworks*. Nesting is a common concept. The focus in the emergent approach is how the nested frameworks work together:

1. Each nested system has its own unique and complete framework.
2. It is no one's job to design or implement someone else's strategy.
3. The parent framework is an external constraint on the child framework.

Nesting does not add layers of management. It is a recognition of layers that exist or a way to clarify functional groups within a layer. It ensures that top management doesn't overprescribe downward, and that lower layers accept the responsibility to set their own strategy in alignment with the higher-level strategy.

Chapter 6 pointed out military levels of war are an example of nesting. All armies include hierarchical structure, for example, divisions, brigades, platoons, squads, as well as functional organizations, for example, quartermaster, artillery, special forces, medical corps. A general's framework for leading a division of 50 thousand troops can't possibly be the same as a corporal's framework for leading a squad of 12; nor could the Colonel of Artillery's framework possibly be the same as the Colonel of a medical corps. Likewise in corporations, CEOs, business unit leaders, and group leaders each have a different framework, as do R&D, HR, manufacturing, and other functions. Governments, NGOs, universities, sports, and religious organizations have similar hierarchical levels and functional groupings. Nested frameworks enable the hierarchies and functional organizations to work together in harmony.

How Nested Frameworks Work

To create a nested system, simply break the larger entity into parts, hierarchically, functionally, or both. Use only the minimum essential nested frameworks because there is a cost of complexity for each one added. Here's the key: each of the new systems has its own *unique* framework that contains at least the minimum essential framework components, including an aspiration, diagnosis, and valid strategy.

Figure 7.1 shows frameworks nested around a focal framework. What harmonizes nested frameworks is that each subordinate, or *child*, framework must be consistent with and responsive to its *parent* framework. In other words, the parent framework is an external constraint on all subordinate frameworks. No child framework can violate any framework above it. Further, the child framework cannot duplicate of any aspect of the parent framework—it must be unique. This uniqueness is what makes the child framework meaningful.

If the child framework violates the parent framework, it destroys unification thus undermining the parent system. If the child is not unique from the parent, then there is no new information, nothing of value, and all that is achieved is to add noise and complication. These two requirements ensure that nested frameworks work properly to solve the killer problems of change and innovation. It follows, then, that it is no one's job to implement someone else's strategy or tactics. The tactics of the parent are not the strategies of the children. The strategy and tactics of each framework must bust its own bottlenecks, while not violating the

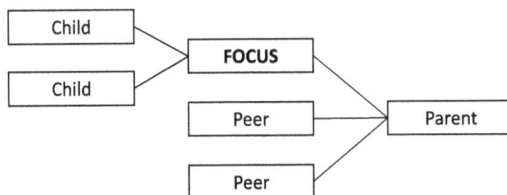

Figure 7.1 Nested frameworks

parent. It follows also that generating nested frameworks by flow-down from strategy themes, as described in Chapter 4, is not valid because these consist of goals, subgoals, and metrics with no strategies and therefore are not minimum essential frameworks.

It may not be natural to imagine CEOs or other leaders having tactics, but there are plenty of areas for them: design of monthly and quarterly cadences and reporting, how to use precious time, ways to avoid being seduced by staff's quick answers to hard questions, how to enable transparency, how not to be too bossy or not bossy enough, or techniques for talking to the press and the investment community. If the bottleneck of any of these is the major bottleneck to success for the company, then it would be the focus of the CEOs strategy, but there will always be a need for tactics for the rest.

Everyone has a parent entity to consider in their endeavors, some entity that provides external constraints. Sometimes, the parent is a distinct and obvious person or group—a boss, a board of directors, or a commanding officer. Sometimes, it's not so clear. For example, shareholders, constituents, and even fans put constraints on leaders in some way.

Parent frameworks are not more important than child frameworks either. The success of one part of a company might be the single most important factor for company survival. Think of a startup venture where a technology group is nested under the CEO. The CEO may coordinate funding and other business needs, but the venture will certainly fail unless the technology group succeeds. Woe to leaders who say that "the only strategy in my company is my strategy," and that everyone else's job is to implement it. Or leaders who tell, for instance, the manufacturing group to "just meet the business needs—I don't want to hear about alternatives, and bottlenecks and manufacturing strategies," are bound to be disappointed.

Example: A New Football Manager

Imagine a football club with a new head coach. This team is flush with money and great players but has underachieved for years. The Head Coach inherits three assistant coaches—Coach Defense, Coach Offense, and Coach Conditioning—each who are somewhat famous and are likely candidates for future head coach positions themselves.

Head Coach's diagnosis is that the main reason for underperformance is the playbook and training are too complicated. Players and coaches seem more intent on showing off their individual brilliance with fancy methods than on playing as a team or winning. Head Coach sets a goal of dropping the complicated playbook and getting back to basics believing the players' greater skill will carry the day. His bottleneck to achieving this goal is that his star players and coaches will resist the simplification. He also believes a slow "cook a frog" approach will not work—these people need to be shaken up. Head Coach's strategy for busting this bottleneck becomes: if players or coaches do not demonstrate willingness to accept the simplicity goal within three weeks, he will demote them or, if possible, fire them. This means monitoring their mindset and actions, not results, for three weeks. The trade-offs is he could lose the support of the team if ownership does not back him when he tries to demote or fire someone. He may also lose star players' playing time.

The three assistant coaches now have a goal (their missions, if they choose to accept them) of quickly instituting the back-to-basics approach in their domain. It turns out that each assistant has a unique bottleneck: Coach Offense has been using fancy plays and approaches for so long that she is not prepared for the fundamentals. Her strategy: borrow from others; the trade-off: risk looking incompetent and losing credibility with players. The bottleneck for Coach Defense is that her best players have scant experience in a basics-type defense. Her strategy: no direct teaching, break the defense into small groups led by older experienced players who are willing to simplify, and let them teach. In essence, add a layer of leadership to decrease the student–teacher ratio. The trade-offs: risk of uneven teaching, angering other players, and the complication of an extra layer.

Coach Conditioning is angry about the change. He pretends to be on board but secretly subverts the process and talks against Head Coach. He has two assistants of his own, one for physical conditioning and one for mental conditioning; both are confused by Coach Conditioning's behavior leading them to goals of figuring out what's going on. Figure 7.2 shows the nested frameworks for the team (plans, tactics, and metrics are omitted). Note that if the bottlenecks of the two assistant conditioning coaches were identical, there would have been no need for two frameworks.

Each coach's framework is unique (the assistants are hardly responsible for firing themselves if they don't do what's expected). Also, while the

Coach Offense

Goal—Institute back to basics offense
Bottleneck—unprepared
Strategy—borrow instead of design

Coach Defense

Goal—Institute back to basics defense
Bottleneck—stars inexperience with basics
Strategy—give up direct teaching; add leadership layer

Head Coach

Goal—back to basics
Bottleneck—stars and coaches do not want to change
Strategy—fire or reduce playing time for those who do not demonstrate a mindset change in three weeks

Coach Physical

Goal—Figure out what's going on
Bottleneck—bad boss
Strategy—ignore boss

Coach Conditioning

Goal—simplify workouts (official, but ignored); make head coach look bad (actual)
Bottleneck—risk of getting fired
Strategy—smile when criticizing the head coach

Coach Mental

Goal—Figure out what's going on
Bottleneck—bad boss
Strategy—align with boss

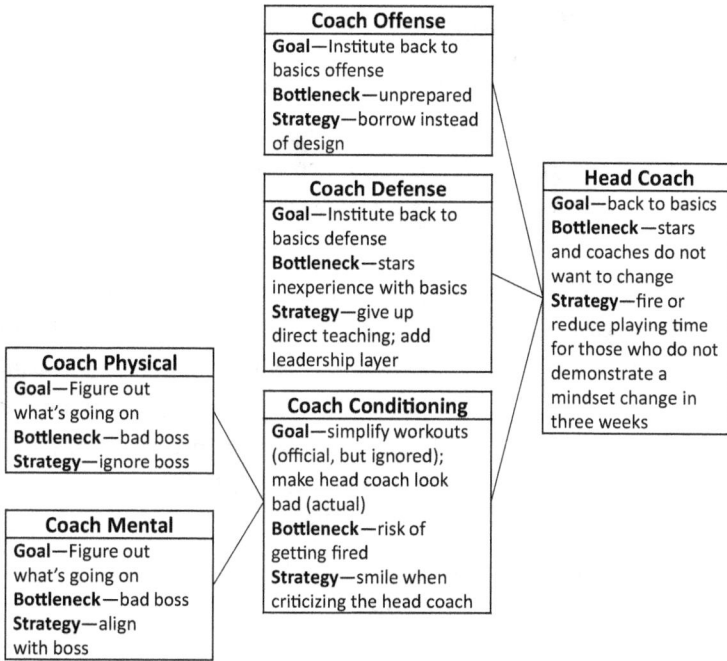

Figure 7.2 The coach's nested frameworks

assistant coach frameworks are (officially) responsive to the head coach framework, their aspirations are not the head coach's tactics. Their aspirations are a subset of the overall aspiration. Another way to visualize nested frameworks is by influence diagram as in Figure 7.3. This view shows more clearly that the parent is an external constraint on the child.

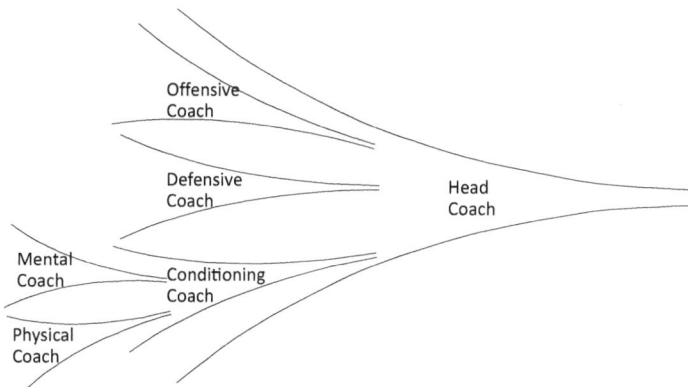

Offensive Coach

Defensive Coach

Head Coach

Mental Coach

Conditioning Coach

Physical Coach

Figure 7.3 Influence diagram view of nested frameworks

🚲 Your Bike Shop Now Needs a Nested System

You defined your new evangelize strategy and Framework 5.2 after 18 months of marginal profitability. This framework requires you to hire a shop manager to take over your shop responsibilities while you are evangelizing. You consider two tactical-rule alternatives: (1) hire an experienced bike person who already knows the business and need not be trained. The trade-offs are they will probably command more salary and they may have their own ideas about biking that are not aligned with your new concepts. (2) Hire someone with some sales and management experience from any field who has the talent and willingness to project your biking value propositions. The trade-off is the need to train them, which will cut a little into the time for evangelizing. Because you are strapped for cash, and don't want any conflicts on approach, you choose the second alternative and hire a young woman with sales experience and some business background. Marie is a go-getter with charisma, which you figure can't hurt business.

The second bottleneck to bust is that Wrenchy and Marie will be running the shop most days, but Wrenchy is not business focused and Marie is inexperienced with bikes. You figure it makes sense to clarify responsibilities and approach in a simple nested structure where each get a framework as in Figure 7.4.

In this design, you have a personal bottleneck in that, although you have shown promise as an evangelizer and marketer, you are still new to it, have little money, and are not sure what will take you to the next level, so you try several tactics and plans.

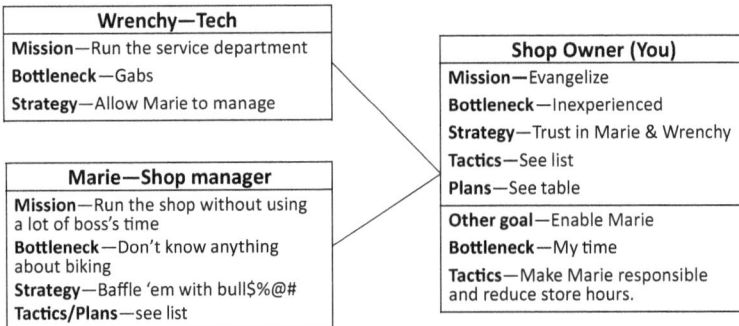

Wrenchy—Tech
Mission—Run the service department
Bottleneck—Gabs
Strategy—Allow Marie to manage

Marie—Shop manager
Mission—Run the shop without using a lot of boss's time
Bottleneck—Don't know anything about biking
Strategy—Baffle 'em with bull$%@#
Tactics/Plans—see list

Shop Owner (You)
Mission—Evangelize
Bottleneck—Inexperienced
Strategy—Trust in Marie & Wrenchy
Tactics—See list
Plans—See table
Other goal—Enable Marie
Bottleneck—My time
Tactics—Make Marie responsible and reduce store hours.

Figure 7.4 Nested frameworks for new evangelize strategy

- Focus on getting press, which is free, versus paying for advertising. Buy advertising only where it entitles you to press opportunities as well. For example, take ads out on local websites only if they allow you to have a periodic blog.
- Write columns that you can leverage in different media venues and that target multiple demographics (safety for schools, exercise for seniors, fitness for hard bodies, biking for commuters, etc.).
- Become a little controversial to improve your newsworthiness (you discover this after writing one column when a little angry): become an activist for bike access and bike lanes, and loudly hold the local government to their promises; goad people into biking even when it's cold outside; embarrass parents who have not taught their kids to bike. In general, become a nuisance.
- Start and lead bike riding groups including one for over-weight kids and one for women enthusiasts.
- Each week, do only one of the following: write a column for the various media, visit at least two schools, or lobby the local or county government. You restrict yourself with this rule so as to leave enough time to prepare properly for each.

You create a small schedule plan (Figure 7.5) that follows this last tactic with dates to coordinate with the school and government schedules, as well as to inform your two employees.

Date	Task	Comment
Oct 17	Schools	
Oct 24	Lobby	
Oct 31	Write	Government not in session
Nov 7	Schools	
Nov 14	Lobby	
Nov 21	Write	School not in session for holiday
Nov 28	Schools	
Dec 5	Lobby	
Dec 12	Write	

Figure 7.5 Your simple schedule

This schedule is a trivial example of a plan, yet it captures an important difference between plans and tactics: the tactical rule—only one task per week allowed—does not explain how to coordinate. The plan does enable coordination by simulating the future. As always, however, this plan is still uncertain. Something may change.

You might add some other plans or subgoals:

- Distribute 100 bumper stickers and buttons each month with the new "Yo. *Bike it!*" slogan.
- Politic for new bike lanes in at least five areas in town, one a month.
- Hold two bike rallies per month.

These tactics and plans fill out the details of your own strategy framework, but they do not provide anything directly useful to Wrenchy or Marie. What about their frameworks? Here's the strategy you and Marie come up with to bust her bottleneck that she is inexperienced with bikes: Dazzle 'em with bull@#%$ until she knows enough to be useful. Here are her tactics, techniques, and plans:

- When stumped by a customer question, call on Wrenchy, but make it sound like I am too busy—kind of projecting that the customer question is so simple that it's not worth my time to answer it. (But don't let Wrenchy gab too much.)
- Convince the boss to put in a couple of flat screens so I can have a few videos running all the time that entertain and educate (the latter for me as much as for the customers).
- Cancel my March vacation and reschedule for November.
- Go to biking conventions in April and May.

You add two tactics to your own framework. First, you give Marie the responsibility to learn. Second, you shorten the store hours, opening at 11:00 instead of 10:00 on the weekdays so Marie can study equipment and technology during that hour. You try to be there then. A trade-off is that you risk losing sales, but you think you can find a way to convince many of these people to come at other times.

What of Wrenchy's framework? There is no bottleneck around alignment on shop vision or on experience. His mission is clear: run the service department. The bottleneck is his predilection for gabbing with customers. His gabbing creates a great vibe for the shop, but he's always falling behind in his work. Wrenchy rarely drives people to buy stuff either. Amazingly, he is not defensive to criticism on this. And Marie is tough. Despite her newness, she has no compunctions about reminding Wrenchy when gabbing gets out of hand—the bottleneck now has a rule.

By defining the components of each of these systems as shown earlier in Figure 7.4, everyone gets maximum appropriate freedom while ensuring integration of their unique frameworks into the whole.

Micromanagement and Minimum Essential

Helmuth von Moltke, the 19th century German general, said, "An order shall contain everything that a commander cannot do by himself, but nothing else."[1] Nested frameworks enable leaders to push decision making more formally to the lowest (nested) level possible. This pushes decisions to the people closest to the actual "fighting," whether war or business. Further, as lower hierarchies learn, new ideas can be adopted at the higher levels—another form of organizational development: upward education.

When the parent supplies only minimum-essential constraints, local leaders can move fast and true without the unnecessary encumbrances of control and command from above. They are free to adapt, yet in a way that is consistent with the overall intent. This is especially true if parent strategies say what not to do, as opposed to plans and goals that say what to do. Minimizing constraint does not mean leadership is laissez-faire. Leadership action with nested systems calls for a delicate balance. Too much top-down constraint squelches the organization's creativity. Too little constraint leads to no common purpose, no guidance, and no unification. The constraints act as stressors: too much stressor and every idea is destroyed; too little and everything survives, which is just as bad.

Nested frameworks are not a license for leaders to abdicate responsibility for their organizations, or to give a few words of direction, or goals, and then take little or no effort to train and develop the people in the lower echelons. Leaders are responsible to ensure the people know how to design and adhere to their frameworks. This is different, and harder at first, than doing it for them. Great leaders with genius can inject their ideas into the systems this way. Only when an organization has the capabilities to design and implement frameworks can a leader, over time, begin to "let go" and give more freedom to operate, and this does not happen overnight.

Jack Welch used the word "boundarylessness" to describe his vision of breaking down rigid and impermeable boundaries between the many functional organizations (silos) of General Electric. He aimed, among other things, to stop groups from sequestering resources and maximizing their own benefits, and instead to get them to contribute to the greater whole. Yet boundarylessness requires defined nested systems boundaries; otherwise, everyone is responsible for everything, in which case, no one is responsible for anything.

CHAPTER 8

The Five Disqualifiers of Strategy

In the fog of designing and implementing frameworks, wouldn't it be wonderful to have simple tests that show whether the strategy component of the framework is, at minimum, functioning as a strategy? The *five disqualifiers* can give this information and are powerful adaptive tools.

Strategy testing is a time-honored practice, and some traditional sets are well known, for instance, those by Michael Porter and McKinsey consulting (see *Strategy Tests from the Literature* {web/supplement} for nine sets of examples). However, most traditional tests apply to entire frameworks, not the strategy component, and many require significant prediction and opinion to answer. For example, "Will your strategy [i.e., framework] beat the market?" Well, if you know the answer is yes, why would you need to do any thinking at all? Just beat the market and get rich and famous. Other tests like, "Does your strategy balance commitment and flexibility?" or "Is there conviction to act on your strategy?" while useful for testing framework alternatives, are quite subjective. The five disqualifiers are less subjective, minimize the need for prediction, and allow for testing the strategy component itself. They also apply to any endeavor or function, not just a business unit, and can be used selectively on the other designed framework components.

What's Behind the Disqualifiers

For a statement to function as a strategy, it must meet the three requirements of a solution to the killer problems of change and innovation: be a free choice, supply real-time guidance, and unify all decisions and actions. How can you know whether a prospective strategy meets the three requirements?

One way is to analyze it using the theory in Chapters 3 through 7 where they were developed. It turns out, however, there are five relatively easy-to-identify characteristics that reveal a failure to meet the requirements. Putting these characteristics into question form yields the *five disqualifiers:*

1. The **opposite** disqualifier: is the opposite of the statement absurd?
2. The **numbers** disqualifier: does the statement include numbers or dates?
3. The **duplicate** disqualifier: is the statement the same as the parent strategy?
4. The **excluded** disqualifier: is there any part of the system to which the statement does not apply?
5. The **list** disqualifier: is the statement a list?

The disqualifiers work in reverse from traditional tests and require a "no" answer to pass; "yes" means the strategy fails, hence the name *disqualifiers.* For instance, a statement consisting of the following three items would be disqualified as a strategy because you would answer "yes" to the question, "Is it a list?":

1. Transform our understanding of customer needs using AI,
2. Discontinue products with lower than 45 percent gross margin, and
3. Cut administrative costs by 30 percent in three years.

The disqualifiers generate creative tension to correct unfit strategy design. If a statement fails even one of the disqualifiers, it is, at best, an aspiration or plan masquerading as a strategy. When there is a significant failure, the statement is likely no more than a cliché or truism. Working by negation, revealing fallacies instead of affirming goodness, allows the disqualifiers to give real-time guidance, making them adaptive.

Figure 8.1 shows the disqualifiers as part of an adaptive feedback loop. If one disqualifier does not catch a failure, then go to the next. You can apply them in any order. In practice, Figure 8.1 is in people's heads, not part of a formal feedback system. To get the most out of the disqualifiers, learn and use them habitually.

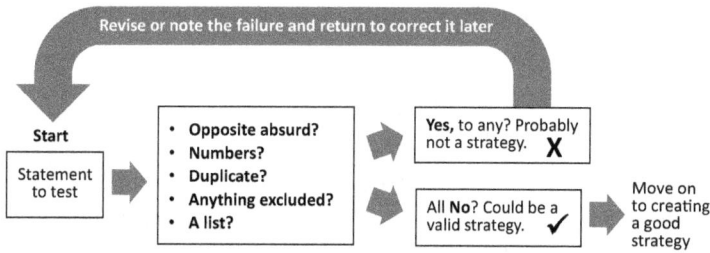

Figure 8.1 Flow schematic for using the five disqualifiers

Not only are the disqualifiers used when designing, but also when implementing strategy. During implementation, the disqualifiers will reveal if a strategy no longer makes sense, either because conditions changed or because the diagnosis was wrong all along. Sometimes, starting implementation is the only way to discover a misdiagnosis.

Applying disqualifiers can become a skill for a team, driving objectivity, collaboration, and creativity. People can "tune their ears" to statements that pass or fail, becoming sensitized to poor strategy functionality. They may even have fun, especially with the opposite disqualifier (recreational strategy). And because less subject knowledge is needed than when using traditional tests, people who are outside of an organization can use them. Managers, commanders, governors, and leaders of all types often need to judge others' work but cannot possibly know all details. Board members, directors, and advisers can often know even less.

To be clear, passing the five disqualifiers does not indicate you have a good strategy—passing only indicates that you have a strategy *at all*. These are disqualifiers, not qualifiers. To judge how good a strategy is requires judging the entire framework. Yet having a functioning strategy is half the battle toward good one. The following explains each disqualifier, showing how they work and examples of their use.

The Opposite Disqualifier: Is the *Opposite* Absurd?

The concept of the opposite is found occasionally in the strategy literature (e.g., Roger Martin and Fredmund Malik),[1] yet it has probably been around for a long time. People use it naturally, almost as folk wisdom, to reveal bad logic, for instance, as Captain (Ret. U.S. Army) Wayne P. Hughes does in *Naval maneuver warfare*:[2]

> *Contemporary American military reformers seem to claim that maneuver warfare is everything good: outwitting the enemy, creating and exploiting an information advantage, moving faster and more adroitly, and shooting more precisely and effectively. In the rhetoric, maneuver warfare is "rapid, violent, coordinated attack." But who would espouse the opposite, a "slow, feeble, disorganized attack?" If maneuver warfare is nothing more than fighting intelligently, then its antithesis is "stupid" warfare.*

The simple question "Is the opposite of the statement absurd?" brings insight into not only whether a statement is a strategy, but whether it communicates information at all! If the opposite of any statement is absurd, then the statement almost certainly has no trade-off. It is *at best* a useful aspiration. But, if it is plainly evident that the opposite is absurd, the statement is probably a cliché or a truism that clogs the airways with noise, allowing people to think they have said something meaningful.

To find the opposite, look for the word (or words) that is intended to give direction, then flip that word to its opposite. Figure 8.2 displays an obvious failure: The opposite of maximize financial return is *minimize financial return*. Who is trying to minimize financial return? Even a nonprofit or a business focused on societal benefit over profit would still not seek to minimize financial return. The opposite of *maximize financial return* is certainly absurd in any situation, and therefore can never be a strategy.

Technically, *maximize financial return* is an aspiration, but not a useful one. It is a truism with no trade-off that gives zero information. To include

Entity	Statement to test	Opposite	Result
Business	Our strategy is to maximize financial return	Minimize financial return	Opposite absurd—not a strategy

Figure 8.2 An obvious failure of the opposite disqualifier

it in a framework as a strategy, a goal, or as anything, is to waste ink or photons by stating the mind-numbingly obvious. Yet you may find it.

Failing the opposite disqualifier means a statement cannot meet the three requirements of a solution to the killer problems of change. It is never a *free choice* to maximize financial return because it is an aspiration far to the right-hand side of the influence diagram (Chapter 3). If maximizing financial return were a choice, everyone could have any financial return that they like, just by wishing it so. You can't know financial return until the results are in, so there is no *real-time guidance* (and knowing if a return was maximized would require knowing the returns from every path not taken). And, even if *maximize financial return* were a useful aspiration, Chapter 4 showed that aspirations cannot be strategies because they do not *unify* decisions and actions on the left-hand side of the influence diagram. Specifying when to maximize financial return, for instance, in a four- versus one-year horizon, might convert *maximize financial return* from empty truism to a useful aspiration.

Figure 8.3 shows a less-obvious failure of the opposite disqualifier. No one would espouse a high-cost strategy, high cost itself is never an objective; therefore, low cost is almost certainly not a strategy. A business may *accept* high cost in return for some other value, such as premium performance, and therefore premium pricing, but the high cost is a trade-off. It would be absurd to aspire to high cost.

Entity	Statement to test	Opposite	Result
Business	We have a low-cost strategy	... high-cost strategy	Opposite absurd—not a strategy

Figure 8.3 A less-obvious failure of the opposite test

Aspiring to low cost may make perfect sense but turning the sentiment into a strategy requires more business content. It requires identifying the bottleneck that is unique to the business and creating a rule that unifies around that bottleneck. For instance, for a company to lower cost whose product line has become hopelessly complicated may need a strategy to *raise* R&D spending. R&D may need to invent more flexible products that replace many specialized ones. The opposite of "raise R&D

Entity	Statement to test	Opposite	Result
Business	Our strategy is to price products for high margin versus high volume	... price for high volume versus high margin	Not obviously absurd—might be a strategy

Figure 8.4 A statement that passes the opposite test

spending" is certainly not absurd. A strategy defined as be low cost could lead to every function in the organization reducing cost with no differential management, which is aimless. The opposite disqualifier illuminates the subtle difference between low cost as a reasonable aspiration and a non-functioning strategy.

Figure 8.4 shows a statement whose opposite is not absurd, and therefore, might be a valid strategy if it passes the remaining four disqualifiers. In principle, it is a free choice to decide whether to price high or low, so long as the decision makers accept the consequences—the trade-offs. Pricing high for high margins may mean losing market share. Pricing low to increase share sometimes irrevocably destroys margins and profitability. Firms have gotten rich by lowering prices (consumer electronics, Model T) and raising prices (luxury goods). That it is an unobvious choice with tough trade-offs is a sign of a potentially valid strategy. *Price for high margin* gives real-time guidance; can be defined and contrasted with low price, so no one needs to wait for results to judge whether they are pricing high; and assuming the pricing rule applies to all the products in the system governed by this framework, it would give unifying guidance.

Ford's Model T mission (Chapter 2) was not low cost, it was *low price and high availability* to get automobiles into the hands of the common people, which has a meaningful opposite—he even sold cars below cost at the end of the Model T lifecycle. His strategies for achieving his mission changed as his bottlenecks changed. For instance, he raised worker salaries to the unheard-of five dollars a day to retain workers because of the monotony of the assembly line, a tactic hardly consistent with across-the-board low cost.

Many commonly used words shown in Figure 8.5 are nearly guaranteed to fail the opposite disqualifier. Some may be useful to describe aspirations, but many are just noise. Unfortunately, these are seductive action

Minimize	Transform	Disrupt	Innovate
Maximize	Get results	Strengthen	Breakthrough
Improve	Grow	Sustain	Capture value
Enhance	Drive	Effectively	Advance
Optimize	Attract	Efficiently	Accelerate

Figure 8.5 Words nearly guaranteed to fail the opposite disqualifier

words that may give illusions of success: "my organization gets it that our strategy is to optimize and grow," "my unit understands that results are all that matter," "my team is accelerating," etc., etc." These words may project excitement to bosses or boards, but don't fool your people and don't fool yourself. Express sentiment in hard-hitting, jargon-free language that shows the tough trade-offs and uncertainties. You may then be rewarded with the discovery that you do not yet have a strategy. The opposite disqualifier will help you ferret out worthless clichés and truisms. Once learned, you may find yourself using this disqualifier all the time—on strategy and communication in general.

One case where an absurd opposite is useful is when people become disconnected from reality and forget the true objectives. They can get stuck in inconsequential details or philosophize at inappropriate times or maybe just be complacent. When these happen, a traditional way to get people's attention is to state the obvious: "your job is to make money," or, "enough with the strategy talk, your job now is to get something done, kapish?"

The Numbers Disqualifier: Does It Have *Numbers* or *Dates*?

A statement with numbers, including dates, rarely functions as a strategy. Numbers usually signify a specific goal, plan, or sometimes a tactic.

Each of the statements in Figure 8.6 is disqualified by a number, date, or both. None of these statements meets the three requirements of a strategy: If it were a free choice to grow 6 percent per year, why not choose 60 percent, or hey, 60,000,000 percent? If it is a free choice to launch in 2026, why not launch it in 2025 and make more money (assuming you would)? And because each is defined for the future, none supply

Entity	Statement
	Our strategy is to …
Business	… launch a new product by 2026
Business	… grow African revenue 40% in the next three years
Business	… be #1 or #2 in cost leadership in our industry
Business	… grow 6%/year versus the industry rate of 3%/year
Sportswoman	… score 100 points this season
Person	… lose 3 kg per month for the next six months
Person	… get married by 2044
Government	… reduce the deficit by 25 billion Euros per year
Government	… increase high school graduation rates by 15% in three years
Government	… achieve a debt ratio equal to the top 10-percentile of benchmark countries

Figure 8.6 Statements that fail the numbers disqualifier

real-time guidance. Some statements in Figure 8.6 have unifying value as aspirations, and often a strategy is stated along with its numerical goal, for instance, "We will grow our revenue in Africa 40% in the next 3 years by focusing exclusively on distributor channels and not direct sales to consumers." The number articulates only the goal, so it does not disqualify the strategy of "exclusive focus on distributors."

Why is the numbers disqualifier needed if the opposite already disqualifies aspirations and plans as strategy? Because the opposite disqualifier cannot catch a statement with numbers. The opposite of a number or date is undefined. There is no opposite to "grow African revenue 40%" or to any of the other statements in Figure 8.6.

Set Points—An Unlikely, But Possible Exception to the Numbers Disqualifier

If the number is a *set point*, then the statement can be a rule, and therefore is not automatically disqualified as a strategy. Thermostats, for instance, control temperature with rules that include a set point. For instance, it is a free choice to set the thermostat to 18 degrees with the rules, "if temperature less than 17 degrees, send heat; if temperature greater than 19 degrees, stop sending heat." The rules gives real-time guidance to the furnace.

Figure 8.7 shows valid rules with set point numbers and dates. In these examples, even though the set point number does not automatically rule out a free choice, this does not mean any of these are a free choice. Practicing golf three times a week may be unrealistic, either due to lack of time or lack of discipline. Few people stick to weight-loss diets. As with the use of the opposite disqualifier, some insight into system capability is needed to judge free choice. Also, even though a set point rule can be a strategy, statements with numbers like in Figure 8.7 are usually tactical rules or techniques. The specificity of numbers usually keeps a statement from being central and abstract enough to unify all decisions and actions.

Entity	Statement
Navy	Stay within 150 nautical miles of enemy cruisers.
Person	Invest 30% of funds into high-risk, high-potential reward stocks.
Business	Invest only in acquisitions predicted to give greater than 25% ROI (no investments may meet this criterion).
Person	Get a golf instructor and practice three times a week.
Organization	Promote to vice president only candidates that have held positions in at least three departments.
Army	All officer candidates will spend at least 6 months as enlisted soldiers.
Business	Cap funding of program WAM-17.56 to 20% of R&D budget.
Person	Aim for fewer than 35 grams of carbohydrates per day to lose weight and avoid Type II diabetes.

Figure 8.7 Set point statements that pass the numbers disqualifier

The Duplicate Disqualifier: Is It the Same as the Parent?

The duplicate disqualifier asks whether the prospective strategy is the same as the parent strategy. If the answer is yes—if it *duplicates* the parent—then it is not a valid strategy. The duplicate arises directly from the proper design of nested strategies in Chapter 7. If the child copies any aspect of the parent, it adds no information. The copied components are correct but useless; they are truisms. The parent framework is an external constraint to the child framework; it is not a free choice for the child to follow it or not. If a strategy different from that of the parent isn't needed, then a nested system may not be needed. Figure 8.8 illustrates the duplicate disqualifier.

The prime minister and commander-in-chief of the country Freedonia states the following strategy for dealing with a border conflict with the neighboring country Tomainia:

We will not retaliate the occasional rocket attack, yet we will maintain position and not back down.

Her diagnosis is that the border conflict is just a ploy that the president of Tomainia concocted because he is losing popularity. She is not willing to give one centimeter of land, because it is legally unwarranted and unacceptable to the Freedonian people. Her goal is to keep emotions cool in Tomainia with the trade-off that a rocket could do damage or hurt her people.

What are possible strategies for her generals who command the border with Tomainia? They cannot simply repeat "do not retaliate against rocket attacks, but maintain position." This is not a free choice because it is already an external constraint on the Generals. If they repeat it, they add no information.

Valid strategies for the Generals would bust the bottleneck of emotional strain on the Freedonian troops caused by the inability to retaliate against attacks, for instance rotate troops often, or increase frontline high-ranking officer presence. Other strategies might involve leading the enemy to false or inconsequential targets or giving troops some super protection. Whatever it is, the General's strategy must be different from, yet still consistent, with the prime minister's strategy.

Figure 8.8 A border conflict

What if There Is No Parent?

Sometimes, it is easy to identify the parent that has evident authority, for example: a business unit leader in a corporation, a coach of a sports club, military officers, or a board of directors (perhaps not if the CEO dominates the board). These parents have the right to impose constraints on their reports, though whether they have the power is another question. A business owner, the president of a country, or individuals in daily life, however, strictly speaking, have no entities above them, so their strategy passes the duplicate by definition. But, as stated in Chapter 7, everyone "answers" to somebody even without a strict external constraint relationship. Everyone must satisfy someone else in some way. One who owes money can't ignore the bankers, movie or pop stars have fans to satisfy, and politicians are beholden their constituents and their donors.

What of Uniqueness to Peers?

Michael Porter demands a "unique value proposition" as part of his tests and advice for businesses. Should we modify the duplicate test to read "same as parent or peer?" There's certainly no harm in including "peer," but the opposite test will likely flag statements that are broad so that they apply to many businesses. Also, Porter's unique value proposition applies to the entire framework, not just the strategy rule, and therefore it is often best used as a framework test (Chapter 17).

The Excluded Disqualifier: Does It *Exclude* Anything?

The excluded disqualifier says, if there is any part of the system to which a statement does not apply, then the statement cannot be a strategy for that system. In other words, if there are any products, people, assets, or other entities that are not a target of the statement, then the statement is disqualified as a strategy. The excluded disqualifier directly audits the unification requirement of a solution to the killer problems. If a statement is not relevant to the entire scope of the system, then it cannot unify all decisions and actions. Figure 8.9 demonstrates the excluded disqualifier.

The business in described in Figure 8.9 has two options to resolve their strategy failure: Create nested systems where "performance improvement" applies only to the framework for the new products, and then design a different strategy for the commodities. A strategy for the commodities may involve something like forward or backward integration to enable a new source of differentiation. An extreme example would be to curtail investment of any kind into the commodities, except that which is required to uphold core values and meet regulatory requirements. The trade-off would

> A business has ten product lines. Six are new and four are late-in-lifecycle commodities. Everyone in the business agrees on a diagnosis that it does not make sense to improve the performance or features of the commodities because the incremental market share or price gain will be minimal. Resources are better spent on the new products that have greater potential for improvement. If this diagnosis is true, then the following statement fails as the business's strategy:
>
> *... outsource manufacturing and instead put our resources into product performance improvement.*
>
> This statement fails because no matter how well it applies to the six early-lifecycle product lines, the strategy is not relevant to the commodities.

Figure 8.9 The excluded disqualifier in product portfolio management

be expected decline in share—a cash cow strategy. If the business does not have the leadership capability to manage a nested two-tier portfolio like this, and can't make the hard choices and say no, the other option is to divest the commodity product lines. A similar logic applies to portfolios of investments, startups in a venture portfolio, and the like.

The excluded disqualifier is the trickiest to apply because it requires the most knowledge of the system. In the example here, it is hard to know when products are maturing without waiting for the decline to show up in the bottom line. When managing a venture portfolio, it is hard to know which startups are getting early traction.

The List Disqualifier: Is the Statement in the Form of a *List*?

The opposite may be the most excellent disqualifier, but the list disqualifier is not far behind. A list of facts is not a theory; a bulleted list of truths on a PowerPoint slide doesn't necessarily add up to a point; and a list of aspirations, plans, rules, policies, initiatives, or anything else—no matter how insightful, inspiring, or actionable—is almost certainly not a strategy. Even a list of central rules that pass the other disqualifiers, and are therefore potentially valid strategies when judged individually, is almost certainly not a strategy in itself. Yet, a vast number of "strategies" consist of lists, especially lists of subgoals, plans, and initiatives. Chapter 4 showed that granularizing aspirations into a multitude of subgoals and strategy themes without a unifying rule does not solve the killer problems.

A list suggests that the bottlenecks are not understood. It signifies that no one did the hard thinking to make trade-offs. Lists are like warming up and never playing the game or jotting down initial thoughts and submitting as a final product. Look out for lists; they are a bane of strategy and communication too.

The most common form of "strategy" lists is like the strategy themes shown in Chapter 1 (Figure 1.1). The list disqualifier isn't even needed to know that such a list of subgoals, plans, and clichés is not a strategy because nearly every item already fails either the opposite, numbers, or duplicate disqualifier. But what about Figure 8.10 where each item is a well-stated rule that is a free choice, gives real-time guidance, and could be a valid strategy? No, the list in Figure 8.10 is still not a strategy (and to be sure, most lists are not laden with such valid rules or even valid aspirations. Most are closer to Figure 1.1.)

While each item in Figure 8.10 might be a valid rule (and look like a good thing to do) when taken individually, the combination of items is probably not a free choice. Launching fewer products may be a free choice, and as such might de-emphasize small accounts, but it may not be a free choice to do both. What if the multinationals demand more product variety from their suppliers? Further, if these two directives conflict, then there is no real-time guidance. Which of the two should be followed? The strategy gives no information on that.

Now, what if each of the items in Figure 8.10 were also consistent with each of the others? Then this list would *still* not be a strategy. The strategy would be the statement that makes them consistent, that is, that unifies them; and the items in the list would be tactics under that strategy, each designed to bust a bottleneck to a subgoal. A strategy designed around a "simplify, even if it means losing market opportunities" concept might be valid if this business had gotten ahead of itself by selling to

Our growth strategy :

1. Launch fewer products but add more features to the products we do launch.

2. Focus the sales force on multinational accounts and de-emphasize local accounts.

3. Eliminate direct sales for all accounts smaller than $400K; distributors only.

4. Promote "reliability" in all advertising, suspending other messages until products show an upward trajectory in online reviews.

5. Add new manufacturing capacity only after we average 80% utilization rate for three years.

6. Stop pursuing acquisition targets and instead invest only in organic growth.

Figure 8.10 Each item is a potentially valid strategy, but the list itself is not

anybody and growing too quickly by acquiring new assets without integration or consistency.

Lists make people feel safe. "Hey, no problem, that initiative is on the list," or "Look, we're making everything better." "Who can criticize? Everyone on the team got their bullet point, we are unified." But when everything is important, nothing is important. And keep in mind, it is easy-peasy to create an appalling list without bullets or numbering, like in Figure 8.11 (this "strategy" fails the other four disqualifiers as well).

One case where a list could be a strategy is when the items in the list are of the same rule. For instance, Figure 8.12 could represent a factory's strategy during a new product line launch. The three items are one thought process, none of the items are independent or have meaning without the others. The rule is about the priority of the three items rather than the individual items themselves. As a single thought process, each element is a free choice, and the list unifies decisions and actions with real-time guidance. Another example of a list that is a strategy is Mao's four war principles in Chapter 6.

> **Our strategy:** We will differentially manage the end-to-end supply chain to support our cash-generation goals. Consistent with our strategic marketing vision, we will segment supply-chain services to match customer value. In today's ever-increasingly competitive global marketplace, we must focus on manufacturing productivity by doubling factory utilization rates and simplifying the product portfolio. We will focus resources on developing strategic growth products and improving customer service levels to over 95%. We will use state-of-the-art data systems to transform the way we work and be agile in everything we do.

Figure 8.11 An appalling list in sheep's clothing

> Our strategy is to utilize our manufacturing resources as follows ...
>
> Priority 1: meeting quality requirements versus throughput,
> Priority 2: automation for increased throughput, and
> Priority 3: automation for cost reduction
>
> We will not work on a lower priority item unless there is a period when nothing can be achieved on higher priorities.

Figure 8.12 A list that could be a strategy

Maxims

One valuable type of list is techniques representing knowledge in a field of endeavor. These *maxims* may also be labeled guidelines, principles, commandments, directives, or tips. Figure 8.13 is one such list.

It is easy to find examples in many fields: W. Edwards Deming's 14 points, John Grisham's Tips for how to Write Popular Fiction,[4] Elinor Ostrom's 8 Principles for Managing a Commons,[5] and Colin Gray's 40 Maxims on War, Peace, and Strategy (lists of many maxims seem common in military theory). These lists, however, are not strategies. They are standalone knowledge collections that a framework may refer to or incorporate. A strategy may be needed to build the capability to adhere to maxims.

1. Build your team, intrapreneuring is not a solo activity.
2. Share credit widely.
3. Ask for advice before you ask for resources.
4. Under-promise and overdeliver—publicity triggers the corporate immune system.
5. Do any job needed to make your dream work, regardless of your job description.
6. Remember it is easier to ask for forgiveness than for permission.
7. Keep the best interests of the company and its customers in mind, especially when you have to bend the rules or circumvent the bureaucracy.
8. Come to work each day willing to be fired.
9. Be true to your goals, but be realistic about how to achieve them.
10. Honor and educate your sponsors.

Figure 8.13 Pinchot's Ten Commandments for intrapreneurs[3]

Summary of the Five Disqualifiers

Figure 8.14 summarizes the five disqualifiers (see {web/supplement} for downloadable version).

The Five Disqualifiers of Strategy

Even <u>one</u> **yes means** the statement is likely disqualified as a strategy

DISQUALIFIER	YES MEANS...
Is the **OPPOSITE** absurd?	At best an aspiration, but very possibly a cliché or truism
Does it include **NUMBERS**?	A goal or plan (if a set point, then likely a tactic)
Does it **DUPLICATE** the parent?	Truism that adds no information
Does it **EXCLUDE** anything or anyone?	Not unified
Is it a **LIST**?	Likely not unified, missing real-time guidance, or lacking trade-offs

Figure 8.14 Summary of the five disqualifiers

Test Your Bike Shop

Your first strategy (Framework 3.1) was *My Thing: invest funds and effort only into high-end and novel offerings as opposed to a full standard product line.* Applying the disqualifiers:

> **Opposite?** Pass. The opposite is the more obvious approach.
> **Number?** Pass.
> **Excluded?** Pass. Gives direction for all resources.
> **Duplicate?** Pass. While responsible to your bank, they do not demand your My Thing strategy.
> **List?** Pass. The statement of the opposite does not make it a list.

This valid central strategy rule came with tough trade-offs: riskier, more borrowing, and more effort. Your strategy changed 18 months later when you realized you had to make a change to address a new bottleneck.

> *Evangelize strategy: be only a full-time ambassador/marketer for the shop and for biking; no running the shop.*

This strategy passes only four of the Disqualifiers. It passes the opposite (well stated as what not to do), and it resulted in tougher trade-offs that you articulated: even more borrowing, risk with new shop manager, even more effort, possibly look like Don Quixote. There are still no numbers. You still have no one to report to but the bank, so you are not duplicating another strategy, and there is no list. But if you labeled this strategy as the bike shop strategy, it would fail the excluded disqualifier. This strategy gives guidance only for you, not Wrenchy, nor Marie, your new shop manager. But you solved this problem by creating a nested system where they each have their own strategies to cover all aspects of the shop.

The Disqualifiers Compared to Traditional Strategy Tests

What makes the disqualifiers and their "no" answers different from traditional tests that require positive "yes" answers? It is because the disqualifiers work at a lower level, adaptively destroying the unfit versus selecting the fit. The disqualifiers look nothing like the result they are intended to enable—one of the telltale signs of an adaptive emergent process. Contrast this with "will your strategy beat the market," or "does your strategy align with the key success factors of your chosen environment?" Knowing the answers to these tests is outcome thinking tantamount to predicting every aspect of the future and knowing nearly everything in the influence diagram. This is the same argument that led to killer problem 4—that what matters most is the least actionable, as illustrated in Figure 3.10.

High-level tests are quite subjective, for example, "Is your strategy contaminated with bias?" Who will stand up and say, "Yes, my strategy is contaminated by bias, it does not form a consistent whole, and there are way better alternatives"?

While the tests from the literature are not useful for testing the strategy component, the best of them are useful for testing entire framework alternatives and useful as fitness criteria in the strategy alternative matrix, as shown in Chapters 15 and 17. They can be ordered in terms of usefulness as shown in Figure 8.15, mostly by how much of the influence diagram that must be specified to answer.

WHAT IS TESTED?	EXAMPLES	ISSUES	WHEN USEFUL
Highest-level, overall outcome	Will your strategy ...beat the market? ...achieve the desired end?	Requires knowing the entire influence diagram.	Never
High-level outcomes	Does your strategy ...align with the key success factors of your chosen environment? ...address those issues or problem areas which are crucially important within the chosen context?	Still require major judgement	Rarely
The process	Is your strategy contaminated by bias? Have you embraced uncertainty?	Can't be answered unless modified	If restated → How have we limited bias? How is uncertainty embraced?
Higher-level framework characteristics	Do the elements of your strategy form a coherent whole? Do you have sufficient resources?	Only have meaning to entire framework; can be hard to judge	Sometimes for auditing entire framework
Lower-level framework characteristics	Does your strategy ...provide a unique value proposition, tailored value chain, and continuity? ...rest on privileged insights?	Usually apply to entire framework	For auditing entire framework
Strategy component	Does your strategy provide clear trade-offs? And explain what not to do?	Require more judgement than the disqualifiers, but are excellent tests	Always

(left axis) Increasing Usefulness

(right axis) More influence diagram needed

Figure 8.15 *Evaluation of literature Strategy Tests (selected from* Strategy Tests from The Literature *{web/supplement})*

Examples of Applying the Disqualifiers

Following are examples of applying the five disqualifiers. Other examples in diverse fields of endeavor are shown online {web/disqualifiers}.

Electro Ltd. Marketing Strategy

Imagine an electronics parts supplier called Electro Ltd. The company has been struggling to get its marketing people to work in a consistent way. For help, they hire Oskar, a consultant from the firm Smarten Duden, GmbH. They show Oskar the one-page strategy created by Electro's vice president of marketing (Figure 8.16).

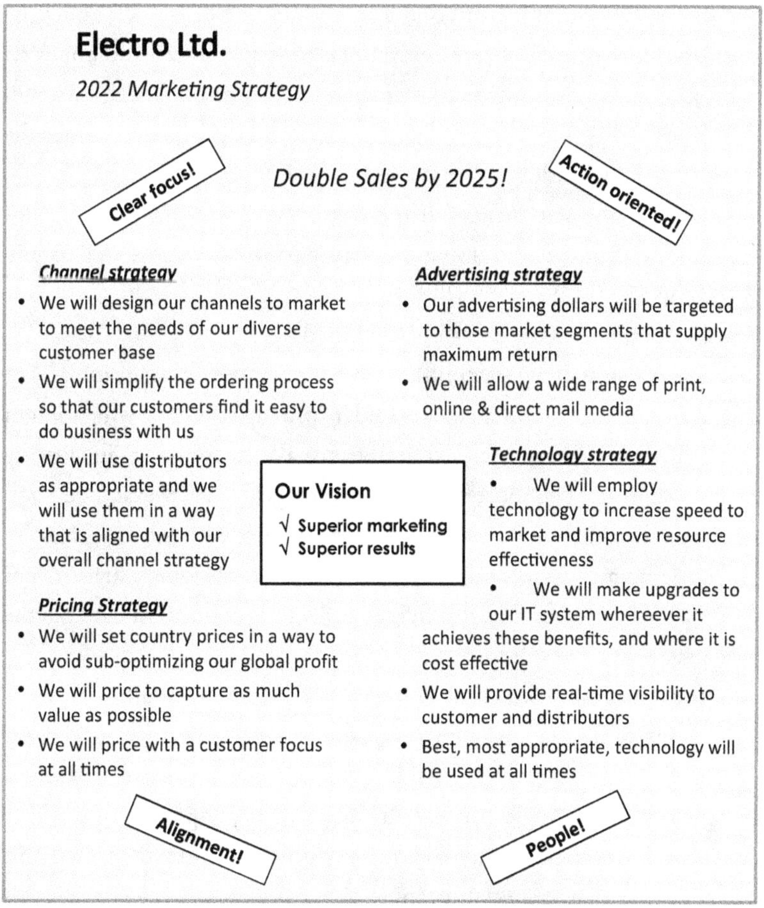

Electro Ltd.

2022 Marketing Strategy

Clear focus!   Double Sales by 2025!   *Action oriented!*

Channel strategy
- We will design our channels to market to meet the needs of our diverse customer base
- We will simplify the ordering process so that our customers find it easy to do business with us
- We will use distributors as appropriate and we will use them in a way that is aligned with our overall channel strategy

Our Vision
√ Superior marketing
√ Superior results

Pricing Strategy
- We will set country prices in a way to avoid sub-optimizing our global profit
- We will price to capture as much value as possible
- We will price with a customer focus at all times

Advertising strategy
- Our advertising dollars will be targeted to those market segments that supply maximum return
- We will allow a wide range of print, online & direct mail media

Technology strategy
- We will employ technology to increase speed to market and improve resource effectiveness
- We will make upgrades to our IT system whereever it achieves these benefits, and where it is cost effective
- We will provide real-time visibility to customer and distributors
- Best, most appropriate, technology will be used at all times

Alignment!   *People!*

Figure 8.16 Electro's initial marketing "strategy"

Oskar studies the document and interviews people throughout the organization. He shares his seven-point assessment with Electro's leadership:

1. Your document is not a strategy. It attempts to be a tactical policy table, but several statements are no more than goals, and others are just noise and clichés. Each one of the four "strategies" fails the **list** disqualifier; nearly every individual statement fails the **opposite** disqualifier. For instance, would anyone in your organization suggest using the "*worst, least-appropriate* technology"? Are there people in Electro who believe that it would be a good thing to "*complicate* the ordering process for their customers"?

2. Two statements have meaningful content: "We will use a wide-range of media including print, online, and direct email" shown under the Advertising heading gives useful real-time guidance. The opposite, "allow only narrow range of media … " is not absurd. "We will provide real-time visibility to customers and distributors" under the technology heading also has a nonabsurd opposite.

3. Most of the statements fail the **duplicate** disqualifier and are not unique. Most would apply to every part of Electro as well as any competitor.

4. Customer service seems to be **excluded**.

5. Some **list** statements conflict, even under the same heading. For example, the three statements under "pricing strategy," which might individually be sensible, collectively make no sense at all. Pricing to "capture 10% more much value each year" (what exactly do you mean by this?) could well be in direct conflict with setting prices "in a way to avoid sub-optimizing our global profit," which suggests not maximizing price for value in each individual country. What does the statement, "we will price with a customer focus at all times" mean?

6. The vision—√ Superior Marketing √ Superior results—fails the **opposite** disqualifier. Do these superlatives really drive excellence? The vision doesn't fail the **list** disqualifier because the two statements seem to be a single concept. It does fail the **duplicate** disqualifier because these points are true for any business on earth. Unless this vision has some special meaning to the organization (does it?), this vision is just noise.

7. Finally, the four sound bites in the boxes—Clear focus, Action oriented, People, Alignment—are a **list** in the same rallying-cry spirit
as the vision, but they are more random. Again, unless there is some
special meaning to these, they are noise.

Oskar explained, "to correct these flaws, you need to articulate the
bottlenecks to aligning the marketing organization, then you can create
coherent policies that will make sense."

Though his message was harsh, his honesty swayed Electro's leadership to accept his approach. Oskar worked them through a framework
design process. He showed how to involve the entire organization so that
the leaders could hear what the marketing people were experiencing, and
so they all could get ownership and pride in the plan. Once people converted the affirmative statements into tactical rules, much of the noise
and confusion subsided. The result was a new one-page marketing policy,
Figure 8.17. They agreed to manage customer service in a separate effort.

Electro Ltd.

2022 Marketing Policy

*If we are to double sales by 2025, we need to work together in a
common way! Here is what we have agreed.*

Channel policy

- Because of our diverse customer base, sell in three channels: distributors, on-line, and direct local sales.
- Err on the side of simple customer ordering processes, even if it means higher return rates.
- Use distributors *only* if customers meet the conditions outlined in our Distributor Policy Table.

Pricing policy

- Set prices to maximize global returns, even if it means losing some profit in individual countries.
- The pricing committee determines global pricing levels.

Our Vision
√ **Standard policy**
√ **Consistent choices**

Advertising policy

- Run each advertisement for at least one-year; historically we are too quick to judge results.
  - Allow a wide range of print, online & direct mail media.

Technology policy

- Strongly resist the temptation to employ new Information technology unless it meets the four requirements established by the Marketing Leadership Team. Too often we have been seduced by the supposed value of copious real-time data.
- Provide real-time order-status visibility to distributors only, not customers

---

Figure 8.17 Electro Ltd. marketing policy after working with Oskar

Oskar then helped Electro design a strategy for implementing the marketing policy. He points out that the bottleneck to bust is that the organization doesn't believe leadership will enforce the policy because others have been ignored in the past. Though reluctant to spend the time (and perhaps a bit insulted), the vice president of marketing agreed to a strategy of spending one day a week auditing and teaching the team until adherence was ingrained. The vice president would not only review adherence metrics, but also perform hands-on reviews of personal at all levels of the organization. It was agreed that unless a senior leader showed this discipline, the organization would not make the change. Oskar convinced leadership that while this strategy seemed inconsequential, it was in fact needed to bust the bottleneck to achieving the marketing aspiration.

Add-Co Growth Strategy

Imagine Add-Co, a business producing specialty additives for construction industry materials. The company is growing well in Europe and aspires to enter frontier markets. Their bottleneck diagnosis is that current Euro products are not quite right for frontier markets and are over-designed and too expensive in several cases. So, they created the following strategy to bust this bottleneck: *develop frontier markets by modifying and cost-reducing Euro products and grow in Europe by continuing to add product functionality.*

Is this a valid strategy? No. It passes all the disqualifiers but one. The **opposite** of modifying Euro products for frontier markets is not absurd. They considered a viable alternative of encouraging Euro product adoption by offering intense product development to frontier customers. There are no **numbers** in the strategy. It passes the **duplicate** because the corporate strategy is the highest level in the corporation and it passes the **excluded** because it includes both markets. The Add-Co strategy is invalid because it fails the **list** disqualifier, even though it is only a two-item list. The list does not unify decisions throughout the functional organizations leading to conflicts between and within Sales & Marketing, R&D (product development), and operations (factory and supply chain).

R&D is overloaded because Euro Sales has traditionally been able to demand new products as desired. But now Frontier Sales needs products and cost reduction, and R&D doesn't know how to prioritize. R&D also lacks experience in frontier designs and needs to invest resources to build capability. Similarly, operations struggles to juggle R&D factory trial time requests for frontier products on top of ongoing development for Euro products and their assignment to reduce manufacturing and supply-chain costs. They also fear being labeled "not customer-focused" if they say no to Euro product trial requests. Further, because of steady and profitable growth in Europe, no one has bothered to model the cost, utilization rates, and working capital requirements of products making joint decisions with R&D and Sales challenging. In Sales & Marketing, people don't want to work on frontier development because it is speculative and very different than Euro business. Salespeople are used to bonuses based on quarterly sales that have been increasing. Euro Salespeople are fearful that their customers will demand price decreases if they hear about "lower-cost" products.

Once Add-Co corporate leadership recognized that the bottleneck to the dual-market goal was organizational conflict, they created a new strategy of bestowing a new product manager position with product-line decision authority. They tasked the product manager with finding the "sweet spot" between (1) adding Euro line functionality, (2) designing and cost-reducing products for frontier markets, and (3) rationalizing the Euro line. Corporate leadership realized that R&D needs more resources and the product manager and a small staff add cost too. These factors led them to add Euro product-line rationalization to liberate cost, working capital, and factory capacity. Figure 8.18 shows the new nested framework design (does not show detailed plans, metrics, or other tactics around milestones for product and organization changes.)

The product manager's strategy is to codify product and resource decisions to give broad guidance to the functions instead of allowing one-off decision making. For instance, the product-segmentation policy table for Euro product development and rationalization (Figure 8.19) identifies allowed resources. A policy table would be created for Frontier products as well. (Note that policy table entries must be tactical rules that pass the opposite and number disqualifiers, not goals. "Price for maximum profitability," for instance, would fail. Clearly, tactics do not have to pass the list disqualifier.)

Corporate

Goal—Enter frontier markets in addition to growth in Europe

Bottleneck—organizational conflicts

Strategy—New product manager position has product-line decision authority (trade-offs: more management, added layers, cost)

Tactic—Fund new costs by rationalizing Euro product line (trade-off: may lose customers)

Product Manager

Goal—Find the sweet spot between (1) adding Euro line functionality; (2) modifying products for frontier line; (3) rationalizing Euro line

Bottleneck—looking like the enemy to Sales & Marketing and envy over new position

Strategy—Codify policy in detail instead of allowing one-off discussions and reacting to requests (trade-offs: new in role so open to criticism? People see it as too rigid?)

Tactic—Euro product segment policy table

Sales & Marketing

Goal—Add Frontier development focus

Bottleneck—Divergence of frontier and Euro tasks

Strategy—Do not mix Frontier & Euro teams (trade-off: adds management)

Tactics—Install a temporary frontier team bonus system, but lobby CEO to eliminate incentive systems completely.

R&D

Goals—Add two programs in addition to advancing Euro product functionality:
- Develop Frontier products
- Rationalize Euro products

Bottleneck—Overwhelmed (despite added budget)

Strategy—Outsource accelerated testing (trade-offs: loss of control, IP risk, cost)

Operations

Goal—Add a supply chain for frontier and support R&D's product development program

Bottleneck—lacking a model of working capital, cost, and factory-time requirement for products

Strategy—Seek agreement with product manager to delay any change until impact is modeled. (trade-off: may appear to hinder progress)

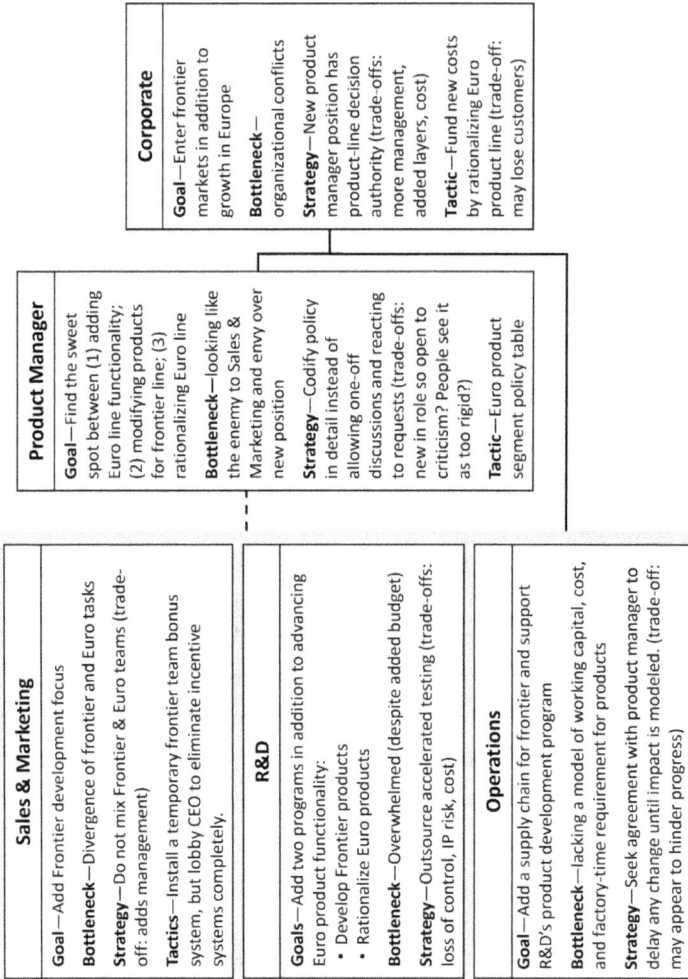

Figure 8.18 Add-Co's simplified nested frameworks

2005 National Strategy for Victory in Iraq

After the 2003 defeat of Saddam Hussain's government, the National Security Council and the White House in November 2005 issued the *National Strategy for Victory in Iraq* to assist development of a stable democracy.[6] Its 35 pages is an astonishing example of lists, 318 items in total, spread among five hierarchical levels, including 49 major arrows, 209 bullet points, 17 dashes, 35 check marks, and 8 numbered *Pillars of Strategic Objectives*. Further, the authors state that they did not show other metrics, classified materials, and "at least five independent lines of action and scores of sub actions," attached to each of the eight *Pillars of Strategic Objectives*, which swells the number of list items further still. (Government organizations, schools, and NGOs seem to be heavily prone to writing long lists).

The document is a framework of sorts. It has visions and missions, and some diagnosis, including beliefs and assumptions about enemies and friends. It includes interpretations of the results obtained in the war so far against overall goals and metrics. What they label as strategies are long lists of predominantly subgoals. They identify "many difficulties" in the way of achieving political and economic stability in Iraq but claim that the "strategy is working," that "solid progress" has been made, and that "failure is not an option" (really?).

Figure 8.20 is a one-half page excerpt showing each level (except the pillars), and three of the major subgoals: *isolate, engage,* and *build*. In other places, these are joined by *clear, hold, restore* and *reform,* spread among the "three integrated strategic tracks—*political, security,* and *economic.*" The *Eight Pillars or Strategic Objectives* listed in an Appendix starting on Page 25 are much the same as the 310 items in the main text.

No matter how sincere the effort, this document is a terrible failure of the opposite and list disqualifiers and not a strategy at all. While an occasional item is a free choice (e.g., the *engage* statement), most are not (e.g., the *build* statement). Yet even if the document were filled with statements that were on their own reasonably free choices, the sheer size of the list rendered hopeless any chance of the overall framework having in it any free choice, real-time guidance, or unification of action in Iraq. There is no apparent effort to determine the dominant bottleneck. It is aimless granularization of goals (Chapter 4) leading to countless useless strategy themes, including the eight pillars, as shown in Figure 8.21. When everything matters, nothing matters.

	CASH COW[a] PRODUCTS	← ON THE BLOCK PRODUCTS → Reach CORE requirement[b] in 1.5 year else move to CASH COW	CORE PRODUCTS	NEW PRODUCTS
Customers		No restrictions		Early adopters only
Respond to customer requests?	No	Only if consistent with approved proposal	Sales & Marketing make proposal to product manger	Customers must have input into design
Pricing	Price must be high enough to achieve 30% above marginal cost	Unless proposal says otherwise, raise prices by minimum 7.5% per quarter to test customer value for the product	If cannot maintain pricing to meet core requirements[b], move to ON THE BLOCK	Price according to target specifications
Order acceptance	Only if opportunistic capacity available[c], no contracts > 12 weeks; no expediting	As part of improvement proposal or normal 14-day lead time.	14-day lead time; expediting requires product mgr. approval	Special order until becomes a CORE product.
R&D product development	None	Only if business team approves a proposal for cost reduction or performance enhancement	Incremental enhancements and new package type/ sizes allowed	As required to achieve the target specifications
Operations resources	No CAPEX; no development; no trials	CAPEX and development resources only if part of approved proposal	Product manager determines CAPEX and development resource priorities with guidance from Operations and Sales & Marketing	

Product-Segmentation Policy for Euro Products

a Eliminate product If no sales in 9 months b Business team determines the profitability, utilization, and working capital requirements for the CORE product segment c As determined by product manager

Figure 8.19 Policy table for segmentation of Add-Co's Euro products

---

OUR STRATEGY FOR VICTORY IS CLEAR

➤ **Our strategy is clear.** We will help the Iraqi people build a new Iraq with a constitutional, representative government that respects civil rights and has security forces sufficient to maintain domestic order and keep Iraq from becoming a safe haven for terrorists. To achieve this end, we are pursuing a comprehensive approach that involves the integrated efforts of the entire United States Government, the Iraqi government, and Coalition governments, and encourages the active involvement of the United Nations, other international organizations, and supportive regional states.

• Our strategy involves **three integrated tracks** -- political, security, and economic -- each with separate objectives, but together helping Iraqis to defeat the terrorists, Saddamists, and rejectionists, and secure a new democratic state in Iraq.

The Political Track
(Isolate, Engage, Build)

-- **Objective:** To help the Iraqi people forge a broadly supported national compact for democratic government, thereby isolating enemy elements from the broader public.

-- To achieve this objective, we are helping the Iraqi government:

✓ **Isolate** hardened enemy elements from those who can be won over to a peaceful political process by countering false propaganda and demonstrating to the Iraqi people that they have a stake in a viable, democratic Iraq.

✓ **Engage** those outside the political process and invite in those willing to turn away from violence through ever-expanding avenues of peaceful participation.

✓ **Build** stable, pluralistic, and effective national institutions that can protect the interests of all Iraqis and facilitate Iraq's full integration into the international community.

Figure 8.20 Excerpt from 2005 National Strategy for Victory in Iraq (bottom page 7)

Isolate hardened enemy elements

Engage those outside the political process

Build stable, pluralistic, and effective national institutions

Restore Iraq's neglected infrastructure

Reform Iraq's economy

Build the capacity of Iraqi institutions to maintain infrastructure

Clear areas of enemy control

Hold areas freed from enemy control

Build Iraqi Security Forces

1. **Defeat** the Terrorists and Neutralize the Insurgency

2. **Transition** Iraq to Security Self-Reliance

3. **Help** Iraqis Form a National Compact for Democratic Government

4. **Help** Iraq Build Government Capacity and Provide Essential Services

5. **Help** Iraq Strengthen its Economy

6. **Help** Iraq Strengthen the Rule of Law and Promote Civil Rights

7. **Increase** International Support for Iraq

8. **Strengthen** Public Understanding of Coalition Efforts

Political track

Economic track   **Victory in Iraq**

Security track

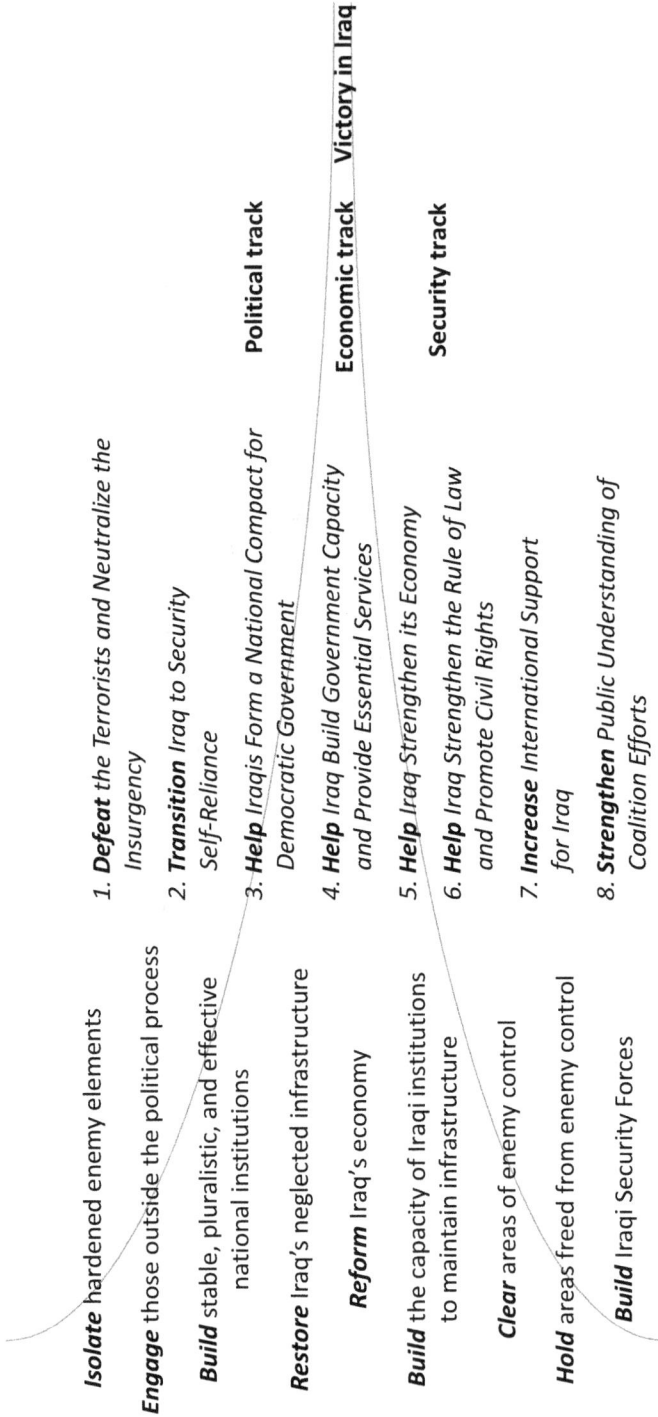

Figure 8.21 *Granularization of aspirations into strategy themes and subgoals in the 2005 National Strategy for Victory in Iraq*

If this is the best strategy and framework that the richest and most powerful country on earth could muster to address one of the most politically important, most far-reaching to humanity, and multitrillion-dollar endeavors of our time, it alone would have been reason to question the theory and practice of strategy.

CHAPTER 9

What Is Execution?

Leaders, strategy writers, and analysts attribute disproportionate blame for success and failure to execution. With strategy so often missing and confused, it is easy to invoke execution as the reason for results. A media pundit says, "Wow! Courier Inc. beat the Street's earnings estimate by 25 cents a share; they really executed!" Well, maybe Courier executed and maybe they didn't. Maybe they pulled sales into the quarter by signing bad contracts or gave discounts that will haunt them in the future or put cost into inventory. Currency may have gone their way, or a competitor may have screwed up. Leadership may have defunded programs for a short-term gain to protect their position. For business unit leaders, pulling in next quarter's sales may be execution if the CEO demands it, but investors might not always see it this way. How often would a constant demand for "*more steam!*" each quarter be viewed as execution? Not to mention, what portion of the results in any given quarter is determined by actions in those three months?

This chapter presents a definition of execution that is a real-time concept, not an outcome, as adaptative action must be. Execution is obviously important for getting good results, but there is little value in waiting till the results are in to judge if people (and leaders) are executing. Management by getting results is management in hindsight, or worse, management by imposition of results, as Deming pointed out.[1] In fact, it is nonsensical to define any approach as "the way to get good results" because it is true for all. Apply the opposite test: heard of any books titled, *A New Approach for Getting Crappy Results and Missing Opportunities—In Three Easy Steps?*

Traditional Concepts of Execution

Complicating things further, the term execution is used in several ways in addition to "get good results." One study concludes that leaders typically equate execution with "alignment" of the organization on their designs,[2] which is certainly a requirement of a leader's framework. But alignment is just one aspect of allowing successful implementation to happen. In other cases, to execute means to implement, that is, *take* decisions and actions as guided by a framework, as opposed to designing the framework. Authors may feel that "execution" of their methods is more invigorating than "implementing," but as said in Chapter 1, there is no need for a redundant term—executing means more than simply implementing.

Execution is sometimes defined as operational excellence, like when an analyst says, "Courier Inc. better stop all this innovation stuff and get back to executing." Or, as one consulting firm said, "It's no secret: innovation is difficult for well-established companies. By and large, they are better executors than innovators, and most succeed less through game changing creativity than by optimizing their existing businesses."[3] The data may be clear and instructive, but this statement also implies that innovation of some type isn't needed for brilliant operation, or worse, that execution isn't needed to innovate. Chapter 2 established that discipline and innovation are inseparable.

Yet the most common misconception of execution remains "to get good results," and sometimes as a catchall explanation for epic successes and failures. A venture capitalist and analyst on Bloomberg Radio said, "Microsoft existed because LOTUS didn't execute, Google existed because Microsoft didn't execute, and Facebook existed because Google didn't execute."[4] (He could have added that IBM PCs succeeded because DEC didn't execute, and perhaps that Amazon exists because Walmart didn't, and on and on. A business school textbook adds that the only difference between Dell's success and Gateway's failure was execution.[5]) In October 2020, amid the Covid pandemic, an investment analyst claimed the stock market was too optimistic as it was valuing the high-flying Zoom, Datadog, and the recent IPO Snowflake for "flawless execution over the long term."[6] These analysts had good insights, but if execution alone can explain the success of Google, Amazon, and Microsoft—whose revenue each exceed the gross national product of two-thirds of the world's countries—or predict the success of Zoom, Datadog, and Snowflake, then execution is every bloody thing under the sun. And like strategy, if execution is every bloody thing under the sun, it's a useless word. Was Zoom's

4× revenue increase in 2020 during Covid due only to their execution? Wasn't Amazon's framework that included investing in their platform for years at the expense of earnings crucial to success despite Wall Street's ire?

Conceiving execution as getting good results doesn't allow for failure. Does an investor who thoughtfully designs a stock portfolio but lags the market for a year fail to execute? Would one who throws a dart to pick a portfolio that beats the market for a year (of course it can happen) have executed? Did every defeated army fail to execute? What if the war was driven by politicians with no realism such that it was lost before it began? The killer problems, including inescapable uncertainty and the time delay between actions and results, mean failure must be part of any concept of execution. "Failure is not an option" is an empty slogan. No leader can enforce it. We forget Deming's Red Beads too easily.[7]

Execution conceived as getting good results confuses cause and effect. A leader gets credit for brilliant execution by keeping prices high over the years, but the high prices drive customers to look for alternatives. When the leader's successor takes over, their customers are ready to switch to an alternative supplier. An army praised for executing a victory loses half of its troops or terrorizes the countryside, creating hatred and animosity for generations to come. What if the soldiers become drug addicts and bring their addictions home and encourage others to use? One can say the ends justify the means only when *all* the ends are tallied.

Execution conceived as getting good results is circular thinking like Figure 9.1, where the outcome you want becomes the method for getting it. As established in Chapter 2, the way to get positive emergent outcomes does not look like the desired outcomes themselves.

Strategists Sull, Homkes, and Sull offer one other description of getting good results in *Why Execution Unravels*.[8] They say that execution is not "sticking to the plan" or other ideas, but rather "the ability to seize opportunities while coordinating with other parts of the organization on an ongoing basis." But again, this is an outcome; you can't know if the organization is seizing opportunities until after they have been seized. And further, unless the basis for coordinating is known before the fact, the many participants, the agents in the system, can't know how to coordinate. Roger Martin argues with Sull et al., saying that people should stop trying to differentiate strategy and execution because strategy and

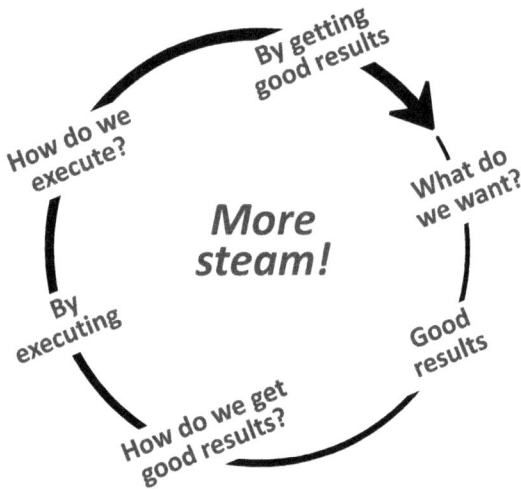

Figure 9.1 Outcome thinking leads to circular thinking

execution are the same thing.[9] He arrives at this conclusion presumably because he defines strategy as the act of making choices. Therefore, choices during framework and strategy design and choices during the implementation of the design are all "strategy." Martin stresses the fundamental truth that a strategy can't be brilliant if it isn't implementable, but then states, "No one can describe 'strategy execution' in a way that does not conflict with 'strategy,'" which would seem to obliterate the need for strategy design entirely.

The Definition of Execution

The following is a definition of execution that is distinct from strategy (and framework) and that retains the link between superior execution and getting good results but adds the ability to judge execution in real time.

> **Execution is doing the work needed to adhere to your framework and fixing the framework it when it is no longer fit.**

Or, more down to earth: Execution is doing what you say you will do, including following the strategy rule, and changing what you say you will do when you realize it no longer makes sense. Therefore, execution is a *quality* of implementing a design, not another word for implementing. It is how well individuals and organizations stress themselves to stick to the framework and its strategy, destroying decisions and actions counter to it. It is how well they stress themselves to maintain awareness of the diagnosis that led to the framework design and destroy the unfit aspects that appear. This is adapting. In nature, organisms continue doing what they do until new environmental stressors force a species to change and adapt. If the species doesn't change quickly enough, it can become extinct.

You don't expect your bike shop to succeed if you sit on the sofa all day eating bonbons, no matter how smart or good-looking you are. Execution requires the work of injecting physical and mental energy. The execution definition doesn't state who does the work, only that someone, or some group, needs to get it done. If a leader engenders success by stepping back and letting their subordinates' energy carry the day, the leader's work to execute could be fighting off the anxiety of wanting to interfere. The definition demands no particular quantity of work either. If tremendous effort is needed—*more steam* all the time—maybe the framework design and its strategy is bad.

The work also needs direction. Busting your butt 24/7 taking disjointed actions won't make a successful bike shop. What is the right direction? What is your guiding light? Since the direction needs to be known in real time, therefore designed before the fact, the direction can't be achieving results or seizing opportunities. The direction must be your framework. The framework converts aspirations on the right-hand side of the influence diagram to strategy and tactical rules on the left-hand side that can be adhered to in real time and to low-level granular plans that can be somewhat adhered to in real time. Since a framework is *your* statement of what to follow, based on a diagnosis, you must believe that adhering to it creates the best chance for good results to emerge—even if it consists of no more than a triad of a goal, a bottleneck, and a rule to bust the bottleneck, and even if it leaves you plenty of freedom. If you stop believing in the fitness of your framework, excellent execution means facing that reality and changing it—destroying it so that a more fit version can emerge. Mao's tacticization (projectization) in Chapter 6 was a failure to execute not because of immediate bad results. It was a failure because of taking decisions and actions counter to the framework—the guiding light—*despite apparently good results.*

There would be no point to the word execution in sports if it meant taking decisions and actions to win. A sports team differentiates its strategy for a match, double-teaming a star with the trade-off of leaving lesser players somewhat unguarded, for instance, from how well the players adhere to the strategy. Such a strategy must be articulated before the fact, or else the players—the agents of the system—cannot act in a coordinated way. Good teams also change their strategy during a match if it becomes clear the strategy is unfit, perhaps because the diagnosis of the opposition's capability or strategy was incorrect. A framework that consists predominantly of lists of prescriptive plans and subgoals will likely not be robust to the future as it leaves little room for players to react to local conditions. Sports teams that "plan" in detail how the game will unfold rarely succeed.

A framework design approach that considers multiple future possibilities will prepare the organization to seize opportunities. If an organization has internalized the dynamics and possibilities of the internal and external ecosystem they will play in and designed a valid strategy rule against which opportunities can be judged, then not only will they be able to pounce on an opportunity when it presents itself, but the organization will also be more attuned to "faint gusts of wind." Chance favors the prepared mind. The prepared mind is a creative mind.

It is just as easy for an artist or musician as for a businessperson or athlete to be undisciplined and fail at execution. It is just as easy for them to take an easy way out, use clichés or accept a shallow solution to a hard problem instead of exerting stressors on themselves to follow their internal low-level rules when making choices (whether they can articulate them in words or not). It's also just as easy in the arts to fail by solving a local problem in a way that doesn't fit with the whole.

That the low-level behavior of adhering to the framework looks nothing like the high-level outcomes it aims to contribute to points to its emergent nature (Chapter 2). One of the disciplines that defines execution in baseball is to resist swinging at certain pitches. The result is more hits, yet the discipline of "not swinging" looks nothing like the outcome of more hits it aims to achieve. In music, the most useful practice on an instrument is often when you can hardly tell what piece is being practiced. "Executing" by playing a piece over and over—which gives apparent quick results—leads to a plateau of very average playing, just as managing by results leads to average results. Your bike shop started making better profits when you adhered to your nothing-but-evangelize rule—not by focusing on profits.

When Something Changes

A framework is no longer fit when you realize it contains fallacies that are big enough to make you change it. The framework may be unfit not only because of a poor initial diagnosis but because of new opportunities or threats due to external dynamics, a new aspiration, a new direction from the parent, or a changed bottleneck. You may discover that the framework is too hard to follow.

When Covid hit the world, many business frameworks were no longer fit for this new reality and they had to adapt and change, a move toward e-commerce for instance. Were those companies whose frameworks had already considered accelerated e-commerce scenarios better able to adapt? Sometimes the required changes are minor (it's important to avoid over-reacting to every little issue), and sometimes they are major; sometimes there's awareness of the need for modification ten months after finishing framework design and sometimes after ten days. If there's no fallacy seen, then the organization must stick to the framework, or as commonly said, "Stick to the (master) plan," no matter how pedestrian this may seem. If not stick to the framewrok, why have one at all?

Flexibility on the Front Lines

There may be no time to debate changing the framework to capture opportunities or avoid problems. People on the "front lines" especially need the freedom to violate the framework when there is something is wrong with it. As discussed in nested systems, Chapter 7, knowing what freedom to give the organization is an enormous challenge for leaders, a challenge illustrated by a story about Vince Lombardi, the legendary coach of the Green Bay Packers.[10] In the final minutes of the 1966 NFL Championship game against the Dallas Cowboys (the semifinal for the First Super Bowl), Hall-of-Famer Dave Robinson improvised a brilliant move—a blitz that forced the Dallas quarterback into a bad throw. The play preserved a 34–27 lead and Green Bay went on to win the Super Bowl, one of five 1960s championships.

Lombardi's response? He told Robinson he wasn't supposed to be blitzing. He could not accept a wildly successful deviation from his framework because, even if occasionally the result was good, there would be countless cases where deviations would not benefit the team. The packers were exceptionally trained, and Lombardi demanded adherence to his framework (did this lead to the ability of players to seize opportunities?). As Robinson recalled,

> *He graded me a minus-2 [the lowest grade] on the play ... even though it was successful, I didn't execute my assignment the way Coach Lombardi wanted me to. As a teacher, Vince wanted me to understand how it was designed and what I did wrong. But it was a play that was meant to be, I guess.*

Lombardi revealed his inner conflict later when on the plane ride home he hugged Robinson and told him the play won the game.

Superior Executors

What capabilities make people good executors (and leaders), and therefore by nature, adaptive and innovative? The obvious one is that they can work, injecting physical and mental energy to drive the endeavor. They are obsessed with the endeavor, as creative people seem to be. Additionally, good executors:

- **Think analytically and critically** to create low-level creative tension that reveal fallacies in the framework. This means using logic and data, seeing patterns, making connections, testing reality, sensing the environment—including calling bull$%@# on themselves as well as others.
- **Must be trained, or learn,** the techniques specific to the endeavor. Not dogmatic "we know what works and doesn't work" knowledge, but rather training that gives people the

ability to make connections, understand the tools, and put history into proper perspective. As Bruce Lee said, "Obey the principles without being bound by them."

- **Are open-minded, and intellectually honest,** while also brave enough to accept the emergent results that the low-level discipline leads to—and brave enough to change direction if they see the framework is faulty. They are open to seizing opportunities but not easily seduced. This also means speaking the truth and being able and willing to hear the truth from others. They will question corporate dogma.

It's easy to be seduced. What if by chance you launch the Evangelize Strategy just as a stock market bubble is forming? Bike and accessory sales go through the roof even before your framework has had time to have impact. You are seduced to believe that you are the cause of these sales, when in truth, you may not be doing so well with the framework. You don't audit to see if your evangelism is causing purchases of $4,000 bikes, $250 headlights, and $199 riding shirts. You believe the metric that says, "profits up, up, up" is due to your actions alone. You spend freely on luxuries, personally, and for the shop. Then when the bubble crashes, so do the sales, and the shop is a mess. Your great results were not execution. Executors and innovators are not easily seduced by wishful thinking, easy answers, ways to avoid hard work, or quick, early victories.

People who execute well become irritated and anxious when the agreed framework is not followed or when the agreed framework can be shown to be wrong. A venture capitalist may be annoyed when a startup in her portfolio fails but will be driven crazy if she doesn't follow her own rules for when to stop investing in a startup.

Under Heavy Stressors

One other huge factor separates people or organizations who are brilliant at execution from those who are average: the ability to keep working and stick to disciplines in the "heat of battle." Brilliant execution means maintaining discipline despite the stressors of mental and physical fatigue, or emotional conflict or fear. It means adhering to the framework and its strategy, if convinced it is valid, even when it is leading to unsettling places. It may mean no panic attack for fear of what Wall Street will say because of a bad quarter.

Stressors can come from success. Euphoria seduces people away from execution as easily as duress. Military strategist Colin Gray quotes Clausewitz warning of the "perils of apparent success," and shows how military success can drive countries down the wrong road, calling it "victory disease."[11] Thom Yorke, the leader of the great English band Radiohead, is more direct: "As soon as you get any success you disappear up your own arse."

Experience as pedestrian as boredom can drive people away from the discipline of execution, especially when processes are proceeding smoothly. It's hard to perform the same tasks repeatedly.

People and organizations can learn to stand tall, conquer their fears, resist seduction, and stick to their framework under destabilizing stresses. They can learn to not revert to high-level "just get results" approaches and management by aspiration, slogans, or threats. Naturally, some people are just plain better at seeing what is going on and helping others to see it—personality, experience, smarts, interest, and effort all matter. And don't be fooled by style. Capabilities come in eccentric forms. The intellectual honesty to face the truth, or to know what is true (at least in one's sphere of expertise), does not necessarily look traditional or conventional. Sometimes the quietest and least-forward people make the strongest statements; at other times, the loudest jerks do.

Does Execution Eat Strategy for Lunch?
How About Culture?

Recall from the Introduction the CEO who says that *execution eats strategy for lunch*? Well, with the concept of execution laid out in this chapter, this is like stating that race car drivers eat race cars for lunch. What good is a brilliant driver if there is no car? Without a framework that includes a strategy and tactics that can be adhered to in real *time*—and detailed plans that are consistent with the strategy—there's nothing to execute on. Comparing strategy and execution is apples and oranges. Sure, sometimes the drivers are the bottleneck, sometimes the cars are, but we can't say that one is categorically more important than the other. And further, the statement, "a great strategy without execution is worthless" also misses the point, as discussed earlier. A framework with a strategy that doesn't address the ability or willingness of the organization to execute during implementation cannot be a great strategy.

By the way, here's another version of the CEO statement: "culture eats strategy for lunch." As before, you need both the right strategy and the right culture. And an organization's execution reveals a lot about its culture: fostering intellectual honesty, facing reality, avoiding seduction, acting when fallacies are apparent, and staying the course in the absence of reason not to, even if there is pain and fear in doing so. This "culture" is the deeply embedded behaviors of individuals in an organization, their internal rules of how to live daily life and how to react to the world around them.

There's no conscious decision or big discussion each time a strong organization faces reality or acts with intensity or intellectual honesty. These disciplines are burned into the minds of the people. And when one person slips, others react. The core of culture is behavior, habitual behavior, not the results of behavior.[12] And one of those habitual behaviors is execution, the quality of implementing. It's empty to say, "they have a habit of getting results;" it is not empty to say, "they get results, repeatedly, because they have habits of low-level discipline."

There is no guaranteed way to know what will bring good results. Executing means sticking to your truth as captured in your framework as best you can despite the demons and naysayers. Sometimes they are right, sometimes they are wrong; you need to be sure. And even then—success may have to wait.

PART II

The Design and Implementation of Frameworks and Their Strategies

Part II puts into practice the theory laid out in Part I and provides adaptive principles for designing and implementing frameworks and their strategies. The tools, design principles, and techniques presented enable creativity and innovation to emerge from the power of disciplined variation-selection-retention *at low local* levels.

An agile-adaptive approach treats change and innovation as a puzzle to be solved. Puzzle solving captures the spirit of the ugly, messy, and sometimes frightening but exhilarating process of making real change and innovating. By focusing on what's needed to solve the puzzle, and collecting information only when the process demands it, the team can keep its energy through tough times.

The objective is not to pick "the answer," a prescriptive plan, easy consensus, or as the authors of *Beyond the Hockey Stick* put it, it is not about, "getting to yes" on the "single proposal brought into the room."[1] It is not, as the authors of *Playing to Win* deride, to "find the single right answer, build unassailable arguments to support it, and sell it to the rest of the organization."[2] The objective is for the team to *internalize* the possibilities for shaping the internal and external world, and through hard debate and analysis, to get the possibilities into their gut. This internalization enables emergence of innovative ideas for achieving aspirations and conceiving new ones. The answer will be the survivor—*the last standing*—after destruction of all weaker and unfit ideas.

The approach applies not only to business units, but to overall corporate strategy and any function within a corporation, including supply chain, manufacturing, HR, R&D, marketing, and product management (it applies to nonbusiness endeavors too). Your aspiration, large or small, starting new or improving an existing entity, determines the scope of the endeavor. The process is the same in all cases. There is little advice for what your aspiration should be or for specific strategy choices for achieving it, only an approach to exploring and making those choices.

Figure II.1 contrasts an extreme version of a traditional stepwise planned approach with an agile, adaptive one. Every strategy or innovation approach ever designed is adaptive in some way and falls somewhere in the middle. Yet when practiced, traditional stepwise approaches tilt toward the planned side. Time constraints and resource cost pressures exacerbate the tilt.

EXTREME PLANNED STEPWISE	ADAPTIVE PUZZLE
Envision the future at the start	Articulate provisional futures, then discover and shape the actual future
Focus on analysis of the topic	Focus on what is needed for actions and decisions
Calculate the future	Internalize possibilities, including risk and upside
Design framework implementation as a follow-on process	Design implementation as part of the framework
Aim for easy and clean	Accept hard and messy
Consider alternatives and multiple futures as afterthoughts, if at all	Integrate alternatives and multiple futures from the start
Make plans and initiatives the heart-and-soul of the framework	Make the strategy rule the heart-and-soul of the framework
Rely on "black box" detailed models or no numbers at all	Rely on visible and understood models, only as complex as needed
Treat words as soft and numbers as hard; absolute assessments	Treat words and many numbers as soft; relative assessments
Design by ivory tower; put on the people	Design by ivory tower and the people; applies to everyone
Manage by results; measure results only	Manage by execution; measure results and causes
Judge success and failure by results	Judge success and failure by results *and* approach
Put pain off	Accept pain in the plan
Follow a recipe	Solve a puzzle

Figure II.1 Comparison of extreme planned stepwise and adaptive approaches to framework design and implementation

I make no claim that the emergent approach fully reaches the adaptive ideal. I hope the principle and techniques presented enable organizations to achieve more of it and avoid backsliding toward trying to plan the future or manage by results. References are cited where techniques align or build on the work of other strategy approaches.

In addition to Part II, there are five online task sets {web/tasksets} that serve as a guidebook for implementing Part II's design principles (Figure II.2). The output of the tasks is an implementation package that includes the final framework for rollout to the organization. Included also online are recommendations for program staffing, several techniques that apply throughout the strategizing process, and templates for use in your documents. Each task is illustrated with the continuing story of the bike shop you have been developing. While tasks are presented in an order, the underlying principles drive the process, not order. Everything is provisional until a compelling framework alternative emerges.

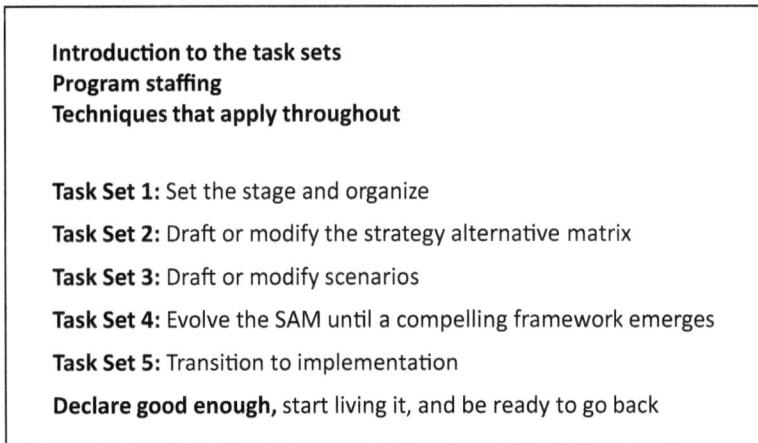

Introduction to the task sets
Program staffing
Techniques that apply throughout

Task Set 1: Set the stage and organize

Task Set 2: Draft or modify the strategy alternative matrix

Task Set 3: Draft or modify scenarios

Task Set 4: Evolve the SAM until a compelling framework emerges

Task Set 5: Transition to implementation

Declare good enough, start living it, and be ready to go back

---

Figure II.2 The task sets of the emergent approach {web/tasksets}

The centerpiece of the emergent approach practice is the *strategy alternative matrix* (SAM), and so we start with it in Chapter 10.

CHAPTER 10

The Strategy Alternative Matrix

The Strategy Alternative Matrix (SAM) is the core tool for framework design (Figure 10.1). It is the "species" that is evolved. It focuses the team on finding the best alternative with the least amount of data and analysis. The SAM brings together framework alternatives (each with a unique strategy), fitness criteria for judging the alternatives, and assessments of the alternatives against the fitness criteria. You evolve the SAM until one of the alternatives emerges as compelling enough—*fit* enough—to carry toward completion of the implementation package that you will use to guide implementation. Yes, survival of the fit to the low-level stressors the team applies to destroy all but the best ideas. The SAM speeds progress by visibly and early focusing all thought and information on discovering a fit alternative. With both words and numbers in a simple format, it enables the right combination of analytical thinking and following your gut—objective and subjective. To ensure the team sees the full picture throughout the design process, don't allow the matrix to become larger than one screen.

Despite a sincere desire not to birth another TLA (three-letter acronym) into the world, it is called the SAM to avoid writing *strategy alternative matrix* a zillion times. Further, it would be more accurate to call it the framework alternative matrix (i.e., the FAM), but because the strategy component is the heart and soul of each framework and, therefore, the key differentiator between framework alternatives, it is called the SAM.

The SAM is a type of *decision matrix*, a tool for solving *optimization problems,* those that demand trade-offs among multiple desired outcomes. When buying an automobile, we value performance, mileage, style, comfort, reliability, and low price, but since none has the best of each of these fitness criteria, we buy one with the best compromise, or "sweet spot,"

		Framework Alternatives for _____		
		Alt 1/Current	**Alt 2**	**Alt n**
	Values			
	Aspirations *Vision* *Mission* *Goals*			
	Diagnosis *Proposition* *Ext. constraints* *Scenarios* *Bottleneck*			
	Strategy			
	Key **tactics, plans,** **& metrics**			
Fitness Criteria	1	Assessment	Assessment	Assessment
	2	Assessment	Assessment	Assessment
	3	Assessment	Assessment	Assessment
	...	Assessment	Assessment	Assessment
	n	Assessment	Assessment	Assessment
		Overall 1	Overall 2	Overall n

Figure 10.1 Strategy Alternative Matrix (SAM)

among them based on our prioritization. All efforts to change or innovate that require strategy are optimization problems, which is why trade-offs are central to strategy design.

Don't confuse decision matrices with techniques that use a geometrical format such as SWOT, PESTEL, Porter's Forces, the Ansoff matrix, the BCG's Share/Growth Matrix, or various 2×2 analysis matrices. These are analysis techniques for making diagnoses and assessments that can be inputs to a decision process.

Beyond driving internalization by forcing integration of the information needed to evolve a compelling framework alternative, the SAM brings these benefits:

Broadly applicable: The SAM can be used for any specific aspiration in any business function and for short- or long-term horizons.

Enhanced visibility: As a communication tool that the team can understand and internalize, the SAM is the antithesis of black-box spreadsheets or obscure models, yet it's not just a simple plus/minus system. Also, it is an excellent communication tool upward to leadership.

Scalable: The SAM can be used for making simple choices or for solving a complicated and multifaceted strategy problem. For major endeavors, the SAM can serve as the front end to more detailed datasets, graphics, models, or even another matrix. The SAM is easily modified.

Financial modeling: While not limited to financial modeling, the SAM easily incorporates financial concepts and can serve as the front end to sophisticated financial modeling if needed.

Documentation (retention): The SAM automatically serves as concise summary of conclusions for the organization during implementation.

The Sections and Use of the SAM

The SAM has three overall sections, shown in Figure 10.2: Framework Alternatives, Fitness Criteria, and Assessments.

Framework alternatives: This section includes qualitatively different partial frameworks. The SAM doesn't require full frameworks; it only requires the information needed to differentiate between alternatives. Therefore, the focus is on values, aspirations, diagnosis, and strategy

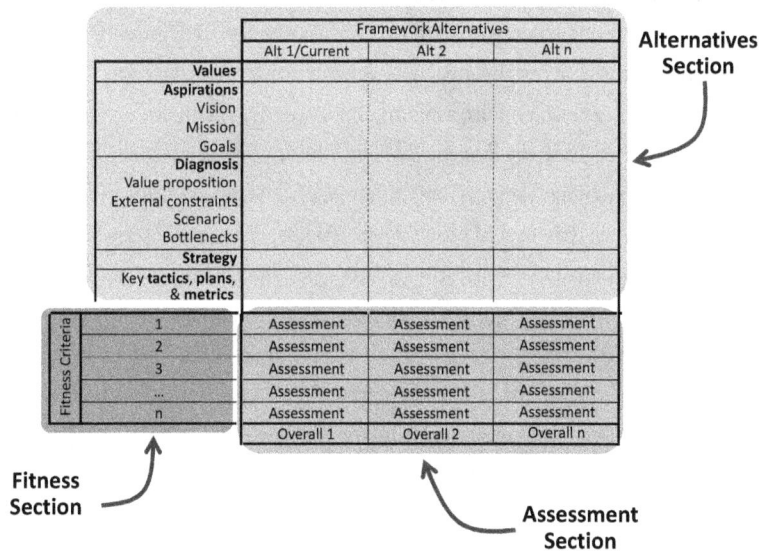

Figure 10.2 The three sections of the SAM

components of the framework. Key tactics, plans, and metrics should be included only if they help inspire or distinguish alternatives, otherwise complete them after choosing an alternative.

In many cases, your aspirations—vision, mission, and high-level goals (if you have all three)—will be common among the alternatives. However, the dotted lines indicate that you may wish to explore different aspirations, usually specific goals, along with the different diagnoses that would lead you to them. Typically, tactics and plans will mostly vary among alternatives, and metrics less so. The strategy *must* be different for each alternative. Values are always common.

Fitness criteria: This section is for judging the framework alternatives, and it includes all the criteria that influence your choice of alternatives, no matter if a criterion is easy or hard to find or model, and no matter if the criterion is "good" or "bad" for a given alternative. Fitness criteria such as cost and sales volume can be expressed in ranges of numbers, but criteria such as complexity, simplicity, diversity, difficulty, or optionality generally require both numbers and words for evaluation. The fitness criteria are derived from your aspiration. Clarity on fitness criteria is key to bringing together the "silos" of an organization.

Assessments: Here, each framework alternative is evaluated, or "assessed," against each fitness criterion. You ask, what will be the result of adhering to a given framework alternative. As shown in Figure 10.3, there are many ways to convey the anticipated future outcome of a criterion given the framework alternative in assessments—words, numbers, graphs, stories, and detailed models. Assessments will be low-level such as "how does this competitive behavior scenario influence our sales projections in upscale markets," not, "is this a good alternative." Assessments are *always* uncertain and ranges of outcomes—multiple futures—are needed. Relative, not absolute, assessments are used across rows, encouraging "approximately correct" thinking and eliminating duplication. Precision is an illusion to be avoided.

The *overall assessment* is the aggregate of the individual assessments, though it will be more interpretation than a sum-up. The winning alternative has the best overall assessment (or, more correctly, the assessment with the fewest bad trade-offs). However, because the objective is internalizing what's possible, not calculating "the answer," the focus when evolving the SAM is individual assessments. Emphasis on individual assessments forces discussion of the trade-offs between competing fitness

Forecasts   Probability distribution

Numbers or ranges of numbers
$1.2–3.7M

Qualitatives / Subjectives
"Customers will fight it"

A Story
The delayed response from
customers in the last upgrade
cycle can be avoided with
earlier communication....

Assessment	Assessment	Assessment
Assessment	Assessment	Assessment
Assessment	Assessment	Assessment
Assessment	Assessment	Assessment
Assessment	Assessment	Assessment
Overall 1	Overall 2	Overall n

Numbers over time
12% to 2012; 15% afterwards

Results of a detailed model

Another SAM

Alternatives	
Fitness	Assessments

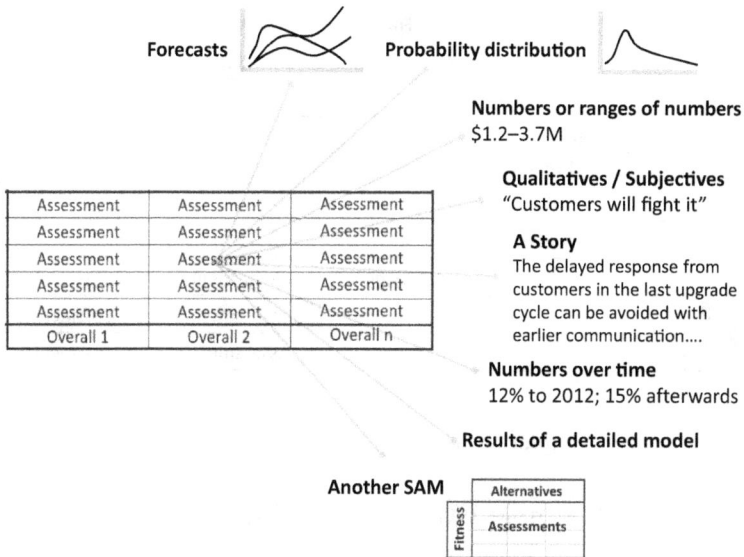

Figure 10.3 Range of information for assessments

criteria of the business's functional silos. It is crucial to get these out in the open. The SAM is complete when a compelling alternative emerges as the last standing, not when all the assessments are made.

Draft the SAM early in the process (in Task Sets 2 and 3), then evolve it—"work it"—and improve it through critical thinking, stories, research, outside feedback, analytical techniques, the five disqualifiers, and experiments and pilots where relevant. These stressors are used to challenge the assessments, modify the fitness criteria, and modify, dismiss, and create new framework alternatives until one emerges as compelling enough to complete for implementation. In the vernacular, you draft the SAM, and then beat the $&#% out of it until it reveals its secrets.

That tough team debate and argument are needed when strategizing (and too often avoided) is a point made forcefully by Carroll and Sørensen in *Why Good Arguments Make Better Strategy*.[1] The SAM is the perfect focal point for the stressors generated by tough debate because it makes visible, with the right amount of detail, the connections between what you can do and how you judge success.

The template shown in Figure 10.1 is a SAM complete enough to cover many situations. Figure 10.4 is a simpler version that assumes the goal won't change, leaving no need for dotted lines between alternatives. Additional versions are available online {web/templates}.

		Framework Alternatives for_____		
		Alt 1/Current	Alt 2	Alt n
	Goal			
	Bottleneck Scenarios			
	Strategy			
	Key plans & metrics			
Fitness Criteria	1	Assessment	Assessment	Assessment
	2	Assessment	Assessment	Assessment
	3	Assessment	Assessment	Assessment
		Overall 1	Overall 2	Overall n

Figure 10.4 A simpler SAM

A Simple Example of Using a SAM

Grandma and Grandpa live in Old City and want to visit their kids in New City, about 100 miles away. How should they get there? Grandpa is a geek, so he creates a little SAM, noting what he feels are the major differences among the three travel options available (Figure 10.5). Grandpa omits several elements for simplicity, including costs like wear and tear on a car, because he feels these criteria won't influence his decision. His SAM is so simple that his frameworks reduce to a goal and three travel choice alternatives. (This SAM is also simple because scenarios are not yet included. Scenarios will be added in Chapter 13). In the automobile buying decision described above, the fitness criteria (the rows) would be the features people care about and the alternatives (columns) would be specific automobile model choices.

Grandpa's matrix makes visible the connection between what the Grands are free to do (the alternatives) and what they care about (the fitness criteria). Grandpa assessed each alternative against each individual fitness criterion—time, comfort, cost, and environment. For example, 1.5 hours travel time for the train alternative, 2 to 3 hours for the highway driving alternative, and 4 hours for the back roads driving alternative. He assessed that the comfort of the train and back roads are superior to the comfort of the highway. Because of the simplicity, Grandpa could add up the individual assessments to get the overall assessment for each travel alternative.

		Goal: Get to New City in Best Way		
		Alt 1: Drive *Highway*	**Alt 2: Drive** *Back roads*	**Alt 3: Train**
	Time	2–3 hours depending on traffic conditions	4 hours	1.5 hours
Fitness Criteria	**Comfort**	Irritating, especially if traffic	Nice drive	Nice view, no effort, can read a book
	Cost	$63: gas ($18), tolls ($20), parking ($25)	$50: gas ($25), no tolls, parking ($25)	$190 for 2 people
	Impact on environment	Feel guilty for using gas and contributing to road congestion	Feel even guiltier for using more gas	Feel good, no added pollution except for short drive to the train
		2–3 hours + irritation + $63 + guilt	4 hours + $63 + more guilt	1.5 hours + $190

Figure 10.5 Grandpa's simple SAM for travel

Which alternative should the Grands choose? If they care more about time and comfort over cost, they should take the train. If they care more about cost and time over comfort, they should pick the highway. Implicit is the assumption that they can afford each option: for instance, if they could spend only up to $100, then the train alternative is plainly not available to them. They could add this tactical constraint to their SAM if it were the case. Clearly, a lot depends on whether the Grands care about the same criteria and agree on the assessments.

Grandpa	Let's take the back roads; it's cheaper and a nice drive.
Grandma	No, your silly table is wrong, the back roads do not take four hours, they take five-and-a-half hours and there is nowhere good to pee on the way.
Grandpa	Well, if you didn't have a Tweety Bird bladder it wouldn't matter.
Grandma	Well, if you weren't such a C E N S O R E D.

This conversation is the Grands "evolving the SAM." If they can deal with such disagreements, including getting data or opinions from each other, they will be able to agree on which column has the best trade-offs, that is, the least bad combination of time, comfort, cost, and environmental impact.

For another simple SAM, recall in Chapter 6 how you hired a bike shop manager which enabled you to focus full time on bike evangelizing. Figure 10.6

Goal: Hire a bike shop manager	
Alt: An experienced bike person	**Alt:** A talented person with some sales experience

	Alt: An experienced bike person	**Alt:** A talented person with some sales experience
Time required to train the person	Less time	More time
Salary they will command	$32.5/hour	$20/hour
Will they follow the evangelize strategy?	Less likely; they have their own bike ideas	More likely; no biking history to sway them
	X	√

Figure 10.6 Simple SAM for hiring bike shop manager

shows the two alternatives you considered and the assessments that led you to hire Marie, a talented but inexperienced sales candidate. The most important fitness criterion was that Marie would be willing to learn the evangelize strategy. Lower cost was a bonus, and a trade-off was that some of your time would be taken up training her.

The Grands' example also illustrates that the SAM contains essentially the same information as the influence diagram—all you need to do is add a *strategy alternatives table* to the diagram, as shown in Figure 10.7 (for simplicity, the influence diagram here omits cross-relationships and double arrow influences between elements). Both the influence diagram and the decision matrix express $Y=f(X)$, with Y being the aspiration and X being the actions and choices to achieve that aspiration, but the matrix is much easier to use.

Figure 10.7 also shows that the SAM does not use the aspiration (the ultimate dependent variable Y) as a single fitness criterion; if it did, a matrix wouldn't be needed. The SAM uses criteria derived from a moderate granularization of the aspiration. It is impractical to assess the overall aspiration directly so we "move back" and break it into more-assessable lower-level chunks. Grandpa asking, "How do I assess time, comfort, cost, and environmental impact?" is much more useful than asking "What travel mode will give us the best trip?" The best trip is defined as the one that supplies the least-bad trade-offs between time, comfort, cost, and environmental impact.

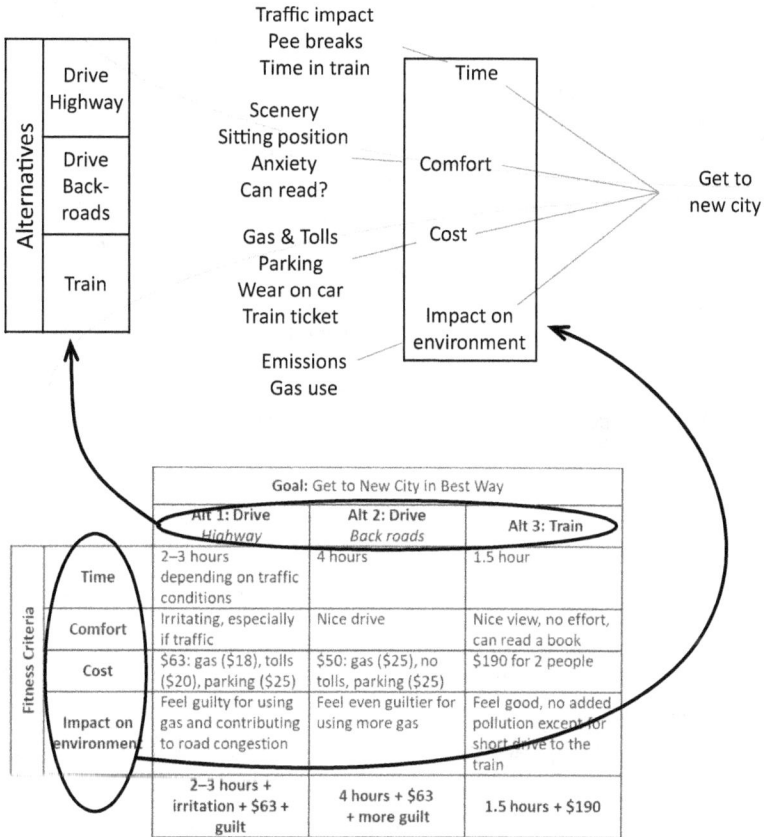

Figure 10.7 Comparison of the influence diagram and the SAM for the Grands

SAM for a More Complicated Endeavor

A simple SAM with simple choices works fine for Grandpa and Grandma, but what if an organization is faced with high-stakes decisions and actions involving many variables? Imagine, for example, Courier Inc., a major player in the transport of specialized freight using personal couriers. Their flagship service is the transport of love potions. They schedule thousands of deliveries each month using trains and fleets of cars and trucks.

Courier wants to expand into the Old City to New City market. Figure 10.8 shows decisions they face specific to expanding into this route in addition to their typical approach to marketing, financing, community

1. Should our couriers use trains, vehicles, or a mixture of transport methods?
2. If vehicles, should we purchase hybrid or electric? Buy or lease?
3. Will our standard marketing approach apply? Do we need a different pitch?
4. Should we continue to guarantee delivery?
5. Which routes are lowest cost? Without delays and with delays?
6. Should we use our own drivers or outside contractors?
7. What level of driver experience should we look for?
8. Do we need new driver training standards?
9. Should we use standard driver policies around hiring and housing (e.g., give drivers hotel rooms or standard reimbursement)?
10. Should we change insurance policies?
11. Should we subcontract out certain shipments to other freight companies?
12. Pricing?
13. Should we invest now in potentially transformative drone technology betting on department of transportation approval?

Figure 10.8 Decisions faced by Courier Inc. for entering Old City to New City market

affairs, legal, IT, and HR. Unlike the Grands, Courier's decisions are not simple choices. This lack of simplicity is why the SAM's alternatives are frameworks and why each framework includes a strategy for unifying the many choices.

Figure 10.9 shows how a SAM might look for Courier's Old City to New City market expansion part-way through their process. Courier designs their framework uniquely for each region to tailor it to local conditions. Note the liberal use of "~" which means "about" or "we are not sure;" question marks and ranges of numbers show uncertainty as well. Courier's choices and actions that make up the alternatives have complicated trade-offs.

The mapping of Courier's SAM to the influence diagram in Figure 10.10 looks like the Grands'. The six fitness criteria were obtained by moving back from the overall aspiration, and the strategy table consists of the four strategy alternatives under consideration. Note that the fitness criteria, the Ys, are not simply a list of financial numbers like cost, price, volume, or capex. We want criteria with much more business information in them, as will be discussed in Chapter 15.

		Alternatives for entering Old City to New City market			
	Values & Aspiration	V: Will not risk reputation of safest transporter of love potions A: Penetrate the New City to Old City market			
	Diagnosis	**Proposition**: Leading capability and reputation; competition slipping **External constraints**: Drones not yet approved for love potions. **Scenarios**: Love potion demand drops; competition starts price war; love potions regulated on trains **Bottlenecks**: Unclear regulatory situation; could train transport be regulated out even if drones approved? Unclear consumer trust of drone transport.			
	Strategy	Invest in train transport only	Train with "reserve fleet" as hedge	Train with heavy drone invest & forgo safety of fleet	Invest in fleet only (Simplicity)
	Key tactics, plans, & metrics	Questions to resolve: Subcontract? Guarantees? Hybrid or electric (if fleet)? Buy/lease (if fleet)? Training standards? Pricing?			
Fitness Criteria	Ease for customers	Expect no change in ease for trains or fleet; drones should be easier in principle, but how can we be sure?			
	Up-front investment	$3–4.5 m per operations team	Add $4 m	Add 8–3 m/y for 3 y to develop drones (**See 12.17 Report**)	**Fleet Model:** predicts $16.5-17.8 m for hybrid
	Operating margin	~50%	~40%	~50% (until drones)	~55%
	Flexibility to deal with regulatory changes	Vulnerable to train loss; cannot capture drones	Can ramp up quickly if train loss	Vulnerable to train loss but can capture drone value	Cannot capture drone; trains irrelevant
	Protection of reputation & customer trust	Expect same result as in all current regions nationally		Will customers accept loss of privacy risk? Will they like not seeing couriers?	Same
	Lobbying expenses	Full-time lobbyist + legal to prove safety of train transport ($1.2 m/y)		Add if decide to lobby for drones—will we help the cause by lobbying?	$0

Figure 10.9 Courier Inc.'s in-progress SAM for entering Old City to New City market

To summarize, in school, we are taught to find the optimum of an equation, that is, $Y=f(X)$, through a nice formula. You know, take the derivative and set it equal to zero. In real life, there are no such equations that can be solved directly. The only way to find the best possible Y is to see how it changes over a range of Xs. In other words, to find framework alternative (Xs), evaluate a range of them against fitness criteria (Ys). Which is why asking "What could an alternative be?" as an afterthought, or evaluating one alternative at a time, are not useful. The SAM can handle these multivalue Xs (the framework components) and Ys (the fitness criteria), make them visible, and accommodate ranges of numbers and words to assess them.

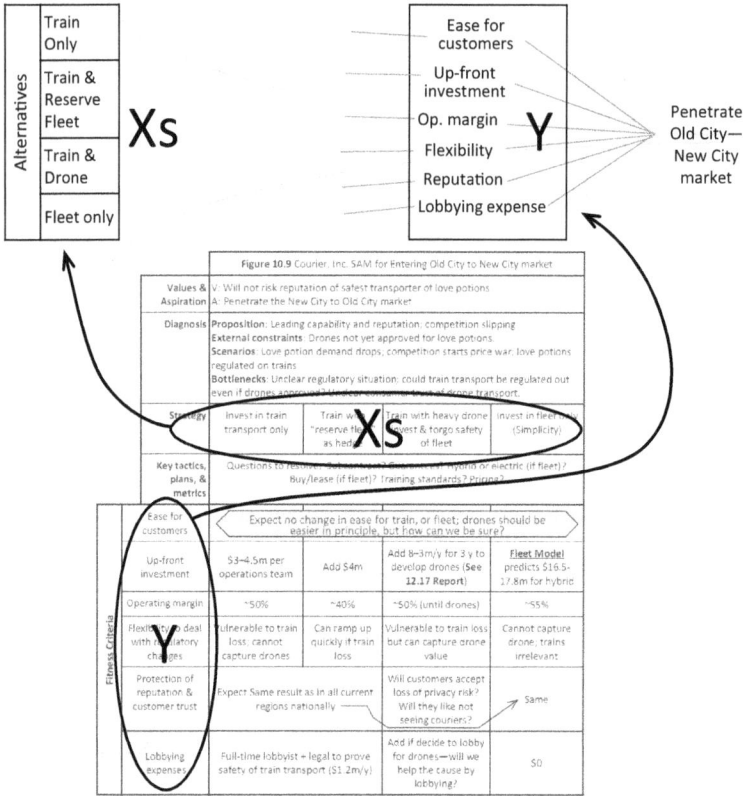

Figure 10.10 Comparison of the influence diagram and the SAM for Courier Inc.

Multiple Futures

Part II is grounded in the fact that there are always multiple possible futures, and that without such uncertainty, frameworks and their strategies would have no purpose. While sounding like something that Brainiac physicists think up to explain black holes and the inflationary universe, everyone naturally thinks in terms of multiple futures. Everyone has at least some tension about their decisions and the world in which they will play out. And everybody knows they need frameworks that are adaptive in at least some different environments than envisioned. Even an adaptive technique as simple as a portfolio would be pointless without multiple futures. Yet, as discussed in this book's Introduction, uncertainty is not always faced head-on. Leaders get mired in the tyranny of the mid-case—habitual, normal distribution-based, "mid-case" predictions, focusing on what they believe is the most likely future (or worse, the future they want). The SAM allows consideration of multiple futures in an integrated way, not as an afterthought.

While creating useful views of the future is not trivial, it is perhaps too easy to imagine futures—like it is easy to create lists of subgoals, plans, and metrics. What is hard to do is, incorporating multiple futures into your framework, designing a strategy that considers them, and keeping the futures in front of you during implementation so that you can react when they reveal themselves.

Besides the sheer difficulty of using them, leaders may feel that considering multiple futures is unnecessary philosophy. They may believe that planning under uncertainty doesn't apply to them for various untrue reasons, such as equating uncertainty with turbulence and ignoring it during less-turbulent times, assuming uncertainty is for other industries because of long-term stable performance, or believing that metrics can solve uncertainty.[2]

Leaders may feel that considering multiple futures is letting the organization off the hook for getting results and is an abdication of responsibility, a point made by Charles Roxburgh of McKinsey in an article expressing frustration with the lack of multifuture thinking.[3] You can almost hear a tough management-by-results boss bellowing, "Predict the right future or I'll get someone who can!" Leaders may also associate multiple futures with a narrow view of the discipline called *scenario planning*, believing it to apply only to massive and long-time horizon problems.

Scenario planning was developed by strategists Herman Kahn at the RAND Corporation in the 1950s and 60s,[4] and Pierre Wack and Kees van der Heijden at Royal Dutch Shell in the 1970s and 80s.[5] Kahn used scenarios to inform Cold War nuclear strategies (he had concerns with mutually assured destruction). Scenarios were used at Shell to inform multidecade, multibillion-dollar oil industry decisions. Scenario planning has since become a class of strategy (framework) planning methods that emphasize conceiving and crafting descriptions of futures.[6] There is no such thing as strategic planning without using scenarios in some way.

Unfortunately, some scenario-planning authors may promote the view that considering multiple futures is only for special, futuristic planning-under-uncertainty situations and not for normal or "linear" strategy work.[7] Surprisingly, some argue that scenarios are not good for extreme uncertainty situations because, in such situations, the future cannot be predicted.[8] But the inability to predict the future is the *only* reason to consider multiple futures and scenario techniques, and the greater the uncertainty (if you can know), the more you need them.

The emergent approach simplifies and scales down multiple future techniques enabling them to become habitual for all aspirations, not just for special situations and not as add-ons to "normal" strategy work. The SAM is key because it integrates multiple futures with framework alternatives. The uncertainty of outcomes you can influence is captured in assessments of framework alternatives against the fitness criteria, often ranges. Those aspects of the future that you cannot influence are captured in the scenarios, that is, the scenarios of the environment. Of course, you may be able to influence and shape the future more than you think.

However, even in a scaled-down way, abandoning the tyrannical mid-case is hard but worth it. The number one benefit is that it destabilizes an organization. Not to undermine people's ability to perform but in the positive sense of stressing people to become vigilant, nimble, and ready to move with speed. You don't need to have one of your futures be the one that takes place to get this benefit; you can't know until it happens anyway.

Scenario thinking is a big part of shooting for approximately correct as opposed to exactly wrong. The likelihood of being exactly wrong is quite high when people believe there is one possible future environment, just as when people believe their own internal efforts will give a single (and desired) result. Organizations that expect the future to be different than planned can prepare by sketching out contingency alternative framework concepts, so they can seize opportunities. It's a bad time to consider alternatives when in the heat of battle and programs start deteriorating. The impulse at such times may be to overcorrect because of embarrassment, fear of criticism, or the need to look tough because "failure is not an option." Even a rough sketch of alternative frameworks designed in the calm before the storm can encourage more objective, less emotional thinking when faced with unexpected challenges.

Forecasting, unfortunately, often has the opposite effect of destabilization. Often no more than graphical depictions of aspirations used for negotiation and publicity, forecasts tend to assuage anxiety. Negotiation and publicity are important, but again, don't fool yourself. Forecasts that do nothing more than support your beliefs are dangerous. There must be projections that are not in line with your desired results (or believed-to-be desired results).

No matter how you consider multiple futures, they must be visible. The SAM provides visibility with a simple and flexible structure.

CHAPTER 11

Agile-Parallel Design

When strategizing, it is natural to gravitate toward well-defined steps with a clear beginning and end and a timeline for everything in between. The ubiquitous stepwise strategy approaches (i.e., framework approaches) satisfy these desires and may look something like the following:

1. Define problem
2. Analyze data
3. Set goals
4. Create strategy
5. Consider alternatives
6. Create action plan
7. Create control metrics

These approaches include usually between five to ten steps with varying degrees of detail (again, some will not have a strategy step because the entire framework being developed is considered *the strategy*). The steps may be shown with chevrons as in Figure 11.1, or "plumbing charts," with many blocks, and they often include back-arrows to indicate when to fix previous sections if new information arises.[1]

In framework design, grouping related activities for simplification is unavoidable, and all good approaches will share certain steps. However, the steps can become recipes, where the design path—often one pass despite the arrows pointing backward—is known at the start. In simple endeavors, recipes reduce uncertainty and save time. It is impractical

Figure 11.1 Chevron representation of a stepwise strategy processes

to design a new chocolate cake for every occasion. Follow Martha's or Roland's recipes, and you have a good chance of making a great one, though little chance of becoming an original chef. It is impractical to design every procedure in a corporation when there are perfectly good best practices.[2]

Set-sequence approaches may suggest certainty and speed, especially if put on a timeline (perhaps to assuage the boss's anxiety). But recipes for designing and implementing frameworks and their strategies will never exist because creativity and innovation will always live on a boundary between the known and unknown. When following a cake recipe, or a best practice, the endpoint and the path for getting there are known, though people's capability to execute—to adhere to the recipe—varies. When strategizing, if the desired endpoint is known, or believed to be known, then the path is unknown. Sometimes the endpoint is only partially known.

An alternative to the sequential approach is a process closer to solving a puzzle. Jigsaw puzzles are solved by starting wherever there is a hint as to what to do—like finding edge pieces or grouping pieces of like pattern or color—and then looking for possible solutions. Mistakes are made. If the top is picked as the bottom or color groupings are misjudged, entire sections may need be moved around to get back on track. Eventually, the picture starts to emerge. Rarely are puzzles solved by starting in one corner and building out a row at a time. Few people would work sequentially saying, "I'm not going to do anything more until I find where this piece goes."

And solving common jigsaw puzzles gives only a hint of the challenges involved in innovating. In real-world puzzles, the pieces don't exactly fit together, and they may unexpectedly change shape and color. Some pieces will never be found. It won't even be clear where the puzzle begins and ends. Certain sections will look familiar as progress is made, but there is no picture on a box top. As an image starts to come into focus, someone may crunch up a section and change some of the pieces. It is unimaginable to solve a real-world strategy puzzle using predefined sequential steps.[3]

Draft It, Evolve It, Finalize It—Then Live It

To solve real-world puzzles, adhere to low-level adaptive design principles. It doesn't really matter where you start. Create a draft and then stress it, add variations and stress it again. Repeat. In other words, *evolve the draft* until a compelling design emerges, like the picture of a puzzle. A compelling design is one that is good enough—*fit* enough—with which to move forward to implementation.

So, in the emergent approach, instead of designing the components of the SAM in sequential steps in series, such as (several components are omitted for simplicity):

1. Goal
2. Bottleneck
3. Scenarios
4. Strategy
5. Plans
6. Done

Draft all the components and then evolve them in parallel:

1. Goal, Bottleneck, Scenarios, Strategy, plans: draft it
2. Goal, Bottleneck, Scenarios, Strategy, plans: evolve it
3. Goal, Bottleneck, Scenarios, Strategy, plans: evolve it
4. Goal, Bottleneck, Scenarios, Strategy, plans: evolve it
5. Goal, Bottleneck, Scenarios, Strategy, plans: evolve it
6. Goal, Bottleneck, Scenarios, Strategy, plans: declare good enough

Parallel design is *agile,* adaptive design, in the sense of drafting a minimum-viable matrix and then putting it out there to see how to make it right. Agile software development is not sequential (Chapter 2), nor is entrepreneurial venturing, and strategizing shouldn't be either. In sequential processes, the barriers to going back and changing earlier work are enormous, especially with a timeline. On top of that, it is not feasible to design individual framework components sequentially because there is no context in which to do so. As the architect, Eliel Saarinen, says, "Always design a thing by considering it in its next larger context—a chair in a room, a room in a house, a house in an environment, and an environment in a city plan." (Developing components one at a time is a form of Mao's tacticization from Chapter 6.) The draft SAM supplies context by providing good-enough-to-start framework alternatives, fitness criteria, and assessments, along with the initial diagnosis that is behind it all.

Figure 11.2 illustrates Courier Inc.'s SAM for penetrating the New City market evolving. Note that some of the assessments may become more numerical over time. Another way to visualize the difference between a linear sequential and an agile-parallel approach is an actual puzzle, as in Figure 11.3.

The Task Sets

The five online Task Sets are broken into 25 smaller more manageable steps, but they are called tasks to stress that they are not one-pass or necessarily sequential (Figure 11.4). The low-level discipline of the approach is to follow the design principles in each task, not the order. Figure 11.5 shows the focus on the SAM in a draft it—evolve it—finalize it model.

Draft the SAM early in Task Sets 2 and 3 after organizing the program in Task Set 1—this should go quickly. The guidelines and principles in Task Sets 2 and 3 are not only for drafting a SAM for a new endeavor. They are much more important for guiding you're evolving the new or existing SAM as a whole in Task Set 4. The probability of getting any aspect of the design right the first time around, except possibly aspirations, is low.

While Task Set 4 is just one task, it is the heart of the approach and may take up 90 percent of your time. Here, you evolve the draft until a compelling framework alternative with a compelling strategy emerges— till one is the last standing. Evolving it means bringing to bear all the low-level techniques for generating new variations and applying stressors to destroy all but the most valuable ideas: get and analyze data, add and modify alternatives and get rid of others, apply the five disqualifiers, make assessments of alternatives, debate what the real bottleneck is, consider different external scenarios, question the fitness criteria, get criticisms from outsiders, apply analytical techniques from the literature, and run experiments and pilots—whatever it takes to get insight that will propel the process forward, including sitting on your butt and thinking.

As described in Chapter 10, the SAM focuses information gathering and research on bottlenecks and possible solutions right from the start. This focus helps the team avoid "looking where the light is," as in the

Week 7

Courier: Alternatives for Old City to New City

	Invest in train transport only	Train with "reserve fleet" as hedge	Train with heavy drone invest & forgo safety of fleet	Invest in fleet only (Simplicity)
Values & Aspiration	V: Will not risk reputation of safest transporter of love potions — A: Penetrate the New City to Old City market			
Diagnosis	Proposition: Leading capability and reputation; competition slipping. External constraints: Drones not yet approved for love potions. Scenarios: Love potion demand drops; competition starts price war; love potions regulated on trains. Bottlenecks: Unclear regulatory situation; could train transport be regulated out even if drones approved? Unclear consumer trust of drone transport.			
Strategy	Invest in train transport only	Train with "reserve fleet" as hedge	Train with heavy drone invest & forgo safety of fleet	Invest in fleet only (Simplicity)
Key tactics, plans, & metrics	Questions to resolve: Subcontract? Guarantees? Hybrid or electric (if fleet)? Buy/lease (if fleet)? Training standards? Pricing?			

Fitness Criteria

	Invest in train transport only	Train with "reserve fleet" as hedge	Train with heavy drone invest & forgo safety of fleet	Invest in fleet only
Ease for customers	Expect no change in ease for trains or fleet; drones should be easier in principle but how can we be sure?			
Up-front investment	$3–4.5 m per operations team	Add $4 m	Add 8–3 m/y for 3 y to develop drones (See 12.17 Report)	Fleet Model: predicts $16.5–17.8 m for hybrid
Operating margin	~50%	~40%	~50% (until drones)	~55%
Flexibility to deal with regulatory changes	Vulnerable to train loss; cannot capture drones	Can ramp up quickly if train loss	Vulnerable to train loss but can capture drone value	Cannot capture drone; trains irrelevant
Protection of reputation & customer trust	Expect Same result as in all current regions nationally		Will customers accept loss of privacy risk? Will they like not seeing couriers?	Same
Lobbying expenses	Full-time lobbyist + legal to prove safety of train transport ($1.2 m/y)		Add if decide to lobby for drones—will we help the cause by lobbying?	$0

Week 3

Courier: Alternatives for Old City to New City

	Invest in train transport only	Invest heavily in drones	Invest in fleet train backup
Values & Aspiration	V: Will not risk reputation of safest transporter of love potions — A: Penetrate the New City to Old City market		
Diagnosis	Value proposition: cost position—capability? Are we sure of impact on reputation and market presence? External constraints: Government regulatory questions. Bottlenecks: Investment? Competitive pricing? Scenarios: Government approves drone delivery of love potions		
Strategy	Invest in train transport only	Invest heavily in drones	Invest in fleet train backup
Key plans, tactics, metrics	Questions to resolve: Subcontract? Guarantees? Hybrid electric (if fleet)? Buy/lease (if fleet)? Training standards Pricing?		

Fitness Criteria

	Invest in train transport only	Invest heavily in drones	Invest in fleet train backup
Up-front investment	~$3m	Launched study	Double tra… investment
Profit	How define??????		
Flexibility to deal with regulatory changes	cannot capture drones		Cannot capt… drone
Marketing?	Any difference in cost or impact expected from other regio…	Depends on whether to lobby for drones	
Lobbying expenses	Full time lobbyist + legal		

Week 1

Courier: Alternatives for Old City to New City

	train transport	drones	? (who determines?)
Aspiration	Grow 20% revenue per year		
Diagnosis	Value proposition: cost position—capability? Are we sure of impact on reputation. Market presence? External constraints: Scenarios: we succeed in beating the competition but it is an aspiration → [no, not only is this in our control to some extent, but it is an aspiration] Bottlenecks: investment dollars, especially for research on speculative project?		
Who do we need to engage on external constraints?	Competitive pricing?		
Strategy	train transport	drones	? (who determines?)
Key plans, tactics, metrics			

Fitness Criteria

	train transport	drones	
Up-front investment	~$3m		
Return on capex ??? or marginal profit? (depends on where the R&D money comes from—call in finance)	How define???????		
Regulatory success	cannot capture drones		
Marketing?	Will we need legal support as well as lobbying?	Depends on whether to lobby for drones	
Legal expense			

Figure 11.2 Courier Inc.'s SAM evolves as a whole

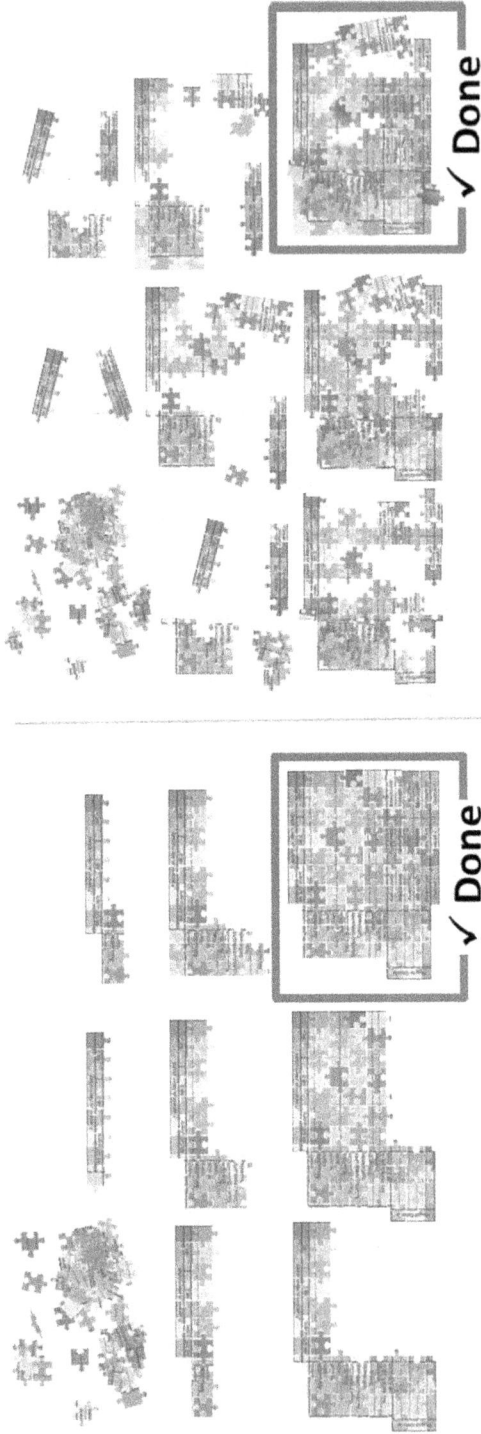

Figure 11.3 Linear sequential vs. real-life puzzle solving

INTRODUCTION TO THE TASK SETS

PROGRAM STAFFING
Leadership and Team Roles
Individual Team Members
Using Consultants
Challenges for Process Leaders
  and Facilitators

TECHNIQUES THAT APPLY THROUGHOUT
Lite Approaches
Naming
Choosing When To Seek Feedback
Data or Hypothesis First?
Be Cautious with Pareto, Ockham, and
  Other Conventional Wisdom
Invest in Housekeeping
Brainstorming Tips—Sometimes Tight,
  Sometimes Loose, but Always Disciplined
Live Capture and Other Facilitation Tips

TASK SET 1: SET THE STAGE AND ORGANIZE
1a Articulate Reasons to Reopen the
    Strategy Process
1b Sketch Your Nested System
1c Design Roles and Teams
1d Capture Initial Ideas
1e Design a Training Approach
1f Draft Timelines and Milestones
1g Complete, Name, and Socialize
    Plan of Attack

TASK SET 2: DRAFT OR MODIFY THE STRATEGY ALTERNATIVE MATRIX
2a Choose Template & Capture Current Framework
2b Discover and Articulate Values
2c Draft or Modify Aspirations
2d Draft or Modify Diagnosis:
    Proposition, Constraints
2e Draft or Modify Your Diagnosis: Bottlenecks
2f Draft or Modify Fitness Criteria
2g Draft or Modify Alternatives
2h Add Initial Tactics, Plans, Metrics,
    or Assessments

TASK SET 3: DRAFT OR MODIFY SCENARIOS
3a Capture Environmental Conditions and Events
3b Construct Scenarios
3c Incorporate Draft Scenarios Into Your SAM

TASK SET 4: EVOLVE THE SAM UNTIL A COMPELLING FRAMEWORK EMERGES

TASK SET 5: TRANSITION TO IMPLEMENTATION
5a Complete Plans, Policies, Budgets & Organization
5b Design Four-station Dashboard and Triggers
5c Complete Charters and Nested Frameworks
5d Make Rollout Decisions
5e Complete Working Documents

DECLARE GOOD ENOUGH, START LIVING IT, AND BE READY TO GO BACK

Figure 11.4 The task sets of the emergent approach

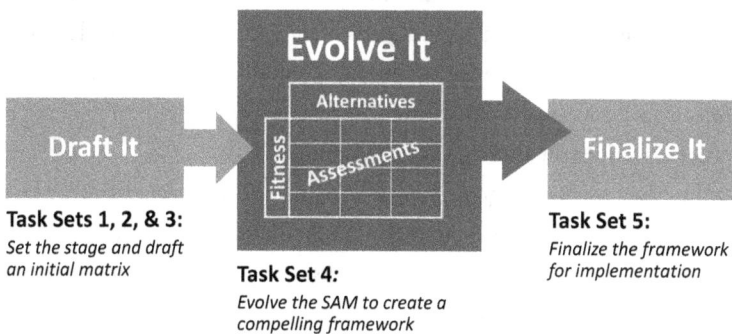

Task Sets 1, 2, & 3:
*Set the stage and draft
an initial matrix*

Task Set 4:
*Evolve the SAM to create a
compelling framework*

Task Set 5:
*Finalize the framework
for implementation*

Figure 11.5 Task Set 4 (Evolve it) is the focus of the task sets

story of the drunk who dropped their wallet on a dark street but searched for it under the streetlamp. The low-level disciplines of the approach help you navigate in the dark alleys.

To avoid analysis of the topic, as opposed to the analysis needed for decisions and actions, *do not* roll out the usual strategy suspects. Lafley and Martin stress this guideline, stating that most strategy programs incorrectly begin with a "deep dive into the data."[4] Delay collecting market share, growth rates, cost structure, financial analysis, and any performing analytical techniques like Porter's Five Forces or environmental scanning until and if the process demands it. Do capture early (Task 1d) what you think about the endeavor, including data and information already available that speaks to the aspiration and bottlenecks.

Task 4 generates plans, tactics, and metrics only to distinguish between framework alternatives, thereby avoiding unnecessary detail. Task Set 5 finalizes the chosen framework alternative, including completing the plans, tactics, metrics, and your final implementation package. Finalizing it ends when you declare your implementation package good enough, or *fit enough*, to move on.

Keeping the SAM on One Screen

When endeavors are large and complicated, it can be tricky to keep the SAM from growing larger than one screen. Aspire to use minimum ink and photons. Merge cells with the same content. Use links if any SAM element—assessments, diagnosis, and framework components—requires a detailed analysis with data and modeling. Show the conclusion in the SAM and double-click to see the details. As the scope of your analysis and synthesis grows, the SAM remains a concise summary, as illustrated in Figure 11.6. The challenge to linking is the discipline to maintain the connection between the SAM and the detailed content. Be reluctant to add details until you are sure you need them.

The other aspect of keeping the SAM simple is allowing time for people to learn what the information in the SAM means. If they internalize what has gone into a diagnosis and assessments, they will not need the details in front of them. You will be able to use shorthand for concepts one they are understood.

Making a Parallel-Agile Puzzle Approach Work

In addition to the SAM and the structure of the task sets, a few other changes in program management enable adaptive agile-parallel design

X SAM grows as you evolve it

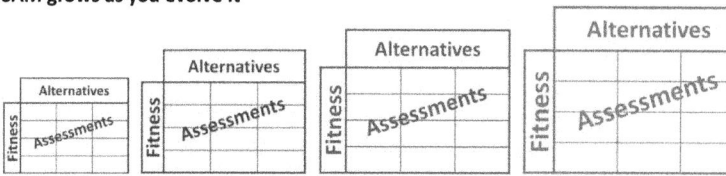

✓ SAM remains on one screen with details linked

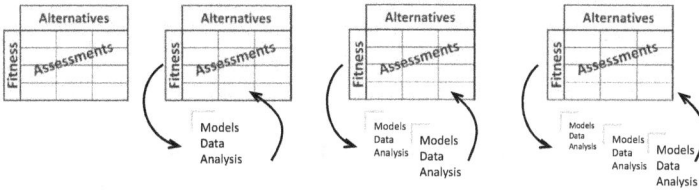

Figure 11.6 Keeping the SAM concise

and achieving the adaptive ideals shown in the Introduction to Part II (Figure II.1).

The nirvana condition is where "strategy processes" are not events and are carried along as the normal way of getting things done, an ideal promoted by many strategists. Think of this as blurring the line between design and implementation. In the best case, the design phase doesn't really end. It just recedes into the background until there is a trigger— enough creative tension—to go back and modify the framework. This is *executing*—injecting the physical and mental energy to adhere to the framework until it is seen to be unfit and needs modification (Chapter 9). Modifications may be large or small (including ending the endeavor) and may take a few days, a few months, or longer, as conveyed in Figure 11.7. Triggered design cycles fly in the face of yearly strategy, a point also made by many. Yearly objectives and budget setting (usually negotiation? mostly based on last-years numbers?) may be important, just don't confuse it with strategizing. If your diagnosis is strong and leadership is attuned to the organization, cycle length will be all over the map.

It is tempting not to distinguish between the design phase and implementation phase at all, because both phases are dedicated to solving the puzzle of how to evolve to a better place. But implementation usually requires a greater expenditure of resources, and some aspects of implementation are irreversible. When building a costly structure or making

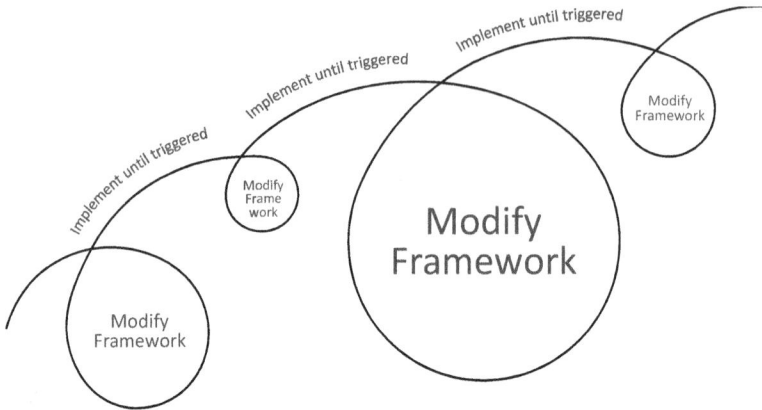

Figure 11.7 Ongoing cycles of framework evolution: some large and some small

a significant purchase, for instances, the cost of being wrong jumps way up. There is also the possibility of looking foolish or weak if implementation is canceled soon after a launch. There is only one chance to make a first impression. These dangers are why pilots, demos, prototypes, experiments, and research can be so valuable. The learning-to-cost ratio is high.

Accept Pain in the Plan

The contrast between planned stepwise and adaptive approaches in Figure II.1 includes the expectation that making a change and innovating will be hard and messy (this doesn't mean it's not fun). First, there's the hard, messy work of design. Not only does the emergent approach include in the framework much of what is often considered implementation— including plans, tactics, and metrics—which adds to the task (a requirement also demanded by strategists to varying extents), but it is harder to put a puzzle together than it is to follow a stepwise method. The ease of stepwise methods comes from not having to integrate the whole. It is less constraining to design the features of a building or the components of an automobile in isolation, though the result will be poor. You lessen the pain of design by identifying prospective solutions to bottlenecks early and by avoiding the rollout of the usual analysis and data suspects. Facing the bottleneck and considering prospective solutions early energizes the team and converts pain into creative tension.

If it is good, framework content is the second source of pain. In other words, the "pain in the plan." ("Pain in the framework and its strategy" is technically correct, but it doesn't make a catchy slogan.) The "plan" should be painful because of the tough trade-offs and sacrifices in any real strategy. The trade-offs may be downright repugnant to some. Some people may feel they are losing. Some people may be scared. The anticipated time (and possibly the cost) it takes to make a real change should give pause; the organization may have to learn new things, create new habits, and accept new rules of what determines success and failure.

It is hard to build consensus on trade-offs when multiple functions and regional organizations are involved. Not an easy consensus based on a lack of awareness of what is being suggested, and not a trivial consensus where everyone gets their personal (and often conflicting) bullet point added to the list of initiatives, giving them the confidence to go back to what they were doing before. But a hard-fought consensus, where the team truly internalizes and accepts the implications of a new framework even if frightening. (The five disqualifiers head off trivial consensus by ensuring that lists of initiatives and goals do not pass as strategy.)

The last pain in the plan is the fear of uncertainty and admitting that no matter how well designed and researched, and no matter how well agreed by the team, the framework may fail. Articulating and acknowledging the range of outcomes helps reduce the fear and gain alignment on risk tolerance.

Desired pain in the plan does not mean the pain of crisis; it means avoiding crisis—and preparing the organization to pounce on opportunities—by unearthing and facing difficult issues in the design phase to the extent possible.

Extend in Time* to Make It the People's Design

*But not full-time

The Introduction to the Task Sets includes a section on program staffing recommendations {web/tasksets} including leadership roles, teams and team members, facilitators, and consultants. Also, discussions of the trade-offs between the benefits of inclusion and the complications of many participants, dealing with geniuses and jerks, and seeking people who can bring one or more of the *three Ws:* wisdom, wealth, or work.

One particular technique for making agile puzzle solving work, perhaps anathema to some leaders and therefore sometimes avoided by consultants, is extending the framework design program in time. Extending in time means getting results sooner by getting the framework into the fabric of the line organization and into all levels—a form of go slow to go fast. Extending is crucial to making strategizing an ongoing effort and not an event. The trick to extending is for the program to be part-time for many involved. And note, extending never means doing aspirations one month, diagnosis the next, fitness criteria the next, and so on in series. Instead, it means drafting a SAM as soon as possible and then evolving it over time.

Extending the design period enables key people to participate. You don't want to staff teams with people that happen to be available. Yet the people with the right capabilities, positions, and personalities have full-time jobs and are in high demand. In small organizations, they may wear multiple hats, as people in regions where you are expanding often do. Further, to implement, you will need a "guiding coalition," as change management specialist John Kotter describes it.[5] In-demand people, especially those on the "front lines," are essential for the coalition. Extending in time allows these folks to work part-time on strategy yet keep their jobs. Temporarily assigning a few people full-time may help, which will also give them a deeper strategy experience, but you can't reassign everyone. If key people can't be made available part-time (even if you restructure some of their current responsibilities), then you are forced to get their perspective by interview or their occasional participation in meetings or sub-teams. These are not great methods and result in little "skin in the game."

Internalization is the key to creativity and innovation and internalization requires emotional connection. When people struggle through the design process, and if they are heard and hear others, then it becomes *their* design—the *people's* design. Then not only will they have internalized it, but they can also have an emotional investment in the chosen framework, loving it and preaching it. The consultants from *Strategy&* refer to these folks as "Pride Builders."[6] They can become advocates and teachers instead of students to be convinced. And this is true even if the core ideas came from just one or a few people, or from the leader.

But there's more. There's *soak*. Never underestimate the value of incubation time to digest and appreciate the implications of new ideas. People need time to digest even what they have said themselves. Those who are driving change need soak time. It's easy to get caught up in the euphoria of wonderful new visions and plans, but what about the next morning? Truly innovative ideas will sound foreign at first. And the "pain in the plan" resulting from tough trade-offs may not be initially accepted. Biases and prejudices don't melt away by telling people that it's bad to have them or running an anti-bias session, though anti-bias techniques may help if used repeatedly. People come to conclusions in their own time by living with ideas, testing their implications by modeling, research, demos, and debate. You don't want them to acquiesce, or just as bad, become advocates for new ideas that they don't yet understand. Extended time allows for experimentation, trials, and research—actions with a theory for learning. And unless there's time, it's hard for the team to have the confidence to revise earlier tasks if new information is discovered.

Finally, extending in time is the only way to achieve simplicity, an ideal that is tough to achieve without multiple adaptive generations of work. The only way to make a framework simple in short time is to make it trivial, or get lucky.

Extending the design period will not automatically give these benefits, but it is sometimes necessary to get them. Figure 11.8 visualizes the difference between a full-time, intensive framework design approach versus extending part-time. Naturally, there are times when there are decision deadlines and extending isn't an option. But if organization is in constant big-decision mode, something is probably wrong with the framework and its strategy.

Do not think of extending in time as *no action*. If the analysis demands implementation after one day of design work, or ten minutes of design work, then do it. But not without a basis for the action. Slogans like "Let's have a bias for action" or "Just go do it," while trying to keep people from jerking around and philosophizing, are not enough of a basis. Just do what? Action is warranted when creative tension based on insight propels

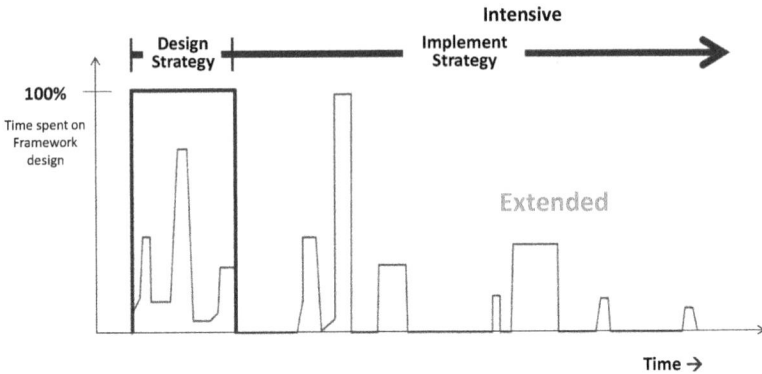

Figure 11.8 Traditional vs. extended framework design timelines

you to stop designing and start implementing. And anyway, busting your butt to create a meaningful framework *is* just doing it.

Consultants may balk at part-time approaches because it makes scheduling their personnel harder. But if they can advise governments and hundred-billion-dollar corporations, they can figure out how to work with you part-time. Consultants also complain that they are let go before implementation because leaders won't pay. Extending part-time may help spread the money out into the implementation phase.

Capable people can work with fewer deadlines and less micromanagement, but you need to judge how much capability the organization has. If you or your leadership fear that teams will lose urgency and stop working hard if they have time, then consider the following.

- Establish rolling deadlines, where after achieving an objective, you determine which objective should be next.
- Teach that perfection means good enough for taking the next step, *fit for use,* whatever the next step is.
- Have leaders learn the process so they can see if the real work at low levels is getting done, even though on the surface at high levels, it's not so obvious. Progress is not linear.

The team can give leadership confidence that micromanagement isn't needed by communicating that they understand the challenge. Early on, communicate bottlenecks, fitness criteria, and scenarios, as well as work schedules. Later, share the alternatives under assessment. Unfortunately, sharing unfinished work comes with risks (see *Techniques* {web/tasksets}).

Of course, at any time you can say, "That's it. No more designing. No more analysis, experiments, or modeling. We're not gaining anything more by design work, it's time to implement."

CHAPTER 12

Values, Proposition, External Constraints, and Aspirations

This chapter provides considerations for drafting values, aspirations, and diagnosis. These framework components are aspects of your endeavor that, once articulated, supply the context for the others. You capture these components in Tasks 2b to 2d. As with all components, you are just drafting at first, and you will modify as you go. As a reminder, the emergent approach gives no specific advice on what your business's or function's aspiration should be, only design principles.

Articulating Values

Companies use values in different ways to express what they care about and the behavior they expect and desire. The strictest are where societal values are translated into policy. At DuPont, behavior and policy standards regarding safety, the environment, people treatment, and business ethics were labeled *core values*. There was no situation in which an employee should sacrifice these codified values for business performance; for instance, violate a safety or people treatment policy to increase production output to make a sale. In other words, no trade-offs. Frequent discussion in "core-value contacts" coupled with defined policy and training drove the right behavior.

A broader use of values is to describe desired culture, like a list of maxims (Chapter 8). "Netflix Culture" is a 4350-word document under the heading "jobs" on their website.[1] It includes 12 *Real Values* (Figure 12.1A), each with several bullet points for further instruction. And while Netflix's document includes the directive "avoid rules," many of their stated values are rules—low-level rules. For instance, *you intervene if someone else is being marginalized* (inclusion), *you make decisions based on the long term, not near term* (judgment), and *you only say things about fellow employees that you say to their face* (integrity). Many of their values are quite subjective and could never serve as strict policy. For instance, *you make wise decisions despite ambiguity* (judgment), *you make tough decisions without agonizing* (courage), and *you make connections that others miss* (curiosity)—these fail the opposite disqualifier. As a whole, Netflix's *real values* document describes a highly idealized company culture. The global bicycle company Trek, also has a long document with "10 Non-Negotiables of Trek Culture," including a "no assholes" policy.[2]

(A) Netflix *Real Values*	(B) Whole Foods *Core Values*
• Judgment • Communication • Curiosity • Courage • Passion • Selflessness • Innovation • Inclusion • Integrity • Impact	• We sell the highest quality natural and organic foods • We satisfy and delight our customers • We promote team member growth and happiness • We practice win-win partnerships with our suppliers • We create profits and prosperity • We care about our community and the environment

Figure 12.1 Netflix and Whole Foods values

Whole Foods' *core values* (Figure 12.1B) are ideals that somewhat resemble fitness criteria, that is, what they care about when making decisions.[3] These core values are much more difficult to codify than safety or business ethics policy. What defines good-enough profits or team-member profits?

Values may be used as an inspiration for embarking on an endeavor. As bike shop owner, you stated *love every aspect of biking and believe it is good for society* in Framework 3.1. This reminded you to go for it despite the difficulties you perceived. Values may also be used to stress the importance of a specific fitness criterion not to be trifled with. The Courier Inc. example, in Chapter 10, includes: *Will not risk our reputation as the safest transporter of love potions.*

Values are not useful if they are obvious and completely fail the opposite disqualifier. *Sustainable growth and profitability* as a value supplies no guidance, nor does *excellence*. Also, any concept that changes is probably not a value. For instance, the "value" for cash generation versus growth or profit may change over time. Express concepts like these as fitness criteria or tactical rules instead.

No matter how you decide to use values, don't include them in your SAM just because they are important. Include them if they influence your choice of alternative, such as they do in the case of the bike shop or Courier Inc. If the need is to get the organization to understand and adhere to the values to improve the organization's culture, create a framework with a strategy to achieve this need.

Diagnoses: Propositions

Your proposition should express why you think you can achieve your aspirations. Courier's proposition for entering the Old City to New City market revolves around their leading reputation for safe transport of love potions, and their success in other markets.

Propositions must state what you can do for your customers. Ask, do we offer something that customers can't get somewhere else at this price or can't do for themselves, and how do we improve *their* ability to get their "jobs done."[4] You want to help your customers bust their bottlenecks. (A government should ask what it can do for the people that the people cannot do for themselves or can do only inefficiently.) Propositions apply to internal customers, too, whatever you call them. If, say, an HR function is given the mission to reduce their cost, unless they consider the overall impact on company personnel—their customers—the mission cannot be achieved properly.

Usually, the term *value proposition* refers specifically to a business's offering to the market. *Business models*, also called operating models, are related to the value proposition. They usually include the mechanics of how revenues are generated and the costs to get them. You can find value proposition- and business model-generation worksheets and "canvases" that lay out the suggested dimensions of a proposition, this in addition to compendiums of proposition suggestions.[5] Some may look like or be called strategy (i.e., framework) methods, and list many aspects of doing business, but even these expanded propositions are only a part of the framework. These expanded aspects may include:

- Target customers/markets segments
- Customer alternatives
- Channels
- The product or service you offer
- What differentiates your offering
- Partners
- The cost to provide the offering
- "People propositions" for all stakeholders (Blue Ocean)

In the emergent approach, you can explore channels, product range, and partners as part of your framework alternatives. Other aspects will be fitness criteria to assess, for instance, the cost of providing the offering. If you are using canvases for all the above concepts, you need to represent multiple alternatives within them. Or you can develop separate canvases for each alternative and link the conclusions for each to the SAM. You might use Porter's Five Forces and similar techniques to analyze your proposition.[6] However, as with values, you only need to capture those aspects of the proposition relevant to the specific aspiration you are designing to achieve.

Diagnoses: External Constraints

There is *always* some external constraint on an organization, some "rule of the game." They can be from the parent framework: Courier's leadership might demand hiring a specific demographic diversity of drivers, restrict doing business to certain suppliers, or set a corporate policy limiting contracts lengths to three years. They can be from regulations from government agencies: Drivers may require particular types of licenses to transport love potions (one of Courier's challenges is they don't know if the government will approve drones for love potion transport). And there are the government laws of doing business.

The organization must be able to adhere to any rule of the game. Courier's leaders shouldn't impose on the project team to "never do anything to jeopardize our reputation as the safest transporter of love potions." It requires significant judgment to interpret this rule, and no one can guarantee to follow it. Protecting Courier's love potion transport reputation is better captured as a fitness criterion, or as mentioned earlier, as a value.

Design Principles for Aspirations

Chapter 1 defined the three types of aspirations—visions (broad), mission (purpose), and goals (specific)—that describe your (believed to be) desired future state. Aspirations lead to creative tension by forcing you to identify the bottlenecks to achieving them and then the strategy and other framework components for busting those bottlenecks. As stated in Chapter 1, it is not required to use all three types of aspiration. Start with one and add the others only if you have reason to do so. Use the one that best captures the spirit of the future state you have in mind.

The idea of designing aspiration could seem strange. If you embark on framework development, isn't there some desired future state already described? Well, if you already know your aspiration and can articulate it clearly, or the boss has imposed a non-negotiable objective upon you, then you don't have to design one. But there are situations where specific aspirations are unclear. You may know there is a new opportunity or threat but are unsure how the new state should look. You may be unclear how to articulate a gut feel or a broad vision of innovation. In some cases, you may not know what's possible. In others, the boss may supply only a broad aspiration, and you need to articulate a more specific one.

Task 1a lists 20 reasons as thought starters for why you would embark on changing your framework under the headings

- New framework not successful enough
- Deterioration and threats
- New opportunities
- Crises
- The boss says to do it

Task 2c is where you draft specific aspirations. The following principles will help you articulate them in a way that can be used successfully in your framework.

Overall Design Principles

The five disqualifiers (Chapter 8) can be used selectively to judge other designed framework components besides strategy. A good way to organize aspiration design principles is by using the disqualifiers to test the free choice and especially the unification requirements of a solution to the killer problems of change and innovation. Aspirations can never meet the real-time guidance requirement, which is why strategy exists in the first place, and why managing by results leads to average results.

The easiest to apply to aspirations are the duplicate and excluded disqualifiers. The aspiration for your system cannot *duplicate* the parent's aspiration because it would supply no new information; all components of the parent framework are external constraints to you, not a choice. Also, no aspect of your system can be *excluded* from your aspiration, otherwise, it will not unify the system; create nested systems if you need different aspirations for different parts.

As for the *opposite*, theoretically, there is nothing that says aspirations must pass this disqualifier. Most aspirations will fail a little. As suggested in Chapter 8, certain statements that fail the opposite might be useful aspirations even though they cannot serve as strategies. However, you should question aspirations that fail. For instance, *be low cost* failed as a strategy for a manufacturing company in Example 8.3 but *be low cost* could be a reasonable aspiration; yet, as discussed in Chapter 8, this statement would be an even better aspiration if it were more specific. Will everyone in the organization lower their cost? Will you spread the cost-reduction goal like peanut butter across every single function without differential management? What if higher cost in one area will lead to a much lower cost than others? For instance, what if higher cost but more flexible supply chains will allow elimination of costs in factories and in sales centers. What if a higher-cost product platform can serve multiple applications, allowing elimination of many other products? Applying the "hey, don't you get it, we're reducing costs here," mentality to every team can drive your organization away from many potentially beneficial approaches and lead to average performance, including loss of high-end customers. It also promotes silo behavior.

Some of the "positive action words" in Figure 8.5 that fail the opposite test and are disqualified as strategies are inadequate as aspirations as well. Words like "optimize" and "transform" have little meaning, especially because they are overused (as marketing) in the consulting-corporate-academia strategy complex. Words like accelerate, minimize, maximize, advance, ensure, strengthen, attract, and eliminate may be useful in aspirations.

Beware of Visions and Missions That Deeply Fail the Opposite

You need to decide if grandiose visions and missions that badly fail the opposite test will inspire your organization to do great things, for instance, the examples from well-known companies in Figure 12.2. While better than the popular "be the world's best" or "excellence," will such missions create positive tension with information that propels and guides the organization, or are they noise?

Grandiose visions and missions may be useful if they represent a big change for the organization. If a company's mission has been "maximize shareholder value," but is changed to "shareholder value *and* good for society," it might catch the organization's and investor's attention (it would be best if the good for society were stated more specifically).

Arguing against aspirations whose opposites are deeply absurd is not an argument against bold missions. Microsoft's 1985 mission, *a computer on every desk and in every home*, was bold, especially the idea of home

---

Fulfill lives, every day (convenience store)

Nourish people and the planet (premium supermarket chain)

Help make every brand more inspiring, and the world more intelligent (label and packaging company)

Operate the best specialty retail business in America, regardless of the product we sell (bookseller)

Unlock the potential of human creativity (streaming service)

Inspire humanity—both in the air on the ground (airline)

Be the best in the eyes of our customers, employees and shareholders (HVAC and Plumbing systems)

Create wildly successful customers by doing whatever it takes to enable our champions to be transformational leaders and their staff to be superstars (IT optimization software as a service provider)

Elevate the world's consciousness (shared workspace and services provider)

Figure 12.2 Actual examples of visions and missions

computers. Yet it had specificity and no superlatives; no buzzspeak like *transform the world with computers*, or *transform the world*. Whether the mission statement impacted Microsoft's great contributions to the personal computer revolution is hard to judge. How many failed endeavors had big mission statements as well?

Sometimes, what are labeled as strategies are missions. For instance, in a well-known article, the following statement was labeled as financial advisement company Edward Jones's *strategy*: "To grow ... by offering trusted and convenient face-to-face financial advice to conservative individual investors who delegate their financial decisions, through a national network of one-financial adviser offices."[7] Though a wonderfully clear rule, this is not Edward Jones's strategy because it is no longer in question; the opposite would be absurd for them. This statement is their mission, or a mix of mission and value proposition or business model. Their strategy would be focused on the bottleneck that limits growth or keeps them from sticking with this model, bottlenecks that would change (as would their strategy) as they evolve. Supposed Edward Jones considered moving away from or adding to its current mission by selling IPO stock recommendations via online subscriptions or some other significant change. In that case, these models could be alternative strategies with not-absurd opposites.

Should Aspirations Have Numbers? (Numbers Disqualifier)

Goals, because they are defined as the specific futures that you aim to achieve, will often have numbers, as will subgoals. You can use SMART (Specific, Measurable, Assignable, Realistic, Time-related) or similar designs for goals, but you cannot assign high-level goals to an individual; they must be the responsibility of the entire nested organization.

Whether visions and missions (again, if you need them at all) should have numbers is an open question. Would Microsoft's vision have been more compelling if written as *a computer on every desk and in every home by 2001?* Hard to tell. In some cases, it's hard to figure out how numbers should be added to missions, for instance, Tesla's *to accelerate the world's transition to sustainable energy*. Most visions and missions do not have numbers.

Should Aspirations Be Lists?

Aspiration lists are as easy a trap to fall into as strategy lists. Aspirations will usually not unify or be free choices if they are lists of more than two or three items. The typical lists of strategy themes (also used in strategy maps) shown in Chapter 1 (Figure 1.1) and Chapter 4 (Figure 4.2) not only fail as strategies but are also very poor aspirations. These long laundry lists, or "dog's dinners," as Rumelt calls them,[8] are just collections of supposedly good things to do. Many items fail the opposite, have no uniqueness, and could apply to any business on earth (probably other planets too), and give the illusion the "everything's covered." If you are a conglomerate and feel these themes are all that is common among your business unit strategies, then you should question why you are a conglomerate.

Some visions and missions consist of short lists that can be useful if they aim to make a single point. For instance, the John D. and Catherine T. MacArthur Foundation mission, "to support creative people and effective institutions committed to building a more just, verdant, and peaceful world." While technically independent, the foundation no doubt sees these three ideals as connected and part of a larger whole. *Just, verdant* or *peaceful* each alone fail the opposite (unjust, paved-over, violent). Yet together, their opposite may not be absurd.

One other type of list that could be an aspiration is a manifesto. Similar to lists of maxims described in Chapter 8, manifestos may include not only tactical policy, but ideals, and perhaps lists of goals. The long Netflix "Culture" document of values and rules discussed previously might be considered an aspirational manifesto that makes an overall point. As a general guideline, however, use lists of aspirations with caution.

How Ambitious Should Your Aspirations Be? How Much to Bite Off at One Time?

Big moves and *BHAGs* (big hairy audacious goals) are often recommended based on case history analysis of successful companies. It's important to keep in mind that many great companies may have evolved to their greatness without an initial vision of the big move, and that data may not always include big moves that failed. Also, there are strategy options for going after big visions in smaller bites (Chapter 16). See Rumelt's warnings about "blue sky" objectives and the need for more down-to-earth "proximate objectives".[9] Note also that the Blue Ocean direction, to aspire to create new business in uninhabited spaces, does not require starting in a massive way.

You may not be able to decide the specifics of your aspiration until you have worked through bottlenecks and strategies. How much you bite off depends a lot on the bottlenecks. It's OK to start with a draft aspiration that you refine as you evolve the SAM.

Note that what are known as *stretch goals* are not big moves or BHAGs. Stretch goals are the idea of adding a modest increment to the "base" goal to inspire even greater achievement in the organization. Stretch goals provide little value and are strongly discouraged in the emergent approach.[10]

CHAPTER 13

Designing Scenarios

Scenarios capture the multiple possible external environments in which you implement your framework design, each with some probability of occurring. As described in Chapter 10, scenarios consist of uncertain conditions and events which you do not influence or can influence only slightly but can impact your results. Therefore, scenarios influence your choice of framework alternatives and their strategies.

Examples of external conditions include economic or competitive environments, weather patterns, or public opinion about an issue. Examples of events include a court ruling, a regulatory change, a competitor's action, a pandemic, or a terrorist attack. External refers to *external to your system*, which means uncertainty about a corporate policy, for instance, could be part of a scenario for a business unit or function in that corporation. Uncertainty about which scenario will occur can itself be the bottleneck to achieving aspirations.

The benefit of using scenarios is not in capturing every possible external future; it is impossible to do so and any effort to try would be a waste of time. No one can know whether they have captured all futures. There is no need to have a contingency for every possible future either. The objectives with scenarios, as discussed at the end of Chapter 10, are to

- Destabilize the organization's belief in a known future,
- Influence strategy alternative design to reflect different futures, and
- Encourage preparation of some contingencies.

This chapter covers the basics of how scenarios work and principles for designing and using them. Chapter 10 pointed out that it's almost too easy to imagine multiple futures, so it's important to construct them with some care. What is hard, and not always stressed in the literature, is the mechanics of incorporating scenarios into decision matrices, in our case, the SAM.

Scenarios are simplified in the emergent approach, enabling them for "habitual everyday use," not only for uber long-term and critical topics (and not only for exploring conditions that could influence achieving yearly or quarterly financials). Consult the scenario planning literature for more sophisticated techniques when needed (see the Scenario Planning section of *References for an Adaptive View of the World* {web/supplement} which includes a comparison of the varied terminology used).

Simple Example of Scenarios

In keeping that they are not only for momentous topics and uber time horizons, even the Grands' little story can illustrate scenario basics. In Chapter 10, the Grands created a SAM (Figure 10.5) to evaluate several alternatives for traveling from Old City to New City to visit the kids. Grandpa assessed that the travel time for driving on the highway was 1.5 to 2.5 hours depending on the traffic, and that the trip would be uncomfortable if there were bad traffic. Two external futures that the Grands care about but don't influence were implied: not-bad traffic and bad traffic.

Now you might say, "But the Grands know that rush-hour or holiday traffic will be bad, so they can avoid it." This is true, but it is the unpredictable event-driven traffic that is interesting. It is the plausible but not-so-predictable futures that require scenarios. The more predictable a future is, the less potential it holds for achieving something new and innovative (Chapter 2). The Grands can avoid known rush-hour traffic, but what if grandpa says, "Traffic, schmaffic, because I avoid rush-hour, we haven't run into traffic in the last ten trips." Then on the eleventh, they find themselves in a five-hour delay caused by an accident, and grandma is so angry she won't talk to him for a week.

You might also point out a confusing observation: The Grands have a fitness criterion to not contribute to traffic and its pollution, yet scenarios like traffic can't be influenced. The reconciliation is that there is an incremental consideration and a moral consideration. If there are 40,000 cars already on the highway, the Grands as car number 40,001 will not materially change traffic congestion or pollution. Yet it is a lie if all 40,001 drivers deny causing congestion or pollution.

It turns out the Grands have become concerned with three additional considerations since they first formulated their SAM. First, while preferring the train when they travel for environmental reasons, they like the convenience of a car in New City when they visit the kids, so they bought a fuel-efficient hybrid for that trip. They also refuse to take the train unless they can buy tickets three weeks in advance to get the lowest fares and to guarantee seats. And last, they are becoming much more concerned about driving in bad weather (ha, an *environmental*-environmental uncertainty), even though bad weather occurs only occasionally where they live.

The Grands now have two external conditions—traffic and weather—that they do not control, and that can influence their choice of travel alternative. They summarize these conditions in Figure 13.1A along with a rough probability of occurrence. Then they construct *safe* and *harsh* scenarios using two methods: simple mapping of conditions and events to the scenarios (13.1B), and a 2×2 cross (13.1C).

Next, Grandpa updates his SAM (Figure 10.5) with the new information, creating Figure 13.2: He adds a fifth fitness criterion that captures their value for a car in New City, he reduces the cost of the

Conditions and Events		Impact on alternative?	Probability of happening?
1	Traffic	Don't want to drive in bad traffic	Once every few months
2	Bad weather	Don't want to drive in bad weather	Mostly in winter

(A)

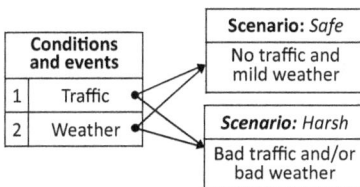

(B)

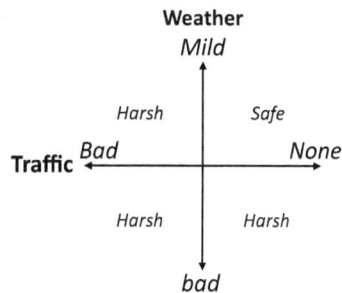

(C)

Figure 13.1 *Two ways to construct the Grand's scenarios from a conditions and events table (A): simple mapping (B) and a 2×2 cross (C)*

Alternative→ Scenarios→	Goal: Get to the Kids in New City in Best Way		
	Drive		Take the train
	Safe (~90%)	Harsh (~10%)	Safe or Harsh (100%)
Time (hrs.)	2–3	4–5+	1.5
Comfort	Somewhat irritating	Highly irritating	Good
Cost	$30	$30 + accident potential	$190
Impact on Environment	OK	OK	Feels good
Car in New City	Yes	Yes	No
	X		√

Figure 13.2 The Grands' updated SAM with scenarios added

driving assessment from $63 to $30 because of less fuel consumed, and he assesses that the impact on the environment is now "OK" with the hybrid car (but still not as good as the train alternative). Then he adds his scenarios by creating subcolumns under his drive alternative. He estimates the *harsh* scenario will occur about 10 percent of the time (i.e., P10). His assessments under the *safe* scenario are the same as before because he assumed safe conditions—in essence this is his "base case" scenario. His assessments of the fitness criteria under the *harsh* scenario reflect what he thinks driving in traffic and weather would mean.

What is seen is the Grands rule out the driving alternative because they cannot accept long and uncertain time, the discomfort, and the accident potential of driving in harsh conditions. They do this even though nice weather is the most-likely P90 case and even though they prefer to drive to New City. They simply will not accept something like a 10 percent chance of harsh conditions.

To accept driving, they would have to relax constraints: either accept driving in harsh conditions an expected 10 percent of the time (or not go at all) or eliminate the three-week ticket requirement. Without the three-week requirement, they can wait till the day before and have a reasonable chance of knowing the weather which will allow them to take the train on short notice if needed (of course, the train may be sold out by then). No one can predict the weather three weeks in advance. No one can predict event-driven traffic, so its possibility of occurring only adds reason to not drive.

Note that Grandpa did not bother adding the *harsh* scenario to the Train alternative because he believed that bad traffic and bad weather would not sufficiently influence train performance. He was willing to accept the consequences if they did. You do not have to design for all scenarios. Note also that percentages are used here for illustration, but unless you have meaningful calculations, words like low and high might be better, or you can use the notation P10 or P90 to represent if such notation conveys less exactitude in your organization.

Scenarios Are Not Assessments of Framework Alternatives

Scenarios capture only those futures that the organization cannot influence or can influence only slightly. Assessments capture the outcomes of implementing alternative frameworks with their strategies, and the alternatives are assessed against the backdrop of multiple scenarios. The Grands' alternatives don't influence the weather or the traffic; they influence their expected results against their five fitness criteria. However, by incorporating the uncontrollable scenarios of traffic and weather, they can more realistically assess how to achieve their fitness criteria, including their risk tolerance for harsh conditions. Using scenarios is not an argument against trying to shape the ecosystem in which you will play. It is admitting that you cannot control some dynamics.

As mentioned in Chapter 10, some literature may view scenarios more broadly by defining them as assessments. In such an approach, the external conditions and events are rolled up with internal events, and the scenarios are defined as combinations of both the outcomes of what you can and cannot influence. So, for instance, a scenario in this approach would be the Grands driving and arriving on time and in comfort because there was neither bad traffic nor bad weather. Another scenario would be the Grands choosing the train and arriving on time and comfort because the traffic and weather had no impact. This broader, rolled-up use of scenarios is common in everyday language, as in, "Hey, we better consider the scenario that we won't arrive on time if we drive."

The problem with the rolled-up view is that the uninfluenceable environment is not isolated in the diagnosis, which means it cannot be studied as easily and can't be clearly monitored during implementation. Separate

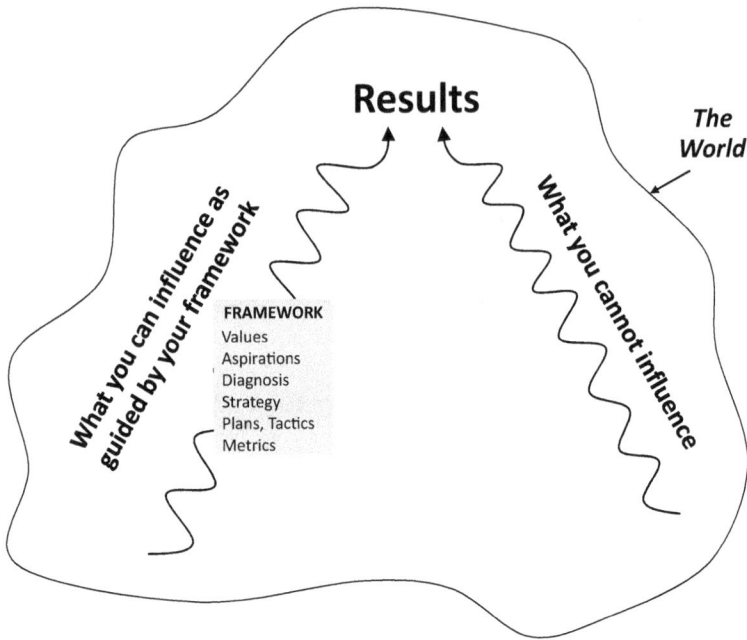

Figure 13.3 Your framework in the context of the rest of the world

what you can do from what the rest of the world does, as in Figure 13.3. If you want to influence something in the environment, say a regulation, and you think you can, then make it an aspiration or a fitness criterion and bust the bottleneck to achieving it.

Scenario Design Principles

Task Set 3 provides a little more detail on the methods for designing and incorporating scenarios into the SAM, including discussions of how many scenarios to use, *Wilson Matrixes* for capturing the probability and possible impact of conditions and events, and the pros and (mostly) cons of the 2×2 cross technique. The remainder of this chapter discusses essential scenario use principles.

Scenarios Usually Comprise Multiple Conditions and Events

The Grands considered only weather and traffic. In more significant endeavors, many uncertain conditions and events can be in play. In Chapter 10,

Courier Inc. included three items as scenarios in their early version of their SAM for expansion into the Old City to New City market (Figure 10.9): price war, loss of love potion demand, and regulation of love potions off trains. Figure 13.4, however, shows that there are several other possible conditions

	Conditions and events	Range of Impact on Alternatives	Probability Estimate of happening
(1)	*Love potions regulated off trains*	Good for fleet and drones; obvious disaster for Train alternative	Most of us think 1 out of 1000; Jaimie thinks 5 out of 100.
(2)	*Rental car companies ban love potions*	Bad if we can't shift to trains or fleet quickly, and competitors avoided rentals.	Lower than (1) because no crowds involved
(3)	*Gas prices through the roof (>17 peso/l)*	Good if trains available; bad if (1) comes true and drones not available	Pretty low, <20%
(4)	*Other bad for driving*	Strikes; construction; public pressure to use trains due to air pollution concerns, low availability of couriers who can drive. With high gas prices, could have impact.	Meaningful probability of several occurring, but wide uncertainty
(5)	*Other bad for Trains*	Schedule delays, strikes, price increases	Unknown—need research
(6)	*Use of drones for transporting love potions allowed*	*Huge impact, changes everything.* Good If we have invested in drones, and used rental cars and train, and not invested in a fleet. Will competition invest in drones, how much?	Increasing, but still very uncertain Some of us believe we can influence the government → **make it a fitness criterion?**
(7)	*Economy does poorly 3–5 years*	Could cut both ways; we could be squeezed on financing, but it also could shut down lazy competition—maybe ignore.	50–50; we won't try to predict it anyway,
(8)	*Aggressive competitors' behavior/ Price war*	Lose pricing power.	Can we erect barriers and influence? Or will entering the market provoke no matter what?
(9)	*Reduced demand for love potion transport*	Some public interest groups are questioning the effectiveness of love potions, and negative press could hurt.	We believe demand growth will remain steady at 3%/y; but the public is fickle

Figure 13.4 Conditions and events for Courier Inc.'s venture into Old City to New City market

Condition and Events		
(1)	Love potions regulated off trains	
(2)	Rental car companies ban love potions	
(3)	Gas prices through the roof (>17 peso/l)	
(4)	Other bad for driving	
(5)	Other bad for Trains	
(6)	Government approval of drones for transporting love potions	
(7)	Economy does poorly 3-5 year	
(8)	Aggressive Competitors	
(9)	Reduced demand for love potion transport	

Fab for Fleet

Train Transport good

We can influence → So make it a fitness criterion

Bad Investment environment

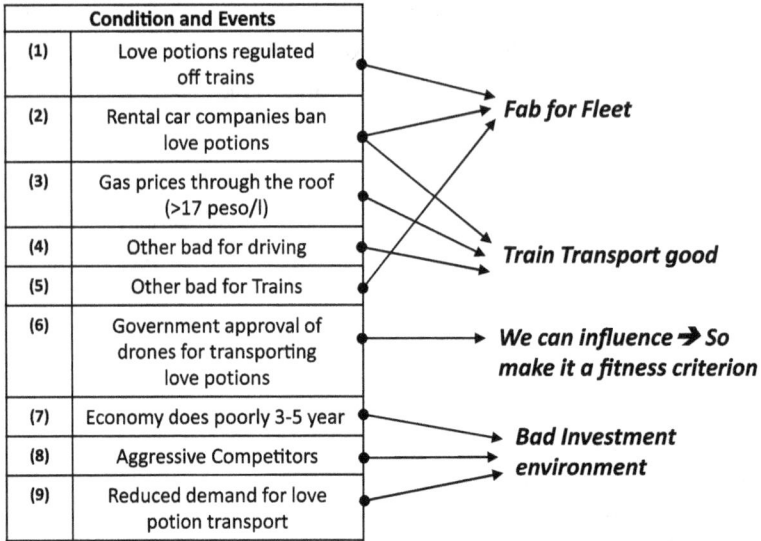

Figure 13.5 Possible scenarios of interest for Courier Inc. using simple mapping

and events to consider that are uncertain. Some are unique to their endeavor, and some are uncertainties for any business. Not also that while they were considering drone approval for love potion as a scenario—a major game changer—they realize now that they can influence this with lobbying and that drone approval should be a fitness criterion, not a scenario.

Figure 13.5 shows possible scenarios constructed from these conditions and events using simple mapping (using 2×2s would be more complicated).

While some conditions and events are so important that they alone can be a scenario, for instance, drone regulatory approval before it was converted to a fitness criterion, scenarios often comprise multiple conditions and events that can be additive and interact. If the Grands, for example, start to believe they can live with moderate traffic or moderate harsh weather but ignore the combination of the two, they may find themselves in an unacceptable situation for driving. For Courier, competitive behavior, the state of the roads, courier availability, and the state of the economy all exist at the same time. A few work stoppages by the bridge and road workers may not make a fleet alternative unacceptable to Courier; but some combination of these strikes, plus high fuel prices, public pressure against single-passenger cars on the highways, chronic road repair, and difficulty getting qualified couriers who can drive—all considered together—might make investing in a fleet of vehicles a complete disaster.

Another reason for combining conditions and events that would have the same potential impact is simplicity. There are only so many scenarios that can be considered when creating alternatives.

Always keep in mind that when you draft possible scenarios, you are not favoring an alternative, or even deciding to use any of the scenarios in your SAM. All you are doing is as objectively as possible capturing possible futures and sensitizing the team to them. You will only be able to fully judge what is important until you are evolving the SAM as a whole.

Aspirations Determine the Horizon for Scenarios

Like strategy, the horizon of your aspiration and the time scale of investments determines the time horizon of your scenarios, not an arbitrary "long-term" view. The Grands have a three-week aspiration and, therefore, three-week scenarios. Courier Inc.'s time frame is about five years. The government advisory organization *Natural England* demands a 50-year horizon for certain scenario studies on England's environment and ecosystems.[1] When the military develops weapon platforms or corporations plan multibillion-dollar factory investments, there better be a many-year horizon. A supply chain team developing framework alternatives in September for supplying February's Lunar New Year products needs a six-month horizon. A product development team might have a two- or three-year horizon because the product has a life cycle of two or three years.

Scenarios Create a Third Dimension

The addition of scenarios to the SAM (or any decision matrix) in principle adds a third dimension because fitness criteria must be assessed against combinations of framework alternatives and scenarios. Figure 13.6 shows the case of two scenarios and three strategy alternatives. Such as case would require, in principle, 18 assessments.

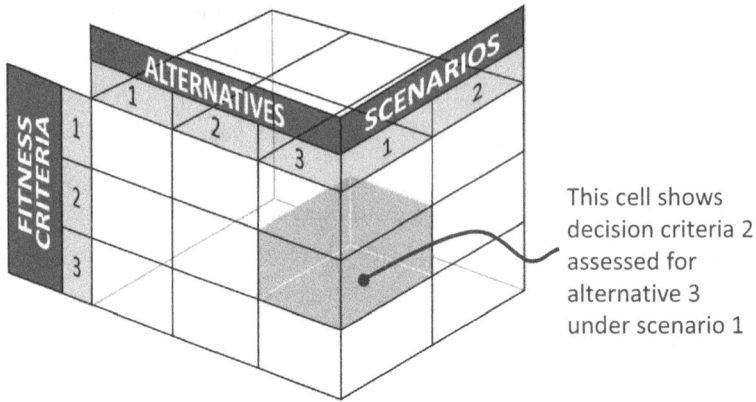

This cell shows decision criteria 2 assessed for alternative 3 under scenario 1

Figure 13.6 Adding scenarios creates a third dimension in the SAM

Working in three dimensions is not practical without some fancy software. An alternative approach is to add sub columns for each scenario, as Grandpa did in Figure 13.2 (or even simpler techniques, see Task Set 3b). He assessed the driving alternative against the *safe* and *harsh* scenarios, a total of 10 assessments, (recall he ignored the impact of the scenarios on the Train alternative). To find the *expected* overall assessment of the outcome, he needs to weight the two sets of five assessments by the probability of each scenario occurring:

Overall Expected Assessment for Driving Alternative =
(2–3 hr + somewhat irritating + $30 + OK + car) × 90% +
(4–5 hr + highly irritating + $30 + accident potential + OK +
car) × 10%

Or, shown in the SAM (Figure 13.7).

Yet not only do you not need math like this, such an expected overall assessment entirely misses the point of scenarios, and you should never do it because of the next principle.

Do Not Average Futures

Averaging different possible futures to get expected values usually obliterates useful information. This is true in scenarios of the external world and

	Goal: Get to the Kids in New City in Best Way		
Alternative →	Drive		Take the train
Scenarios →	Safe (~90%)	Harsh (~10%)	Safe or Harsh (100%)
Time (hr.)	2–3	4–5+	1.5
Comfort	Somewhat irritating	Highly irritating	Good
Cost	$30	$30 + accident potential	$190
Impact on Environment	OK	OK	Feels good
Car in New City	Yes	Yes	No
	× 90% + × 10% = Overall Drive		

Figure 13.7 The Grands' SAM showing the calculation of the expected outcome

in making assessments of outcomes you can influence. It is nonsensical for the Grands to average nice weather and harsh weather to get kind-of-OK weather. This average conceals the "highly irritating" and "accident potential" outcomes that keep them from choosing the driving alternative, despite these outcomes having a small impact on the weighted average.

For another example, say a business is exploring alternatives for replacing a critical machine in a factory. If they believe the cost of one alternative could range anywhere from $10M to $30M, it may be nonsensical for them to average the $10M and $30M cost to get an expected $20M cost. What if a $30M cost would thrust the business into bankruptcy? Then it would hardly matter that $20M was the expected cost. Likewise, it would be entirely senseless for Courier Inc. to average government approval and government denial of drones for love potion transport. Averaging has meaning only when assessing many outcomes.

Even though averaging cases to get an expected point prediction defeats the value of using multiple futures, averaging is often the first impulse, especially when assessments are numerical. If a high case is 30 and a low case is 10, assume 20. Yuck. This is the tyranny of the mid-case.

Each Scenario Does Not Get Its Own Strategy

A McKinsey article *Overcoming Obstacles to Effective Scenario Planning* says, "Access the impact of all scenarios and develop strategic alternatives for each of them." No! Only one framework alternative, with its one strategy, can be implemented and executed on at any time. The strategy and the other framework components are "at the mercy" of all scenarios, of all futures, whether it's possible to discover and articulate them or not. The Grands, because they insist on buying their train tickets three weeks in advance, cannot cherry-pick the scenarios and say, "We will drive if conditions are safe and take the train if not." They must decide on one or the other alternative three weeks ahead (or again, relax the constraint).

Imagine using the one scenario-one strategy in gambling. In the game *craps*, if a player's first dice roll is a 7 or 11, they win; if their first roll is snake eyes (1+1), they lose. The outcome of a dice roll is an event that is uncertain and uncontrollable (or is supposed to be). One scenario-one strategy would be like saying, "I'll make a bet if I roll a 7 or 11," which is silly. You must bet before rolling the dice, and your bet is at the mercy of both the 7/11 *and* the snake-eyes scenario.

You can choose a strategy alternative that ignores all but one scenario (there's always some assumption of the external world you will implement in—stated or not), but futures don't go away just because they are ignored. Either you believe the ignored futures are low-enough probability to safely ignore, or you are willing to accept the consequence of being wrong. These could both be perfectly reasonable choices. In many cases, the approach is to design strategy alternatives that are robust to multiple scenarios (Chapter 16). One particular technique is to have contingency strategies that you can switch to when triggered by the realization that a different scenario is coming true, in the spirit of an IF-THEN rule. But this implies you still have time to make the switch. If Courier wants to launch the new route but is still unsure when and whether drones will be approved, they have no choice to invest in alternative fleet or train options.

Do Not Use Scenarios as Forecasts

When treated as forecasts, scenarios become damaging, a point stressed repeatedly in the literature (read the first chapter of Schoemaker's *Profiting from Uncertainty*).[2] Scenarios are needed because of limited ability to forecast and the danger of point predicting. The Grands would destroy any sensible planning if they tried to forecast what the weather would be in three weeks. Even worse would be if they correctly guessed the weather several times and started to believe their abilities. In a more serious example, in 2010 the government of North Carolina commissioned a study on how future sea-level rise will impact their vast low-lying coastal areas. They were not pleased with the study's conclusion that sea-level rise will likely adversely affect more homes and regions than previously believed. Their response was to pass a bill in 2012 that, among other stipulations, restricted use of sea-rise projections in policy decisions until new projections were made.[3] Accepting the accelerated projections would force limitations on the development of coastal areas, restrict rebuilding of roads and bridges, and add requirements for flood control, all very tough economic pills to swallow.

But seeking the perfect single forecast of sea levels is a terrible approach in strategizing for policy. No one can know the *exact* sea-level rise over the next decades. The question is whether it makes sense to simply dismiss the significant evidence for an accelerated sea-level rise scenario presented in the range of outcomes that the study provided. Dismissing this evidence is like betting your home on a craps game because no one can prove to you that you will lose.

Everyone has the right to ignore scenarios at their peril (well, at others' peril in the case of North Carolina), but to pretend that there are no other futures nearly guarantees failure. Obviously, waiting for a forecast that pleases you is absurd.

Avoid Normal Probability Distribution Thinking

It would be rare to use a mathematical probability distribution in strategizing, but it's valuable to keep in mind the characteristics of various distributions. Mid-case thinking derives from the paradigm of the normal distribution with a small standard deviation. The peak of the distribution is viewed as far more probable to occur as the "tails." But scenario planners and the growing body of knowledge on the failure of prediction referenced in the Introduction to the book show that such distributions are not good representations of the future.

The future is often better described by flatter or modal distributions as in Figure 13.8. In flat, or *long-tailed* distributions, even if you could know

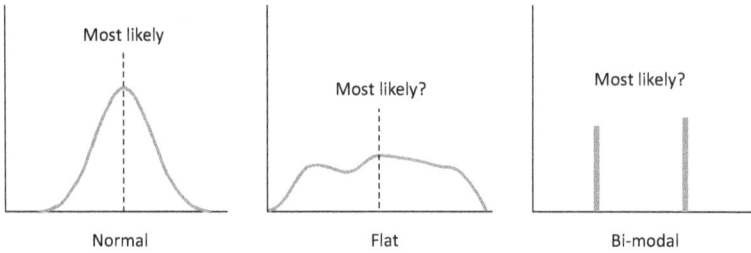

Figure 13.8 Probability distributions

that a given case is the most likely one, it does not mean it is necessarily *very* likely. What if the Grands lived in an urban area? The probability of bad traffic might be equal to the probability of no traffic, a 50–50 proposition that looks nothing like a normal distribution. Courier Inc.'s scenario of regulatory approval for drone transport is either off or on—bi-modal—not a continuous distribution at all. For the business making the essential equipment purchase, the probability distribution of costs might be quite flat from $10 to $30 million, reflecting that they don't know what the cost will be within that range. None of these examples have useful most-likely mid-cases. Mid-cases are imagined.

Some scenario planning authors will label high-probability conditions and events as *predetermined*. For example, these authors sometimes call demographics predetermined, using birth and death rates, but did these rates hold during the two 20th century world wars? How many extremely likely futures did not occur because of Covid-19? The concept of predetermined opposes the spirit of scenarios. Courier might think love potion transport by rail is unassailable, and it might be, until it isn't. It is better to classify future conditions and events as relatively high or low probability.

Small probability but possibly large impact environmental forces are often referred to as *wild cards*. Nassim Taleb's black swans are in this category. If the Grands live in a rural area, then bad traffic could be a black swan because it is so rare but also impactful on their ability to make a comfortable and timely trip. Taleb uses the term *fat-tailed* distributions to describe the potentially highly impactful black swans on the tails. Usually, when people talk of wildcards, and when Taleb talks about Black Swans, they are again referring to the roll-up of the probability of occurrence *times* the potential impact of occurrence, not only the probability of occurrence (this is what makes fat-tailed distributions as opposed to just long-tailed, or flat, distributions).

It is most sensible to include only those low-probability scenarios that also have a potentially high impact, if, of course, you can know the potential impact. The regulation against love potion transport by rail might have a low probability of occurring, but if it occurs, it could destroy Courier Inc.'s venture. This could happen if they choose a rail-only alternative and can't easily switch to vehicle transport for love potions, because the drivers require months of training on handling the potions, and the vehicles need to be specially outfitted. But again, the objective in the emergent approach is not detailed calculation, but internalization by making scenarios visible and understood.

Don't Ignore Upside Potential

An uncertain future is not necessarily a pessimistic one. If the Grands must drive the Brooklyn–Queens Expressway in New York to get to the kids, a traffic-free ride might seem like winning the lottery. For a CEO running a fledgling security and surveillance company, the 9/11 terrorist attacks were likely an unexpected boost. For those in the government who drove military action in Iraq—either in the belief that war would promote democracy and diminish terrorism, or because they expected political or financial gain from war—the 9/11 attacks were a gift on a silver platter. Those who invested sensibly in FAANG (Facebook, Amazon, Apple, Netflix, and Google) and companies of similar ilk in the early 2010s, may not have anticipated the amazing growth of web-based commerce and social media. Too often, scenarios focus on downside potential (risk) and ignore upsides. If the government approves drones just in time for Courier Inc. to avoid massive investment in traditional transport, it would be an enormous competitive advantage.

A scenario is itself neither good nor bad. It can have potentially good or bad implications for strategy alternatives. What makes a scenario useful is how well it captures the possible external conditions and events.

CHAPTER 14

Finding Bottlenecks

Because bottlenecks link strategy and overall aspirations (and link tactics and smaller-scope aspirations), they play a starring role in the emergent approach. Bottlenecks are the glue that holds frameworks together, which means finding them requires knowledge of the entire system. It may be just as challenging to find bottlenecks as it is to find strategies to bust them, but once you've found the bottleneck, you're halfway to finding the strategy.

Bottlenecks are discovered and articulated, not designed—they exist whether discovered or not. They are a property of the dynamics of the system. There is no simple discovery formula, and the only way to be confident of your bottlenecks is to evolve the SAM as a whole, or even begin implementation. There are, however, several techniques and guidelines presented in this chapter that can aid in discovering bottlenecks.

Starting Bottleneck Discovery

The **strategy ← bottleneck ← aspiration** triad is again helpful for facilitating discovery, as shown in Figure 14.1 for Courier Inc. debating bottlenecks to entering the Old City to New City love potion market. Think both backward, asking what is in the way of achieving the aspiration, and forward, by generating rough strategy ideas that stimulate ideas for bottlenecks. Don't worry if initial strategies fully pass the disqualifiers. As always, when brainstorming, focus less on correctness and more on what the words mean.

Other approaches to bottleneck discovery include traditional exploratory techniques, such as five whys, fishbones from lean six sigma, and heatmaps (see Figure 17.4). These techniques may be simple and are often applied to problems with fewer variables, but the simplicity may help focus thinking.

Possible Strategies	← Possible Bottlenecks	← Aspiration
	Uncertainty of drone approval for love potions	
Fleet vs train		
Fleet "on the shelf"	Uncertainty of regulation of trains for love potions	Enter Old City to New City transport market
Train with "fleet in waiting"	Competitive response ... will a price war kill everyone? Will a price war spread to other markets?	
Invest in drones		
Wait until/if drones approved	The cost of a vehicle fleet in waiting?	

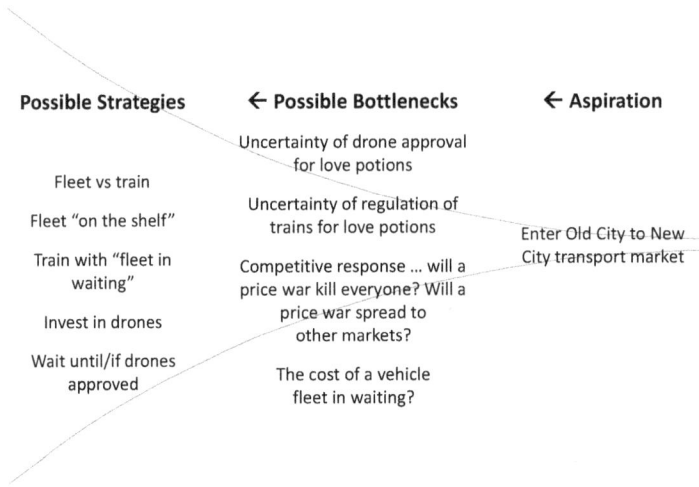

Figure 14.1 Courier Inc. exploring bottlenecks

Where to Look for Bottlenecks

Bottlenecks come in all shapes and sizes and can be real or imagined. They can be **people-related** when aspirations are a poor fit for the culture of the organization, or when these is lack of motivation, mind-space, confidence, or capability, including the capability to design strategy and their frameworks. People may not understand the framework and its strategy because it poorly articulated and communicated. Lack of interpersonal alignment can be a bottleneck, as can entrenched adversaries who may be unreasonable, uninformed, or just ridiculous, but sometimes adversaries can be either won over or gotten around (they may also be right.) Sometimes the bottleneck is the fear of stepping on powerful people's toes; it is hard to cross your sugar daddy or sugar mommy. Sometimes it is a sacred cow.

Intelligence-related bottlenecks can include lack of insight or uncertainty about elements of the ecosystem: competition, market dynamics, customers, technologies, public opinion, and governments and the regulatory environment, that is, uncertainty about scenarios. For the Grands, the bottleneck is an inability to forecast uncontrollable environments. For Courier Inc. a possible bottleneck in Figure 14.1 includes inability to forecast the love potion regulatory scenario.

Process-capability bottlenecks can include entrenched approaches that no longer work, or a lack of understanding of what the processes must achieve. They can be a lack of **methods** for differential management, life cycle management, or other basic business practices. They can be a lack of **digital capability.**

Lack of common **language** can be a bottleneck (in addition to the definition of strategy and other framework components). People might have divergent views of what defines a product's position in its life cycle, (i.e., growth, mature, end-of life) or what defines a specialty product that is supposed to receive unique supply chain, pricing, or customer service treatment.

Bottlenecks can be **asset related** including lack of intellectual property, equipment, or inability to procure need products or services. Existing asset locations and designs may be a problem. Sometimes there is not enough **capital** (too much money can be a problem too). The bottleneck may be that resources have too many strings attached or come at some other excessive cost.

Complexity itself can be the bottleneck. Organizations, techniques, offerings, or communications can be too complicated to manage or control. There can be too many—or too dissimilar—technologies, projects, products, and services. Organization structures, managing systems, and policies may be too complicated. Complexity can exacerbate any other bottleneck. For instance, factory automation that on paper improves cost and output over manual methods may not be helpful if complicated to operate and maintain.

Guidelines for Evaluating Bottlenecks

No matter where or how you look for the bottleneck, the following guidelines will help you zero in on the one you need to bust with the strategy. Like the five disqualifiers, these guidelines don't confirm you have found the right bottleneck; they provide stressors to eliminate (destroy from the team's thinking) the wrong bottlenecks until a fit one emerges.

Guideline 1: The bottleneck should not be extremely easy or impossibly hard to bust.

If the bottleneck is too hard to bust, it may mean the aspiration should be revised because it is impossibly hard to achieve. On the other hand, a bottleneck that is ridiculously easy to bust may not be what's truly in the way of the aspiration or may indicate that the aspiration is not ambitious enough, and again, you should reconsider it. The following examples illustrate these two extremes.

Aspiration: Reduce operating cost of the Navy by 10 percent.
Bottleneck: The government requires projection of naval force in too many regions worldwide.

The validity of this bottleneck depends on the willingness of the government to reduce the number of regions in which its naval forces must operate. If the government is adamant, then the "too many regions" is not the bottleneck because it is an unbustable external constraint. If, however, the country is in financial and hegemonic decline because natural resources are declining or its population no longer values projecting military power, then convincing the government to eliminate regions from the Navy's responsibility might be feasible, and number of regions could be the right bottleneck. Here are other possible bottlenecks for the aspiration of reducing the cost of the Navy by 10 percent:

- Officers create their own objectives by flowdown into strategy maps, which creates silo behavior and limits the ability to create desperately needed integrated approaches between departments.
- Too many weapon systems exist because no one has the courage to tell top brass that some are inferior.
- The government keeps several inefficient and unneeded bases because of political pressure from representatives in those districts.
- There is little coherent direction from the government. Their "strategy" is a list of conflicting subgoals.
- Leveraging designs with the army and air force has gone too far leading to expensive designs with lower performance.
- Personnel are not trained in techniques for economical operations.

The next example is different.

Aspiration: Reduce operating cost of the Navy by 10 percent.
Bottleneck: Officers are not sufficiently aware of the cost imperative.

If all you have to do is communicate the imperative, then this bottleneck will be ridiculously easy to bust. What if, however, the officer corps hears the same story year after year from the arch admirals and politicians: "It is imperative that we mobilize resources to the fullest extent to significantly reduce cost!" What it they are rarely forced to materially change how they operate and can comply with a little window dressing and delay a few programs (even if these actions are marketed as tough leadership choices)? In this case, communicating and getting the officers to believe the cost-reduction message could be the bottleneck.

Guideline 2: The bottleneck cannot be just a different way of expressing the aspiration or a symptom of the problem.

A bottleneck that repeats the aspiration using different words adds no new information. For instance,

Aspiration: Improve the salesforce capability.
Likely incorrect bottleneck: Salespeople are not meeting their yearly objectives.

Not meeting yearly objectives is just another symptom of poor salesforce capability. Actual bottlenecks in the way of improving the salesforce might be:

- Lack of training.
- Lack of online tools.
- Salespeople lack incentive to change or have negative influences that discourage them from improving.
- Salespeople are rewarded in a way that is contrary to the profitability of the company, creating conflict with other functions.
- Recruiting the wrong salespeople.

Guideline 3: The bottleneck must be in the way of the full aspiration.

Because the aspiration determines the scope and horizon of your endeavor, it also determines the scope and horizon of the bottleneck (which, again, in turn determines the scope and horizon of the strategy). If the aspiration is wide-ranging, the bottleneck must be in the way of succeeding in the entire wide-ranging scope. Guideline 3 is identical to the *is anything excluded* disqualifier (Chapter 8).

If there appears to be more than one bottleneck, you may need to create multiple nested systems. For instance, in Figure 8.9, "outsource manufacturing and instead put all resources into product performance improvement," was disqualified as a strategy in Chapter 8 for a portfolio that included both early- and late-life cycle (commodity) products. The diagnosis was that improving commodity-product performance gave little return and therefore these products should have a different framework with a different aspiration and strategy.

The need for two systems, however, may have also come from different bottlenecks. If the aspiration for both new and commodity products was to grow, the nested systems may be needed because the bottleneck to growing would be different for each. For instance, the development team for the early life cycle products may not have the right skills for doing what it takes to grow the commodities. In this case, the strategy for the commodities would have to bust the bottleneck of not having the right skills, while the strategy for the early life cycle product would be related to the company's traditional bottlenecks to product performance improvement.

Dealing With Multiple Bottlenecks

Make every effort to find the dominant bottleneck in a system, so that the strategy to bust it will have the greatest leverage. Finding the dominant bottleneck is key to avoiding lists of initiatives as your "strategy." Yes, every system will have lesser bottlenecks that matter as well, and you can bust these with tactics (Chapter 6). If in the salesforce upgrade example mentioned earlier, lack of incentive to change is the dominant bottleneck, but training is lacking too, there can be a tactical program to bust the training bottleneck. And in the section just above, nested systems enables maintaining a dominant bottleneck for each system with its own framework. However, if you truly believe that there are two or three major bottlenecks of equal weight and you don't want to call one dominant or use nested systems, then try to find a strategy that busts all of them.

When the Whole System Is Broken—Finding Root Causes

Systems in which many bottlenecks are seemingly in play and many symptoms of failure are visible can be called *systemically broken*. Everything is a mess and leaders may be caught in a perpetual game of whack-a-mole, dealing with symptoms as they arise. In such situations, it may be challenging to discover the real cause—the root cause—of the problems, and therefore what is the bottleneck to fixing that root cause. The bottleneck may be that divergent beliefs about causes have paralyzed everyone. The bottleneck may be that there is no one powerful enough or with enough moral authority to force the tough trade-offs that are needed, or it may be that the poor leadership that has enabled the systemic failure is still in place. Strategies to bust such bottlenecks may be built around:

- Finding small problems to solve to show progress and build credibility (but be sure to not think the big problem is solved).
- Stabilizing to stop the bleeding so everyone can catch their breath, then start to go deeper.
- Finding someone with the authority to make change.
- Simplifying.
- Taking the drastic actions needed and accepting that certain groups will be alienated.

Historical/Past Causes

An added difficulty to diagnosing bottlenecks is that past causes of current performance are no longer changeable. You cannot change history. And since an unchangeable cause fails to meet Guideline 1, a past cause cannot be the bottleneck. Because of the cumulative nature of evolution, many of the causes of a good or bad current situation are past and unchangeable.

If someone is unable to get along in society because they were utterly neglected by parents throughout childhood, what is the bottleneck to getting along? No one can change their childhood. The person needs to identify in adulthood what is preventing them from altering their ways, and figure out how to bust that bottleneck, or find an environment where their behavior is acceptable. In business, bad past decisions can't be changed either. Dell, and to a lesser extent, Microsoft missed the mobile revolution, but instead of trying to compete with Apple and Google in phones, which may have involved impossible bottlenecks to bust, they let go and went on to thrive in other areas. For instance, the massive success of Microsoft's Azure Cloud Services. On the other hand, while Walmart allowed Amazon to take a great lead in e-commerce, they seem to have enough scale, supply-chain scope, and resources to bust the bottlenecks to compete with Amazon.

Examples Where Guidelines Are Met

Three examples from earlier in the book illustrate bottlenecks that meet the three guidelines. The street intersection example in Chapter 5 illustrated the difference between external constraints, the bottleneck constraint, and the strategy rule (the self-imposed constraint).

> **Aspiration:** Facilitate safe and efficient flow of traffic through the intersection.
> **Bottleneck:** Cars must share pavement.

The bottleneck buster of a traffic light takes investment, maintenance, and has an aesthetic downside, but is certainly easy enough to install and therefore the bottleneck is not ridiculously difficult or easy to bust (Guideline 1). Sharing pavement is not a restatement of the aspiration (Guideline 2). And, because there are no other causes of accidents presented, shared pavement addresses the entire aspiration (Guideline 3).

In the example where you are the head of the city council trying to stem the exodus of small businesses (Chapter 1), your mission was to reduce regulation that was driving businesses away.

Aspiration: Reduce onerous and unnecessary regulation.
Bottleneck: Council members are unwilling to listen to your logic.

This bottleneck was not too easy to bust because other council members still deeply value the regulations, yet it was not viewed as impossible to bust either because you were able to articulate strategies for doing so (Guideline 1). For example, you considered a strategy of "horse trading" the deregulation you desire for other changes that the planners valued. The bottleneck was not a restatement of the aspiration such as "our town has 85 percent more regulation than other similar towns," (Guideline 2). And, in the absence of evidence to the contrary, the bottleneck was believed by you to apply to all the small businesses that mattered (Guideline 3).

Note that "reduce regulation" was explained in Chapter 1 to be an invalid strategy for stemming the exodus of businesses because it was not your free choice to do so. The opposite disqualifier would have caught this because the opposite of reduce regulation—increase regulation—would have been absurd to you. But "reduce regulation" also fails as strategy because the bottleneck of too much regulation is impossible to bust directly and therefore fails Guideline 1. A strategy designed to bust an unbustable bottleneck cannot be a valid strategy.

The third example of a bottleneck that meets the three guidelines is your Bike Shop. At the beginning of your venture, the aspiration-bottleneck combination reflected your fear of launching a shop without the support of the national chains.

Aspiration: Launch a bike shop without the national chains.
Bottleneck: Overwhelmed by the number of decisions for launching a shop.

This bottleneck appeared quite difficult, but you believed the My Thing strategy might bust it (Framework 5.1), so Guideline 1 was satisfied.

Guideline 2 was satisfied because expressing how overwhelming the task seemed is nothing like the aspiration. And Guideline 3 was satisfied because launching the shop was your only mission.

After 18 months you busted this bottleneck and became a capable businessperson, but the shop was not profitable enough. You determined a new bottleneck in Framework 5.2:

Aspiration: Launch a bike shop without the national chains.
Bottleneck: People do not understand the value of biking and of the shop.

This bottleneck also satisfied all three guidelines: while not easy, you had evidence that you could bust it with the evangelize strategy (Guideline 1); customers "not understanding" is not a restatement of the aspiration (Guideline 2); and again, your bike shop remains your only mission (Guideline 3).

CHAPTER 15

Designing Fitness Criteria and Making Assessments

As introduced in Chapter 10, fitness criteria are for judging alternative frameworks and their strategies. Making an assessment is asking the question, "what do we project the performance against our fitness criteria if we implement an alternative?" By assessing, you not only distinguish between alternatives but, much more important, exert stressors on the alternatives so they evolve to become better. Like other elements of the SAM, you will not get fitness criteria and assessments correct right away. Use the principles and techniques presented here to draft and later refine the criteria as you evolve the SAM.

Before discussing principles for fitness criteria and assessments, consider reasons for avoiding the use of aggregate financial numbers.

Avoid Aggregate Financial Numbers

The idea when using aggregates like return on investment (ROI), internal rate of return (IRR), economic value add (EVA, also called economic profit), and net present value (NPV) is that the many predicted future inflows and outflows of money—revenues, costs, CAPEX, change in working capital, taxes, and so on—can be put on the same basis and aggregated into a single number that predicts total return on resources employed. The framework alternative with the highest expected projected return is considered the winner. Aggregates differ in part because some incorporate the time value of money (i.e., discounted cash flow) and some include a reference point (e.g., the cost of capital in EVA), but the arguments against using them apply to all, so NPV is used here to represent any of them.

Figure 15.1 shows how NPV would be used to distinguish between alternatives in a SAM. In Figure 15.1A, NPV is used as a single fitness criterion, as an output from a spread sheet; in Figure 15.1B, the fitness criteria are the typical components of the NPV calculation (the assessment cells could be graphs of the time series used in the calculation). The detailed version in Figure 15.1B makes the calculation more visible. Figure 15.2 shows the elements of NPV in influence diagram form. In all cases, the assessments will be over some period at some frequency; quarterly over five years, for instance.

Here's the problem. It is not that NPV is a false representation of money-related performance; who wouldn't want to know the future cash flows of a strategy alternative? It's that calculating NPVs is not useful in practice. You can't know the future cash flows. Creating years of projections for all the elements easily becomes a making-up-numbers exercise because there is so much uncertainty. The spreadsheet creator may be the only one who understand the calculations (and maybe not even the creator if the spreadsheet gets convoluted). The team and the organization may lose the transparency of the assumptions and modeling, leading to *black box* models that hinder internalization. The input and output are visible in black box models, but how the model transforms the input into the output remains unknown.

Further, forcing assessments to be numbers to calculate an NPV results in oversimplification, and loss of information and subtlety. Concepts like reputation, customer opinion, and especially flexibility, complexity, or distraction are difficult to put into standard spreadsheet calculations and therefore tend to be considered "soft" and less important. When strategizing, numbers are also soft because they are describing the future. Uber-love of numbers can even lead to damaging conservatism; for instance, ignoring the cost of complexity and undervaluing flexibility because they are difficult to put into numbers with credibility. Several of the references cited in Part II stress in different ways that frameworks cannot be designed or evaluated solely with numbers.[1]

Avoiding NPVs for fitness criteria doesn't mean spreadsheets and calculations are unimportant. Calculations are needed for specific assessments such as costs, sales funnel revenue projections, capital expenditures (CAPEX) estimates, borrowing and tax strategies, impact on customer's quality and process, or constructions like the risk cube.[2] Pull the conclusion (including ranges of results) of these models into the SAM. It may

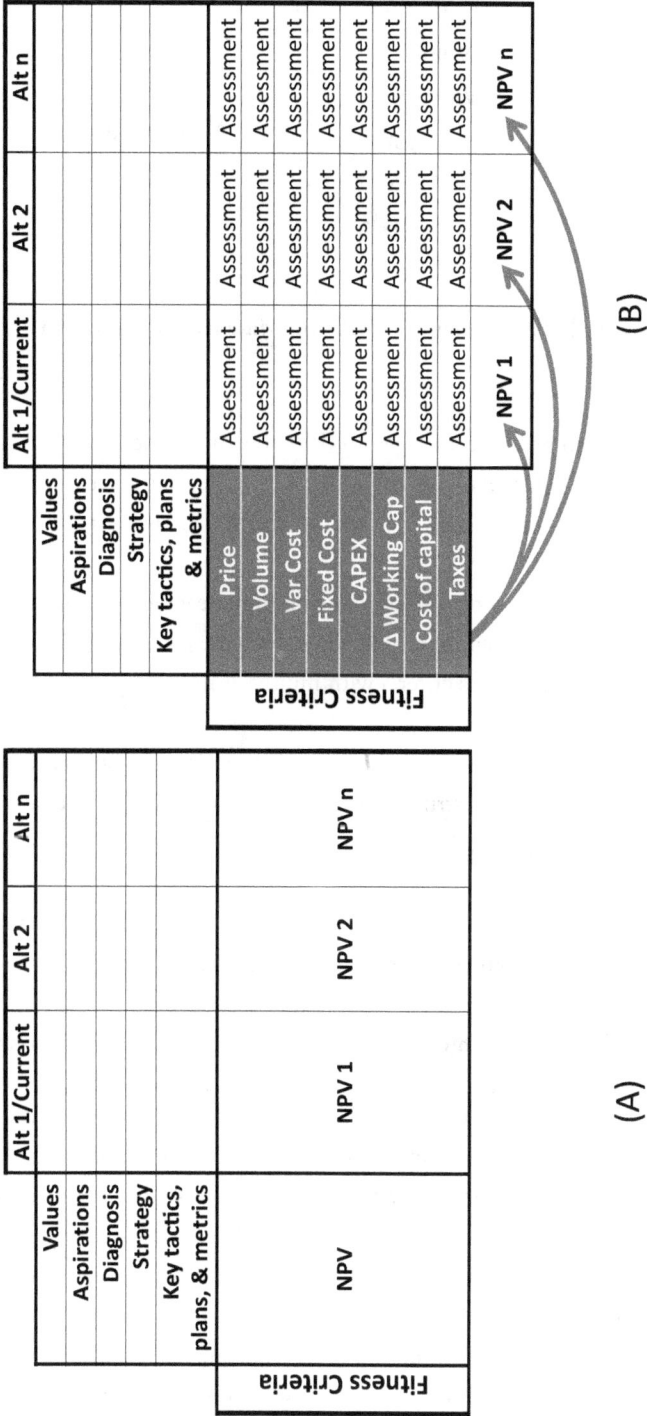

Figure 15.1 *Using NPV as the overall assessment*

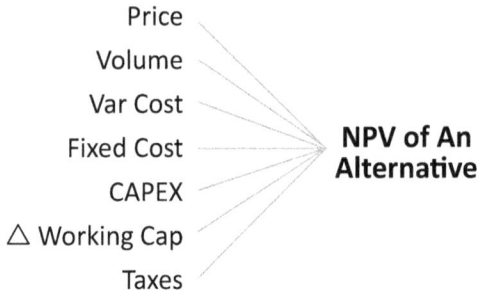

Figure 15.2 The elements of NPV in influence diagram form

be helpful to generate a range of NPVs to explore the impact of various assumptions when evolving the SAM as a whole, but don't let this be the focus of evolving the SAM. Oversimplification is always required to get to all numbers.

For a functional organization, using multiyear projections of the elements of NPV is even more ridiculous. Imagine projecting the outcomes of the following fitness criteria with multiyear number projections:

IT: usability, training requirements, integration of systems, adaptability to business structure or product line changes, dependence on single suppliers

Supply chain: robustness to weather disruption, visibility and simplicity for customers, complexity for business, lost sales, redundancy

Product development: customer utility, competitive response, cannibalization, confusion to customers, manufacturability

Aggregate financial numbers can be useful for benchmarking historical performance, particularly EVA,[3] in which case they are metrics, not assessments. It may be meaningful to show that Company A has, over the last 10 years, returned 12 percent more on invested capital than Company B, or that Company C has performed in the bottom 10th EVA industry percentile, assuming the comparison companies are chosen properly. Be careful, however, not to twist this around and say that the *reason* that a company underperformed was that they did not aspire to high-enough numbers, or, that they used NPV not the more stringent EVA. How many chronically underperforming companies in the bottom 10th EVA percentile aimed at the bottom 10th percentile? How many chose not to do better? Imagine arguing that a sports team failed to have a winning record over 10 years because they did not intend to win more games. Sure, great stars may have ambitious goals, but we hear less about marginal players who have them too. Goals are overrated.

Choosing Fitness Criteria

Courier Inc.'s fitness criteria from their SAM (Figure 10.9), shown in influence diagram form in Figure 15.3, is an example of getting beyond the simple elements of NPV and other aggregates for judging framework alternatives. Each criterion can be mapped to an element of NPV, but there's more richness of what they believe will drive the economics, that is, what will drive the NPV of the venture to enter the Old City to New City market. Their criteria are better connected to their proposition and external constraints.

Courier asked, "What are the key influences on the elements of NPV?" and "What is the key to good pricing and volume and low costs and investment?" Other financial criteria that may be relevant to Courier's venture include estimates of cost of drone development per year, cost of a new marketing campaign (and the danger of diluting the message in other markets if they use a different approach), cost of a fleet in waiting, and the like.

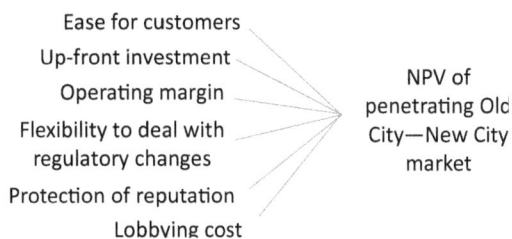

Ease for customers
Up-front investment
Operating margin
Flexibility to deal with regulatory changes
Protection of reputation
Lobbying cost

NPV of penetrating Old City—New City market

Figure 15.3 Courier's fitness criteria from Figure 10.7

Customers
- In tune with customer's expectations, needs
- Make customers successful
- Market attractiveness, newness
- Channel access
- Adjacency potential

Competition
- Crowded
- Moat, pricing power
- Not-in-kind impact
- Disruptive technology

Diversity
- Viewpoints
- Optionality
- Flexibility

Other Stakeholders
- Will the organization like it
- How sellable
- Will the boss accept it
- Responsive to parent framework
- Responsive to mission and purpose
- Value to society

Aggressiveness
- Difficulty, can the organization adhere
- Is too much or too little demanded of the organization
- Will it provoke competitors
- Extent visionary
- Time to benefit
- Recklessness, timidity

Complexity
- Number of organizations and functions involved
- Organization structure change required
- Number or newness of markets, technologies
- Number of, dissimilarity of products and services
- Hard to explain

Opportunity Cost
- Resource pull and distraction from other initiatives
- Impact on other parts of the company
- Builds foundational capability

Figure 15.4 Thought starters for fitness criteria beyond traditional financials (customers can be external or internal)

Financial numbers like costs, CAPEX, prices, margins, and cash flow are of course important, but don't fear using fitness criteria that have a dominant qualitative dimension when it is best. Figure 15.4 lists thought starters for fitness criteria beyond traditional financials to show the range of considerations. See there that you start thinking about the organization early, not waiting till you have chosen an alternative. Criteria such as sustainability, feasibility, and attractiveness are absent from the list because these are at too high a level to assess directly. Note that opportunity cost is explored also by including the "current" alternative in the SAM.

Robustness to scenarios is also not included as a fitness criterion in Figure 15.4. The range of your assessments is the determination of robustness to scenarios. However, you do have the option of assessing your fitness criteria against one scenario and then using "robust to other scenarios" as an additional criterion (see Task 3c).

Additional Considerations for Fitness Criteria

Use these guidelines when drafting your initial fitness criteria in Task 2g and when modifying them while evolving the SAM in Task Set 4.

Think of the criteria from both internal and external perspectives.
Put yourself in the shoes of your customers, suppliers, competitors, parent
organization, and your reports, especially those on the "front lines." What
will these criteria mean for them?

Don't let the difficulty of assessing a criterion deter you. Include
any fitness criterion if its assessment materially influences the probability
of achieving your aspirations, and if its assessment differs materially from
one alternative to another. This discipline will help you to evolve to new
places. Never accept statements like "but we can't get data on that," or
"but that's difficult to model," or "we don't have a financial measure of
that," or "we don't understand it," or any of similar ilk. If you let these
difficulties sway you, you will look is where the light is, and you will
find detailed answers for just part of your problem. Instead of an approximately correct assessment of the full dimension of the problem, your
answer will be exactly wrong. And the more you work on the well-lit
criteria, the more exactly wrong your result will be. Ironically, those who
resist including hard-to-quantify items like complexity or distraction as
fitness criteria are unwittingly proposing a precise assessment of the omitted item: they are assessing that the impact of complexity or distraction is
zero—exactly the number 0!

**Omit an influence if its assessment will be nearly identical for all
framework alternatives**; for instance, a cost that clearly will not change
(in geek, the derivative of a constant is zero). Such omissions eliminate
noise and ink. Because the framework alternatives will evolve, however,
you may not know which fitness criteria will be identical for all alternatives until you have evolved the SAM. So, be cautious about eliminating
any criteria early.

Try to work with 4 to 8 criteria. The problems with using an aggregate
concept as a single fitness criterion is clear but moving too far back and
having too many criteria is also a problem. You will drown in noise and
digital ink. While it is always best to question how many criteria you
need, generally 4 to 8 fitness criteria will be a manageable number. The
number can be modified with the use of subcriteria. In general, people
may be more attuned to the problems with under-aggregating than to
those with overaggregating.

Choose criteria that are (mostly) independent. Follow the MECE principle: Fitness criteria should be Mutually Exclusive and Collectively Exhaustive. Independent fitness criteria (i.e., reasonably orthogonal) make the SAM simpler.

Principles for Making Assessments Against Fitness Criteria

Assessments of alternatives against fitness criteria are stressors that drive creative tension by revealing gaps and contradictions in the SAM. New ideas will emerge by narrowing uncertainties using low-level logic, analysis techniques, debate and argument, research, and experiments. These stressors will enable you to judge the alternatives, and more critically, reveal where more knowledge is needed to create better ones.

As a reminder from Chapter 10, there are no restrictions on what can go in an assessment cell (Figure 10.3); cells can be numbers, words; they can be the representation of models, studies, detailed analysis, or graphics; use links to place only the result in the SAM. The focus should be on internalization and understanding through visibility and simple models versus single forecasts, point predictions, or obscure calculations.

The following principles will enable you to get the most out of assessment techniques.

Avoid Weighting

Avoid weighting for reducing the assessments of fitness criteria to a single number. The well-known idea is to assign numbers to each fitness criteria according to importance—a weight. Then, turn every assessment into a number and sum the products to calculate an overall weighted-average assessment. If Courier used weighting, it might look like Figure 15.5.

Courier's SAM looks nice and neat with the numbers; but instead of reducing the subjectivity and adding rigor to assessments, the weighting adds a hidden layer of subjectivity, further clouding the approximations and subjective assessments that are already there. Weighting reduces

		Courier Inc. SAM for entering Old City to New City market			
Values & Aspiration		V: Will not risk reputation of safest transporter of love potions A: Penetrate the New City to Old City market			
Diagnosis		**Proposition**: Leading capability and reputation; competition slipping **External constraints**: Drones not yet approved for love potions. **Scenarios**: Fab for Fleet, Train Transport good, Bad Investment Environment **Bottlenecks**: Unclear regulatory situation; could train transport be regulated out even if drones approved? Unclear consumer trust of drone transport.			
Strategy		Invest in train transport only	Train with "reserve fleet" as hedge	Train with heavy drone invest & forgo safety of fleet	Invest in fleet only (Simplicity)
Key tactics, plans, & metrics		Questions to resolve: Subcontract? Guarantees? Hybrid or electric (if fleet)? Buy/lease (if fleet)? Training standards? Pricing?			
Ease for customers	20	4	7	4	8
Up-front investment	10	9	7	5	3
Operating margin	20	6	4	7	7
Flexibility to deal with regulatory changes	20	3	7	7	2
Protection of reputation and customer trust	25	7	7	5	9
Lobbying expenses	5	2	2	5	10
Overall Assessment		**5.4**	**6.2**	**5.6**	**6.9**

Figure 15.5 Courier's SAM using weighted averages

anxiety, but all you will accomplish is to reduce the potential for the team to internalize, learn, and communicate.

It's fine to rank fitness criteria importance with numbers. And there are nonnumerical techniques you can use too, for instance,

- Group into "higher" and "lower" importance or some other words (you don't want "low importance"),
- List in order of importance, or
- Differentiate with colors or shades of grey.

Resort to aggregate numbers and weighting only after you are sure that you cannot distinguish alternatives by learning and simple summing the collection of assessments. You might use aggregates and weighting as a check or audit as part of your process, including a pro forma earnings or cash flow analysis, but this is icing, not cake. If you start with aggregations, disaggregating is hard. Resist the impulse to aggregate!

As a rule, avoid overall assessments until you need them, even without weighting. If this seems counter intuitive, remember that the aim is internalization, not "the calculated answer." You want to internalize in detail how fitness criteria respond to alternatives.

Assess Cells Only to the Extent Needed

In principle, all cells should be assessed because every fitness criterion matters. If Grandpa does not assess the environmental impact of driving versus the train because it is hard to do, but Grandma strongly cares about the impact their travel has on the environment, then Grandpa's strategy process has failed. He must take a stab at the assessment. Remember, a blank assessment cell is the same as assigning exactly the number 0 to it. You may not know if something matters until you try to assess it.

But this doesn't mean every cell needs to be assessed to the same degree or that all uncertainties need to be narrowed. It's irrelevant to the Grands if the weather and traffic are bad 10 or 80 percent of the time because 10 percent is bad enough to influence their decision. If up-front investments for Courier Inc.'s drones always dwarfs lobbying expense, narrowing the uncertainty of lobbying expense may not matter. They might even eliminate it from the fitness criteria.

At early stages, focus on narrowing uncertainties that are keeping you from distinguishing between alternatives. You will probably not need big spreadsheets or complicated models to do this. Scan at early stages, including making rough assessments of how external scenarios will impact the alternatives against the fitness criteria. Have the team describe in words how they would make assessments, including where the key uncertainties are and how they might narrow them. You won't fully know what matters until you evolve the SAM as a whole anyway.

Use Relative Versus Absolute Assessments

Assess alternatives relative to each other across columns, not as absolutes within a column. Because there is such a wide range of possible outcomes, there is usually little value in attempting to determine the absolute outcome of implementing a framework and its strategy, or the absolute outcome of a specific decision or investment. It is more valuable to assess whether alternatives are better or worse than others. Relative assessments also remove factors that do not change from alternative to alternative, increasing the signal-to-noise ratio and allowing what is important to stick out.

Say the Grands always have a $200 lunch when they travel to New City because they like to eat fancy. Should they include this money in the assessments? Not unless they will spend a different amount depending on travel mode. Otherwise, the spending doesn't influence the decision. It only adds noise and dilutes the information that matters. The back-road cost ($50) is in fact 17 percent of the train cost ($290), but if you add the meal cost to both routes (the absolute cost of the trip), the backroad only shows to be 51 percent (250/490) of the train ride. The only case in which the Grands should care about the absolute cost of the trip is if they have a spending limit, say $400. Then the absolute numbers would tell them that they need to either eat something less fancy and take the train, or drive.

But most important, in real situations, it is essentially impossible to know the absolute value of an alternative. Point predicting that a given framework approach with a given strategy for say, launching a new product line, will have an NPV of X million dollars is simply impossible. The outcomes can be all over the map including exceeding all expectations or losing all the investment (or losing even more if good money is thrown after bad to salvage a disaster). Instead, compare alternatives and eliminate all the common elements—including any cash flows you use in your assessments—to highlight what is different. If you must use NPVs for some reason, and a cost is the same in all alternatives, do not include this cost in the calculation; in other words, use a differential NPV.

Further, absolute assessments are impossible for qualitative information. How would the Grands determine an absolute value for comfort or the pleasantness of the view? Likewise, how would Courier Inc. make an absolute assessment of the value of their "flexibility" and "ease for customers" fitness criteria?

A fair question is, however, if assessments are made relative to each other, how do you know the most-fit alternative is *fit enough*? How can Courier Inc. know that the alternative assessed to make the most money and do best for their customers will make *enough* money and do well *enough* for customers? There is no foolproof way to know. You can guard against "not good enough" by including a full range of alternatives, including a status quo case. You can attempt to make an absolute evaluation on the best alternative as an additional exercise, but there will be enormous uncertainty in the answer. Imposing a "failure is not an option" rule is not a way to guard against not good enough (Execution, Chapter 9); this is just wishful thinking. Your best defense against not good enough is always to internalize the endeavor deeply.

Do Not Use Accounting Numbers With Allocations for Calculations

Pulling numbers from the accounting system for assessments in the SAM is easy, but often unhelpful. The whole idea with these systems is to "account" for all inflows and outflows of money, so you can pay your taxes properly and satisfy your fiduciary requirements to communicate performance. Accounting for all flows is also true for activity-based or standard costing.

Because cost accounting needs to attach all the money to something, when you contemplate a change, for instance removing a product or platform from your offering, the accounting system may tell you that all the fixed costs attached to the product or platform will go away. But often the costs will not. For instance, eliminating a product will not eliminate the cost of the C-Suite, insurance, buildings, factories, the IT, HR functions, or the R&D time used to create it, even though these, and other costs, may be allocated to that product. And misleading allocations isn't the whole problem. Accounting systems say nothing about cross relationships. If you are a paint producer, and red paint costs triple that of other colors, you can't just remove red from your lineup to improve profitability (sometimes this is called cutting off the tail of the profitability curve). B&Q or Lowe's would hardly be interested in carrying your paint line without red. Therefore, red paint can't be less profitable than other colors; in fact, profit per unit of red paint (sales price minus its cost) has no meaning because removing red paint cannot be isolated as a decision from the rest of the system. Instead, the profitability analysis needs to be made at the next level of analysis where the costs and revenue of one complete paint line are compared to another. You can, of course, compare the costs of two different formulations of red paint.

Eli Goldratt identified the failure of using accounting allocations for analysis in his 1984 *The Goal*. He taught that unless you were improving throughput to sales at the bottleneck (his constraint), you weren't doing anything except massaging numbers in a misleading way. Yet 35 years later, the authors of the 2019 book, *Throughput Economics*, still see the need to show how using allocations distorts decision making and interpretation and promotes silo behavior.[4]

Work across the SAM to eliminate the noise of allocated costs and be sure that you know which costs get added or eliminated with decisions by getting to the raw data. The same goes for working capital and CAPEX.

Integrate Risk and Upside Directly Into Assessments

Risk is not just uncertainty; it is the downside potential in anything you care about when taking a decision or an action (including no action). Downside potential is defined as the probability of an outcome times its believed negative impact. Risk, therefore, is the assessment of the downside potential in your fitness criteria—what you care about—if you implement a given framework alternative. The risk of Courier Inc. provoking an aggressive competitive response is the probability of it occurring times the impact of it occurring, an impact on pricing power, for instance.

The opposite of risk is upside potential, or just *upside*, which is the probability of an outcome times its positive impact. For Courier, the upside of investing in drones could be the expected market value of drones times the probability of government approval. Impacts and probabilities are always uncertain and so risk and upside always exist and are always uncertain.

The measure of risk and upside is the range of your assessments. Manipulating risk and upside from a framework design point of view is the act of narrowing assessments through understanding and insight. The key is that risk and upside cannot be separated from each other nor separated from the entire system. When asked about risk, Jeff Yass, founder of the Susquehanna international investing group, said, "Risk schmisk, the biggest risk is that you have a losing strategy when you think you have a winning one."[5] The point is that risk and upside are properties, that is, attributes, of any system, just as is the expected average performance of a system. For this reason, "managing under risk" is identical to "managing," just as "planning under uncertainty" is identical to "planning."

In the absence of new knowledge or capability, any decision to reduce risk means a likely reduction in upside—a trade-off. If you don't want to accept the downside potential of a 35 percent drop in stock prices in any given year, then buy a portfolio of high-quality bonds and treasuries, which means likely giving up any possibility of anything like 35 percent growth in a year. When people say, "We need to take more risk," they are expressing that there is not enough upside. Why else would anyone want to accept more downside potential?

To reduce risk while maintaining or gaining upside potential, the capability of the system needs to improve. If the project team developing Courier Inc.'s drones for love potion transport tells management, "You can either have drones fast, good, or cheap," they are explaining that there are trade-offs among these three properties of the system. A drone can be had in one year if money is no object, or if the quality of the drone is not such a big deal, and so on. Yet, if leadership improves the capability of the project team, with either better or more people, better research and training, new techniques, or regular beatings, they can raise the overall capability of the system and the trade-offs among speed, quality, and cost can be at a higher overall level. The whole risk-reward profile of the system elevates such that the risk is lower and the upside is higher (time, except in the case of just trying harder, is therefore intimately linked with risk and upside). Likewise, when Blue Ocean theory says, make the "competition irrelevant" at "lower cost," they are not decoupling cost from market success, they are saying a blue ocean approach has a better revenue-cost profile.[6]

Capturing Risk and Upside in the SAM

Figure 15.6 shows options for incorporating the assessment of risk and upside in the SAM. The first (A) is a more traditional approach. Here, the "base case" (40 percent margin on love potions for fleet, 50 percent for trains) is assessed as a point prediction, and then a risk level is assessed (high for fleet, low for trains). The risk and upside could be numerical too.

Fitness Criteria		Fleet	Trains
	1		
	Margin on love potions	40%	50%
	Uncertainty	High risk	Low risk, good upside
	...		
	n		

(A)

Fitness Criteria		Fleet	Trains
	1		
	Margin on love potions	22 – 43%	46-62%
	3		
	...		
	n		

(B)

Fitness Criteria		Fleet	Trains
	1		
	Margin on love potions		
	3		
	...		
	n		

(C)

Fitness Criteria		Fleet	Trains
	1		
	Margin on love potions	~40% most likely, but a big downside	~50% most likely, but a big upside
	3		
	...		
	n		

(D)

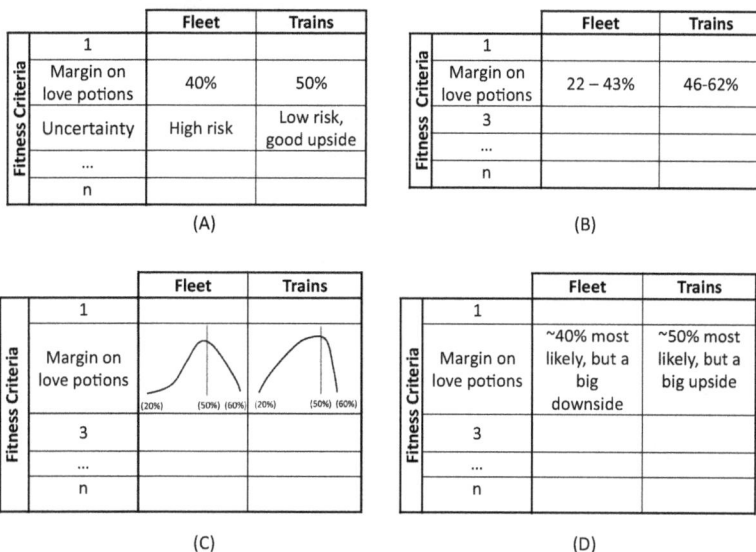

Figure 15.6 *Options for capturing downside (risk) and upside potential in the SAM*

In (B), the uncertainty is captured as a simple range, but you would never use precise numbers like this unless they are spit out of a model. In (C), there is an actual probability distribution. A sophisticated model might create a distribution, or you might "eyeball" a distribution to represent skewness or some other characteristic shape. In (D), there are simply words, which is best unless you have ways of generating meaningful numbers. Figure 15.6A is aligned with the concept of *risk-adjusted return* (more correctly, risk- and upside-adjusted returns) but is not recommended because it promotes assessing uncertainty as an afterthought or a separate thought process, and that you can point predict. Figures 15.6B, C, and D avoid these pitfalls. Naturally, in all cases, the more uncertain an assessment is, the wider will be the range of numbers or words that describe it.

If there is a level of risk that is unacceptable to your endeavor, then identify this in a fitness criterion, and do not accept an alternative that is assessed to lead to this downside (it's possible no alternative will meet the requirement). In other words, be explicit about your risk tolerance. Otherwise, do not give risk more weight than upside with the illusion that it is more rigorous to do so. Capture the future as honestly as possible.

CHAPTER 16

Design Principles for Strategy Alternatives

Even though a strategy does not entirely define a framework, since it is the most important component, articulating possible strategies is core to drafting framework alternatives. This chapter provides guidelines for constructing strategy alternatives for the SAM and discusses using exemplars—generic strategies and case studies—as inspiration. As you work, adhere to the principles for strategies that have been laid out so far, as summarized in Figure 16.1.

As usual, it is simplest to start with the **strategy←bottleneck←aspiration** triad and work backward, as shown in Figure 14.1. Placing alternatives directly in the SAM works well too, as shown in Figure 11.2, especially because you see the rest of the diagnosis (see the bike shop SAM design

---

The strategy must be a **free choice, supply real-time guidance**, and **unify** (chapter 5); if it does, it will pass the **five disqualifiers** (chapter 8)

The strategy must have a **trade-off to bust the bottleneck** (chapter 5)

Everyone in the organization must be able, or nearly able, to **adhere to the strategy** (chapters 2, 5)

The most elegant strategies state **what not to do** (chapter 5, 8)

The strategy should be **somewhat abstract** to give people freedom to innovate in their local areas (chapter 5)

Each framework alternative can have only one strategy; if more than one is needed, use **nested systems** (chapter 7), or use **tactics** to bust bottlenecks to smaller-scope aspirations (chapter 6).

Strategy is at the **mercy of all scenarios**, articulated or not (chapter 13)

Figure 16.1 Design principles for the strategy component of a framework

in Task Set 2). The triad may be easier when you are still exploring multiple bottlenecks.

Use Lafley and Martin's (*Playing to Win*) technique and ask, "What must be true for each strategy alternative to be a terrific choice?" (they call alternatives *possibilities*, and they call the process *reverse engineering*, which nicely captures its spirit). But keep in mind that while many factors can contribute to an alternative being a terrific choice, there's one thing that must be true: busting the bottleneck. A framework that includes 50 good things but doesn't bust the bottleneck is not a good alternative, so be sure the bottleneck is part of your answer. Lafley and Martin test for bottlenecks in a later step (they call them *barriers*), but in the emergent approach, focus on bottlenecks early because this is how you find strategy.

Lafley and Martin stress that listing what must be true is "not intended for arguing about what *is* true" because that only opens opportunities for skeptics to kill ideas. Instead, "skeptics can express everything they believe is needed to come true without giving up their doubts." Asking skeptics to also give their view of the bottleneck early will force them to express why they are skeptical, which is valuable because then you can debate the reality of the bottleneck and how to bust it.

When drafting, adhere to strategy design principles including the disqualifiers but use them lightly if strict adherence is getting in the way of ideation. As with the components discussed so far in Part II, you will only find your compelling alternative with a compelling strategy until evolving the SAM as a whole in Task Set 4.

Guidelines for Alternatives

The following guidelines will help you find a set of alternatives that enables exploration of a full range of possibilities. Or as stated in Chapter 10, a full range of *X*s to find your best *Y*.

Include your current-state framework, even if you know it to be ugly or inadequate, and even if you are confident that you will need a new one. Ask, "What will the future be if we keep doing the same thing?" The current framework serves as a reference state from which to compare new alternatives, encouraging relative assessments. Comparing with the current may also discourage hockey-stick projections because you need to explain what is so different in a new framework. You might even find your current framework, with a few tweaks, is not as bad as you thought. The grass is not always greener on the other side. However, because you must improve to stand still, continuing your current-state framework does not necessarily mean maintaining current performance. Of course, an entirely new endeavor will not have a current state, instead, you are comparing alternatives to "continue doing nothing."

Make alternatives qualitatively different. Be wary of alternatives that are different only by a degree of some parameter—for instance, a portfolio of five versus a portfolio of seven initiatives. Instead, focus on the rule that determines which initiatives to include. You might include a tactical constraint within this rule that puts pressure on how many are allowed, perhaps due to resource constraints. The numbers disqualifier would reveal that five or seven initiatives doesn't define a strategy, yet alternatives like "invest in new technology" versus "aggressively invest in new technology" both pass the numbers disqualifier but they are not qualitatively different. Instead, describe the essence of what makes an aggressive approach different from a modest one, perhaps the aggressive case includes more speculative technology. To stretch thinking, you may ask for extreme or outrageous ideas, and then look for ways to make them more realistic while retaining some of the benefit of the extreme.

Don't shy away from exploring alternative aspirations if your aspiration is not clear (Chapter 12). You can explore multiple strategies for two or more different aspirations (and therefore bottlenecks). Doing so may stretch the team's thinking around what's possible.

Don't fixate on a specific number of alternatives. While it's difficult to work on more than three or four simultaneously, don't target a specific number of alternatives (see discussion about choosing the number of scenarios in Task 3b). If you need six to capture the full range of possibilities, then start with six. You might be able to simplify with subcolumns. For instance, Courier Inc. could create an invest-in-drones alternative with subcolumns for with and without hedging with a fleet.

Finding Inspiration From Exemplars

The business literature, including the writings cited in Part II, is filled with case histories of success and failure. The literature also provides considerable specific business advice for customer, market, and regional targets, positioning, aspirations, and many other aspects of product and service offerings.

You can use these as exemplars to inspire strategy alternatives. Once again, the spirit of the emergent approach is to find your own strategies and frameworks by internalizing the external and internal worlds in which you will implement, but exemplars might spark a new idea for an alternative or help you articulate more clearly one that is still murky in team members' minds. It is recommended to explore exemplars only after you have drafted strategy alternatives on your own.

Generic Strategies

Generic strategies are strategy exemplars with no specific content, which makes them potentially applicable to any endeavor. They can become actual strategies when you add your content. While not the first to describe generic strategies, Porter's *differentiate*, *focus*, and *cost leadership* are well-known.[1] Porter taught that hybrids of these, getting caught in the middle, was a mistake, so don't try to be all things to all people (recall the discussion in Chapter 8, Example 8.3, and Chapter 12 that the sentiment of "cost leadership" needs to be recast to be an actual strategy). Here's a sampling of other generic strategy ideas.

> **Blow it up versus improve what you have.** Blow it up and start again—a *clean sheet* approach—applies when you have hit a dead end. This could apply, for example, to a technology development, an organization, or a product line.
>
> **Keep options open versus commit to one approach** to achieving your aspirations. There are many variants of this generic:

- Portfolios (create or invest in multiple possibilities and then eliminate the less successful, as opposed to a big bet on one)
- Hedge, buy options, lease versus buy
- Real options

- Invest stepwise, keep asking "what is the price to see another card?" (using a poker analogy)
- Leave headroom. When building a factory that can be modularized, for instance, spend for excess utilities and extra space to enable easy accommodation of modules for expansion later

Isolate new development groups versus integrating into existing units. The story of Xerox PARC is now famous, where a host of modern computing technologies were first developed including the mouse, the laptop, laser printer, and Ethernet protocol.[2] PARC was isolated from the core business and there are those who believed the isolation contributed to creativity.

Many versus few. This generic includes ideas such as having many manufacturing or distribution centers that are close to markets, specialized, or redundant as opposed to large, centralized facilities for efficiency (for instance, BASF's integrated Ludwigshafen site). The article *Competing on Platforms* recommends selling through multiple channels as opposed to concentrating on one to avoid dependency on Amazon and other dominant online platforms.[3] The trade-off is that multiple sites adds cost and complexity.

Smaller bites versus all at once. If your aspiration is a vision or mission of "going big" (Chapter 12, aspirations), there is still the option of building toward *big* in smaller bites. For instance, a 2021 Boston Consulting article proposes that traditional banks should consider breaking down modernizing for the digital world into "smaller, more manageable initiatives."[4] Dave Ramsey, the popular personal finance advisor promotes paying off small-amount loans first regardless of interest rate as opposed to paying off highest interest-rate loans first.[5] Rumelt demands "proximate goals" in Good Strategy/Bad Strategy.

Cook a frog versus shock and awe. Put a frog in hot water and it says, "Oh, $%!#," and jumps out, as the old story goes. Put the frog in tepid water and slowly turn up the heat and it's cooked. Frog cooking may help avoid the organization immune response, including not scaring the boss, or used to avoid a bad customer, supplier, or Wall Street response.

Eliminate instead of adding: A Blue Ocean article argues that streamlining your offering will often do more good than adding to it.[6]

Textbooks and other sources[7] may refer to standard business techniques as generic strategies, for example, forward integration, backward integration, horizontal integration, acquisition, joint ventures, retrenchment, divestiture, and liquidation. These may also inspire ideas.

Generics Must Pass the Five Disqualifiers

Like any strategy, for a generic strategy to be valid, it must pass the five disqualifiers. Generic strategies generally have no *numbers* and are not *lists*, so they pass these two disqualifiers. Each of the generics described above has a viable *opposite* stated explicitly and therefore a trade-off. For examples: The redundancy of "many" and "keeping options open" while reducing the likelihood of failure comes at a resource cost. Taking "small bites" while raising the likelihood of success of each milestone, in principle, adds time and possibly cost. The opposite of Ramsey's "pay off small loans first" is the obvious "pay off high-interest loans first," but his view is that small early successes build confidence and momentum that enable people to get out of debt.

"Blue Ocean strategy," that restricts new developments to markets where there is no competition, can be a generic strategy alternative if there are meaningful red ocean possibilities. However, if you have decided that you will explore Blue Ocean possibilities only, then the opposite of Blue Ocean is absurd, and you should treat it as your mission. If the parent framework specifies Blue Ocean only, then a Blue Ocean strategy would fail the *duplicate* disqualifier for your framework, and it should be an external constraint. If you want Blue Ocean for new developments, but you already have several successful established units in competitive markets that you don't plan on exiting, Blue Ocean then fails the *excluded* disqualifier, and you would need to limit Blue Ocean strategy to new ventures and initiatives in a nested system.

Could *disruption* be a generic strategy? Yes, if defined as targeting less-demanding market segments ignored by incumbents with lower-price but good-enough offerings, and then aim to gradually take share in higher-value segments as you improve. Absolutely not if you define disruption as upending established companies or industries. The first has a meaningful opposite (wait till you have higher-performance and -priced products), the second does not. Beat the competition or upend an industry are just broad and useless aspirations with no information content.

The Danger of Exemplars

Using exemplars may create the illusion that you have insight. Putting aside that studies of success may be biased because it is easier to get the histories of great companies than the countless more that failed or that had only middling performance, your strategy needs to grow organically out of your work. You cannot scan a list of generic strategies and pick one. This is like starting with the answer or lazily filling out forms.

It's hard to tell who the mainstays of business books copied, companies like Google, Dell, Amazon, Intel, Facebook, Netflix, Tesla, Southwest, Walmart, Microsoft, and Apple. Did they follow exemplars? How many were just struggling to implement their ideas until finding their eventual success? General Electric was perhaps the most common exemplar 20 years ago but it's not clear that the great companies that came after copied GE. For that matter, did it make sense for GE to copy itself over the last 20 years? They have struggled mightily during this time, even nearing bankruptcy. By the time you would have the clarity to create a "generic model" for great companies, their greatness is already done.

Discover your own reality and future using design principles. Use exemplars to stimulate thinking while recognizing the limitations and possible dangers of doing so.

Designing for Adaptability to Multiple Futures

Several generic strategies explicitly address multiple futures by building in flexibility and resiliency, that is, adaptability; not only the *keep options open* category, but *many versus few* and *start small versus go big*. Schoemaker argues, "Almost any investment can be made more flexible than first imagined."[8] He also encourages thinking in terms of "reversibility."

However, there's no requirement that your strategy considers every possible scenario. You can choose a strategy alternative that ignores all but one scenario (there's always some assumption of the future environment—stated or not). Either you believe the ignored futures are low-enough probability to ignore safely, or you are willing to accept the consequence of being wrong. Both could be perfectly reasonable choices. The commit/go for broke generic strategy ignores some futures, but it's assumed that the payoff for success is worth it. If a company believes there is a considerable asymmetry where the upside of a venture is much greater than the risks of, say, aggressive competitive response that brings everyone down, or that value-chain partners may not want to participate, then it may be perfectly rational to ignore these scenarios. Grandpa ignored the scenario of trains not running in Chapter 13 because he judged it to be low-enough probability or impact. But always remember that futures don't go away just because they are ignored.

Top poker pro Antonio Esfandiari said his days of folding pocket kings (two kings as down cards) in Texas hold 'em are "long gone."[9] He no longer considers protecting against the scenario of an opponent developing aces or better. He says, "You got it? You got it." His rule, *never fold pocket kings* (well-stated as what not to do), is to accept the trade-off that sometimes he will be beat, in exchange for never being bluffed out by a weaker hand. By the way, poker shows the benefit of separating what you can influence and scenarios that you cannot. No player can influence an opponent's hand. A player can assess an opponent's hand, but with uncertainty. And they can, with their own betting actions, influence opponents' bets, including folding.

Contingency Alternatives

Developing contingency alternatives comes with the (modest) trade-off of spending up-front time. Contingencies can be thought of as *on-the-shelf alternatives.* The trigger to switch to a contingency alternative is when scenarios or internal developments turn out to be different enough—positively or negatively—from diagnosis and assessments such that a change in framework is needed. The trick is having the discipline to monitor how the world is unfolding.

Contingencies are in some ways a substitute for flexible framework alternatives. If Courier Inc. is unwilling to invest in a "fleet in waiting" to hedge against the scenario of new regulation banning train transport of love potions, they can instead invest in a contingency framework of how to quickly create a fleet if that regulatory scenario were to play out.

With contingency alternatives you can be ready to pounce because you don't wait to start thinking about what to do after the problem or opportunity is upon you. When things start to go bad—or good—may be the worst time to consider alternatives. Predesigned options keep you from having to create new direction in the heat of battle. Or, as Scenarioist Jay Ogilvy says, "Scenario planning gives executives a way to rehearse different futures in the relative calm of a meeting room rather than in a war room set up for emergencies."[10] The impulse may be to overcorrect in tough times because of embarrassment or fear of criticism or needing to prove toughness and that there's no such thing as failure. In great times, euphoria may lead to greed and overextension. Contingency alternatives need not include every little thing. A rough sketch provides grounding in more objective and less emotional thinking later when the impulse is to freak out.

CHAPTER 17

Evolving the SAM as a Whole

Evolving the SAM is the heart of the emergent approach. Here you abandon completely any reliance on sequence. Instead, let the creative tension caused by the discipline of the method tell you where to go. Revisit Chapter 2: creativity *emerges* from internalization. Internalization comes from the disciplined application of low-level stressors to an evolving entity to see how it responds, enabling the elimination of what is unfit. At this point, the evolving entity is the SAM.

The chances of having drafted a fit-enough SAM with a compelling-enough alternative in Task Sets 2 and 3 is effectively zero. There will be unfit gaps and contradictions in many forms: missing assessments, framework and fitness criteria design principles violated, assessment ranges so wide they don't help distinguish alternatives, strategies that don't bust bottlenecks or have no trade-offs, bottlenecks that do not relate to aspirations, lack of variety in alternatives, and models and projections whose results make no sense.

Destroy these unfit gaps and contradictions by thinking, hard argument and debate, modeling, analysis techniques, the five disqualifiers, research, experiments and pilots, and learning from customers and other ecosystem participants. Take the lump of clay that is your draft (or existing SAM that needs improvement) and work it and shape it. The matrix evolves to greater fitness as you repeatedly add variations and then exert stressors. As you learn and internalize, new variations of ideas will occur to the team. Be open to these results, even if they are counterintuitive. Keep going until a compelling framework with a compelling strategy emerges. Don't pick a winner; let the winner come to you. The winner will be the *last standing*. This is how you solve a puzzle with no picture on the box.

You won't ask high-level stressors such as, "Will this alternative work?" or "do customers' think the product is a good idea." Instead, use low-level questions like, "Will everyone be able to adhere, or nearly adhere, to the strategy and tactical rules?" or "Do our fitness criteria give equal representation to good and bad?" or "are customers putting resources towards testing the product?"

How long does it take to work the SAM? Might be two days, might be two weeks, might be ten months. It depends on the scope of your aspiration, its difficulty, and the team's skill. You may decide quickly that further analysis will not bring value, and that implementing some or all of a framework alternative is the only way to make progress. As discussed in Chapter 11 and shown in Figure 11.6, you can move to implementation and be triggered to stop and modify the framework at any time. And you will never have a perfect picture with all the pieces of the puzzle or all the information or data; there is no such thing.

Getting Away From Just "Talking to Yourself"

It can be a challenge to obtain feedback and input from those that are outside your team, including customers or suppliers or even peers in other departments or your own people on the "front lines" if they could not be included in the design teams. You may have to suspend disbelief when discussing ideas, and team members may have to suspend disbelief as they debate them. There are techniques in the literature for putting yourself in other people's shoes and imagining how they would see the environment.[1]

When getting feedback, the key is not to be easily swayed by high-level opinions, such as "that alternative won't work" or "great idea." You can't keep people from giving such opinions, but you can ask them why they hold them. Discuss the low-level details. Go back to asking what must be true to make the alternative a good one and ask what the bottleneck is. If the bottleneck is a technical capability, ask why the capability can't be developed or bought; if it is resources, ask why resources can't be augmented; if a market doesn't exist, ask why it can't be created—dig deep. Avoid the high-level opinions of habitually optimistic people as well as habitual skeptics. Assess alternatives with equal levels of excitement and skepticism.

Apply the same approach to people outside the company. It's well established that asking customers their high-level opinion about what your next product or service should be is of lesser value than asking them what job they are trying to do and why they do it.[2] Ask them low-level details of how they use your products. What are their pains and challenges when trying to get the job done, and what desired outcome(s) are they aiming for? Henry Ford and Steve Jobs made it clear that they would not ask their customers what the next product should be. As Ford said, "They would tell me they want a better horse." Yet they wonderfully understood their customers. Stakeholders may struggle to articulate why they feel the way they do; so it may take time and effort to draw their answers out. You must evolve to this understanding, just as you evolve your overall understanding of the endeavor.

Techniques for Evolving the SAM as a Whole

Most of the emergent approach's low-level tools and techniques have been presented in the previous chapters: design principles for the framework components, bottleneck discovery guidelines, the principles for designing fitness criteria and making assessments, and the five disqualifiers. Following are tips for evolving the SAM where you consider all its elements simultaneously.

Making assessments is core to revealing gaps and contradictions because assessments are where your alternatives, fitness criteria, and scenarios come together. Minimize focus on overall assessments, i.e., the high-level answer, because it can encourage picking a winner. Instead, do everything you can with individual assessments and let the overall answer emerge. (One case where you will use overall assessments early is to capture the impact of scenarios as described in Task 3c.) Also, as discussed in Chapter 15, avoid using weighting and financial aggregates to bring assessments down to all numbers.

Aim for Horizontal Divergence and Vertical Consistency

Figure 17.1 provides a guideline that applies to the entire SAM. By diverging horizontally, you explore a wider range of possible alternatives,

		Framework Alternatives		
		Alt 1/Current	Alt 2	Alt n
	Values			
	Aspirations			
	Vision			
	Mission			
	Goals			
	Diagnosis			
	Proposition			
	External constraints			
	Scenarios			
	Bottlenecks			
	Strategy			
	Key tactics, plans & metrics			
Fitness Criteria	1	Assessment		Assessment
	2	Assessment		Assessment
	3	Assessment		Assessment
	...	Assessment		Assessment
	n	Assessment	Assessment	Assessment
		Overall 1	Overall 2	Overall n

Make the verticals consistent

Make the horizontals different

Figure 17.1 Evolving the SAM as a whole

that is, a wider solution space (the Xs in Chapter 10). This raises the probability of finding good alternatives and avoids undue focus on any single one. By consistency in each column, you ensure coherent alternatives and valid assessments of each. When you vary an aspect of an alternative—a plan, a strategy, a diagnosis, and especially an aspiration—the discipline of vertical consistency will create tension for adjusting the other components as required.

If you are having difficulty creating divergent alternatives, the facilitator can allow some drift by temporarily loosening adherence to design principles and the disqualifiers. But trying to come up with divergent ideas by "thinking outside the box" is not usually a fruitful process—new ideas emerge.

Future Histories and Premortems

Future history is the process of imagining the future that would result from implementing a framework alternative under different scenarios. History implies a story or narrative rather than the more technical assessments described in Chapter 15. This technique may help loosen up the team. You can ask outsiders to the team to make stories too. Telling stories is a good way to keep people from making overall conclusions. It's not a story to forecast how drones will lead to $100 million added earnings for Courier, a high-level prediction. A story will describe how drones will help people, how customers will manage with them, how the technology will be developed and trialed, what public opinion will be, and why regulators would accept them to transport love potions, and what they will cost.

Complimentary to future history is the concept of the *premortem,* championed by psychologists Gary Klein and Daniel Kahneman,[3] where you identify what could go wrong. Related is the idea of playing devil's advocate. Like asking what is in the way of success versus what needs to make an alternative good, premortems may enable finding bottlenecks.

Don't Hesitate to Elevate or Relax Constraints

Because you will make trade-offs between them, fitness criteria are not constraints. But you may realize that you care so deeply about a fitness criterion that you elevate it to a not-to-be violated mission, tactic, core value, or even a strategy rule. You may also demote any presumed constraints to fitness criteria if they are more malleable.

Courier Inc. may at first have a tactical rule of hiring only certain types of couriers, then later relax this constraint, demote it, and instead capture the quality of their couriers as a fitness criterion. The quality of couriers would then be a trade-off with other criteria they care about, like cost. At first, the Grands placed the cost of their trip as a fitness criterion and were willing to trade-off cost against time, comfort, and environmental impact. In another case, they removed cost from the fitness criteria and elevated it to an external constraint by setting a dollar cap on their spending.

If you discover that the constraint provided by a strategy rule is simply not appropriate for the entire organization and therefore fails the *excluded disqualifier,* relax it to a tactic that applies to only part of the system or create a two-part nested system.

Simulate Alternatives with Draft Plans, Projections, and Policies

Exerting stressors by simulating and reality testing your alternatives can bring them to life. Gifford Pinchot III advises in *Intrapreneuring* to start simulations early but warns not to "believe any of them." Your work here is not to predict the future but to sample it and explore it. None of the plans, tactics, and roadmaps need to be completed in detail when evolving the SAM. Complete them in Task Set 5 after choosing an alternative. All you need here is enough detail to gain insight.

Plans—future actions and milestones—need little discussion because they are so common. Filling out plans allows you to more fully answer the question, "what has to be true for the alternative to be a good one." Plans always have names, dates, and completion details attached to them. Because each milestone requires resources, time, and interdependencies, articulating detailed plans creates excellent stressors on alternatives. If an alternative lacks sufficient resources and time, it is a contradiction that needs to be fixed. Software is widely available for visualizing timelines, linkages, and dependencies. When evaluating timelines, be sure to consider organizations outside your unit or function. For instance, a product manager may need to consider,

- Is R&D "scheduling an invention" that the product requires?
- Are manufacturing and supply chain including the time to learn how to make the product and time to scale?
- What are supplier's development timelines? Are they overly optimistic?
- What determines customer timelines?
- Is time for obtaining funding and CAPEX approval considered?

When dealing with other organizations—customers and partners in particular—be sure that the person you are working with, your contact, represents the view and commitment of their larger organization. Your contact may be overly optimistic or trying to make a sale to you or their own organization. The project may be "their baby" and are making a bet that everything will fall into place. If you can't find out, just be sure to go in with eyes wide open and retain some optionality.

Road maps are a type of simulation used to coordinate the actions of participants in an endeavor. For example, a producer of CPUs, SSD drives, or OLED displays will publish a road map of specific models they plan to launch or discontinue in the next several years. This allows customers, suppliers, and other players in the ecosystem to plan their own product lines. Drafting a road map may reveal timing inconsistencies in your alternatives. **Staircase models** are a type of simulation used to layout predicted progress in an organization that are sometimes confused with strategies.[4]

Forecasting is modeling that is a massive discipline unto itself. The point to consider here, however, is that, as discussed regarding multiple futures in Chapter 10, be sure your forecasts are not just supporting your beliefs. If you use optimistic forecasts to sell your program to the outside, be sure to use neutral forecasts for yourself. Forecasting, like plans, is an important part of coordination between functions as well. For instance, forecasting demand.

Budgets and financial modeling. Like other functions in a business, it is a process failure if finance people are engaged to evaluate an alternative only after you have chosen one. If they have not struggled through design with you, they will not know how to judge the alternatives using their financial models. And if they do correctly identify a problem, a budget constraint you were unaware of, for instance, then you have wasted precious time.

If you feel they are needed, now would be the time to challenge alternatives using aggregate financial numbers like NPV. You can vary the range of your assessments to see the response to the NPV. Use Monte Carlo methods for a more sophisticated approach. But keep in mind the loss of information needed to turn everything into a number (Chapter 15).

Staffing and organization structure. Focus on changes needed for implementation. The conventional wisdom "set strategy then design the organization" is an outdated holdover from the paradigm of separate one-time design and then implementation. Strategy and organization structure should evolve together; both are part of the framework.

Flowdown of nested frameworks and individual objectives. Companies may have individuals setting their objectives based on a flowdown of some sort, including use of Balanced Scorecard or OKRs (objectives and key results). Having the extended design team, or a smaller team, draft what their objectives would look like is an interesting simulation of alternatives. Be sure to remember that because of the granularization problem (Chapter 4), without a framework and its strategy, it is impossible for the various nested organizations to properly create objectives because they will not see the needed trade-offs. "Strategy themes" cannot supply this guidance.

Tactical rules are for busting bottlenecks to smaller aspirations (Chapter 6). While you can wait to complete all tactics, articulating them while evolving the SAM may also bring insight. The last section of Chapter 8 showed two examples: Electro Ltd.'s marketing policy table is a set of tactical rules that could give insight into the feasibility of a framework alternative because it shows how marketing wants to engage with customers. Likewise, Add-Co's product segmentation policy table shows how they wish to use their development and production resources.

Audit/Test of Framework Alternatives

To help think about what's "good enough," a collection of audit questions that can enable debate is shown in Figure 17.2. One of the most important questions asks whether you have talked to the right people. Take Sherlock Holmes's advice: "Nothing clears up a case so much as stating it to another person." For additional questions and questions more specific to business units specifically, see the *Tests of Strategy from the Literature* discussed in Chapter 8 and found online {web/supplement}. Recall that most literature tests are not tests of the strategy component but are best used as fitness criteria (Chapter 15) or tests of frameworks. Several of the literature tests are included (somewhat reworded) in Figure 17.2. As discussed in Chapter 8, the best tests from the literature are lower-level questions on the left-hand side of the influence diagram, as shown in Figure 8.15. Another way to visualize audit questions is to map them onto the SAM, as in Figure 17.3.

The greater the rigor you demand by stressing your thinking using these audit questions to resolve gaps and contradictions, the greater potential for seeing new ideas. To zero in on the issues you have been fighting, make your own table or figure including low-level questions specific to your endeavor (Figures 17.2 and 17.3 are available for download {web/supplement}; you can customize them as well).

Framework Components	Are we convinced of our **strategy←bottleneck←aspiration** triad?
	Do strategy alternatives pass the five disqualifiers? (And therefore, have trade-offs)
	Do the strategy and tactics explain what not do to?
	Will everyone be able to adhere, or nearly adhere, to the strategy & tactical rules?
	Do we have the proper nested frameworks? Are we sure we understand the parent framework and other external constraints?
	Are we following the specific strategy and business advice from experts that we agreed to follow?
Fitness Criteria & Assessments	Have we made relative versus absolute assessments? Have we fought the urge to bring everything down to a number by aggregating and weighting?
	Have we fought the urge to point predict the future? Have we avoided bell-curve-like assessments and mid-cases?
	Have alternatives been assessed against every relevant scenario in some way?
	Do our assessments give equal representation to "good for us" and "bad for us"?
	Are we clear about the pedigree of the data? (No data is better than bad data.)
	Can we tell a story about each alternative? Can we write it as a narrative?
SAM Overall as a Whole	Do we have horizontal divergence and vertical consistency?
	Is their *pain in the plan*? What is the pain? Is there uncertainty? (If yes ... good.)
	Do we use more advanced tools when assessments or other elements require it?
	Will the management team be able and willing to lead the new framework with conviction?
	Is the compelling framework simple? (And not because of taking shortcuts.)
Procedural	Have we argued our views, even if frightening to do so? And even though it creates conflict?
	Do we need a pilot or an experiment?
	Are we convinced that people with the right capability and insight have beat up the SAM, including customers (the parts you can reveal to them)? How are we convinced we are not just talking to ourselves? Who has played "devil's advocate?"

Figure 17.2 Examples of audit questions (stressors) for the SAM

An excellent practice suggested in Figure 17.2 is to write out the arguments for the chosen framework design as a narrative, including discussion of the alternatives rejected. Presenting PowerPoint or talking through the SAM may not demand the same completeness or flow of logic. The document can be in the spirit of a white paper. Avoid giving a historical account or a travelogue of how you got there unless relevant to the decisions.

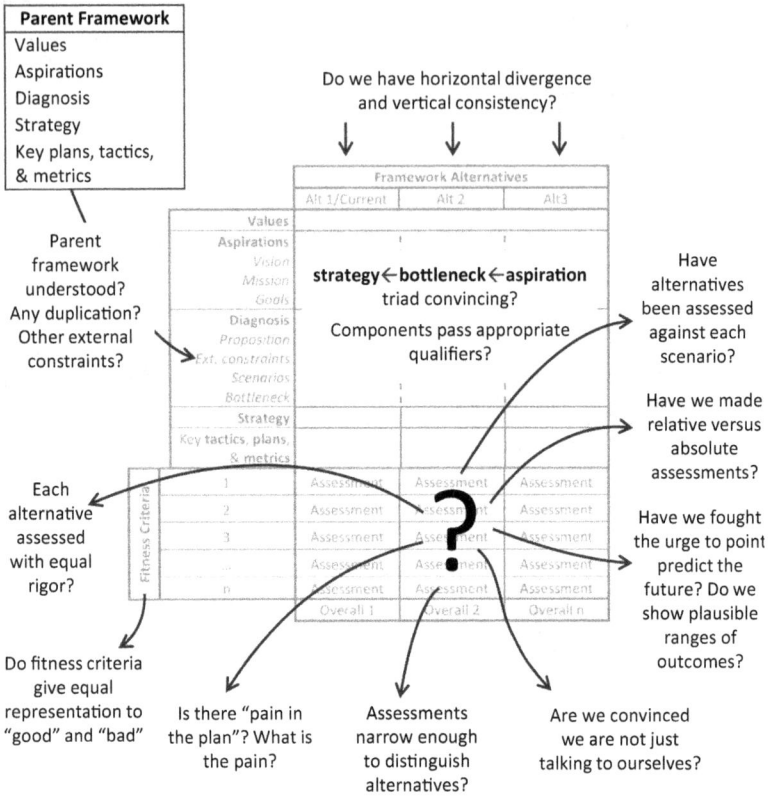

Figure 17.3 Example audit questions (stressors) mapped onto the SAM

Bring in Additional Techniques

You can make good progress at creating variations and then stressors to destroy the unfit ones using the domain knowledge you already have coupled with the techniques and principles presented so far. Your endeavor, however, may require more varied and sophisticated analysis and discovery techniques to create the variations and stressors you need. And you may need expert advice about your business or function.

Figure 17.4 is a selection of additional techniques roughly categorized from the simplest and least time-consuming to the more complicated that require significant skills, time, and resource commitment (see *Additional Techniques from the Literature* for some references and commentary {web/supplement}). Some techniques are widely applicable, some apply to

Type		Examples
Ways of working and collaborating		Sit on butt and think, reading/watching, interviews (stakeholders, subject matter experts), debate, whiteboarding, brainstorming {Web/Task Sets}, "sticky note" exercises, secret voting, Cynefin facilitation modules, agile techniques, bias busters
Analysis and Modeling	Structured analysis and development	Five disqualifiers, Strategy←Bottleneck←Aspiration triad, influence diagrams, value proposition and business model canvases, "what must be true," basic financial modeling, future histories and pre-mortems, Theory of Constraints
	Visualization & diagnostics	Surveys, flow mapping (a key element of Lean Six Sigma), heat-maps, cause and effect methods (e.g., Five Whys), diagnostic question sets and maturity models (Oliver Wight, SCOR, i2i, 8-shifts), benchmarking, jobs-to-be-done
	Exemplars	Generic and situational strategies, case studies, business models, specific strategy advice (e.g., Blue Ocean, Christensen and Raynor disruption, Porter's uniqueness, make big moves, customer and market choices)
	Ecosystem analysis techniques	Scenario techniques, Porter's Five Forces, BCG Growth Share Matrix (and descendants like industry attractiveness), PESTEL, capability analysis, lifecycle analysis, market pyramid
	Heavier research	Critical literature and patents reviews, crowdsourcing, reverse engineering, piloting and experiments
	Advanced modeling	Real options, game theory, Monte Carlo, advanced forecasting, AI

Increasing Resources and Difficulty

Figure 17.4 Sampling of additional techniques from the literature

specific functions, and some are specific to markets and business design. It is impossible to categorize these techniques perfectly and there's overlap between them. Within each category there is a range of difficulty as well. The emergent approach techniques are included to help illustrate the categories.

Spending more time and money doesn't necessarily lead to better truth, but it may raise the probability. It is better to use simple tools and techniques that everyone understands than complicated ones that few understand. And as discussed earlier, use models early if you can, but don't believe the early results—learn from them.

The Emotional Side: Bias and the Courage to Destroy

Bias is one of the dimensions of creating frameworks and their strategies that consultants and academics address with various techniques, sometimes called "bias busters." Consider also that a powerful way to reduce bias is to work at low levels where less prediction is required. The connection to the overall assessments is not immediately apparent when working at low levels, so opinions about the overall are somewhat taken out of the discussion. A trial jury that audits the detailed evidence of a case against the statutes has less potential for bias than one debating the high-level question "is the defendant guilty or innocent?" Courier Inc. has less potential for bias if they focus on details like the customer experience, competitive response, and whether they have a valid framework, as compared to debating if entering the Old City to New City market is a good idea or not.

Consider another emotional challenge—having the courage to destroy. You have to "kill your darlings." Innovation requires giving up on ideas and constructs that were once seductive, but it can be emotionally draining to destroy or give up design work you have completed, bringing a sense of loss, waste, even embarrassment. Leaders who condone destruction may fear looking idiotic and weak. It's easy to destroy small stuff like a bad assessment, or a fitness criterion you conclude is not right, or a strategy alternative that you have spent some time on but no longer makes sense. But what if you start to see problems with the whole diagnosis or the aspiration on which everything is based and destroying these means throwing out weeks or months of work and starting over again? The more you have completed something, the harder it is to throw it away. And if you are on a timeline—for good or bad reasons—going back and starting again is brutal. But destruction of the unfit is the only way to evolve to a strong framework.

It can be even harder to abandon propositions and assets that made you successful in the past. It's hard to know when a proposition is past its prime and is now just a sacred cow.[5] The ability to abandon a new venture after significant time and resource expenditure can be just as difficult, even if the evidence is against continuing. The barriers may be real, for instance, you may be unfairly blamed for failure. But often, the barriers are the emotional sense of loss and the emotions of eternally unrealistic hopefulness. And on the other side of the coin, sometimes courage is needed to keep what you have. You may be discounting what you have just as you may be overestimating it.

Good Enough to Move On to Implementation

A framework alternative is compelling enough—fit enough—when it has the clarity and depth to propel the organization forward with the guidance for making decisions and taking actions. You see this when the alternative is resistant to all the stressors you throw at it and when you feel good about how it responds to audit questions like Figures 17.2 and 17.3. A good result may be that the do-nothing alternative was the most compelling, and you move onto something else. A frustrating result is when no alternative is compelling enough but you must still start to implement. You may be out of time, either because your boss says so, or because of some other deadline. The worst result is when you think you have a fit alternative, but you don't.

Sometimes, due to fatigue or a less critical eye, the team is unwilling to continue, and you may not have the power to urge them on. Not to mention, the team also might be right. Sometimes everyone is simply out of ideas. If any of these are the case, then try to run a pilot with the alternative you have versus a full launch.

What is *not* needed is every assessment or analysis completed. Banish any thought of perfect or "optimized" frameworks with optimized strategies. It's not that you sometimes must make a decision without all the data or all the puzzle pieces, you *always* have to make a decision without all the data and pieces. Not only could you never collect all potentially relevant data, but once again, *there ain't no data from the future*. And the future is all that matters. All you can hope for is a picture of the puzzle that is clear enough to give conviction. Approximately correct; not exactly wrong.

There should always be a tension between "study more" versus "move on." Study forever and all potential is lost; study too little and risk never seeing the potential. But paralysis comes from bad analysis. Meaningful, hard hitting low-level analysis will tell you what to do. If the work is truly internalized, as are all the connections between parts of the SAM and components of the frameworks, and if you are working at low levels, then you will have powerful intuition about when it's time to move forward. And as always, you will come back if you find faults in later tasks, or if triggered to do so during implementation.

CHAPTER 18

The Four-Station Dashboard

Everyone has likely heard the maxims *what gets measured, gets improved, what you measure is what you motivate,* and others of similar ilk. Sure, there is truth in these statements. Metrics can create valuable stressors—creative tension—to ensure the organization executes during implementation, including adaptive course correction while there is still time to do something about it. Metrics stress by revealing the difference between what is and what is desired.

Yet how is it that most companies that go bankrupt likely measured their earnings, cash flow, and other numbers right on through the day they had to lock the doors? (Sure, some companies did not monitor metrics, yet most know their basic numbers well enough.) Countless metrics are maintained in sports with maniacal precision, yet somehow, some teams and individuals get no more competitive. People weigh themselves repeatedly yet remain overweight. Children are hyper-tested in school, but complaints persist about the quality of their education. The U.S. national debt is reported daily, yet it now climbs by several billion dollars a day.[1] And in a tragic example, metrics of U.S. military performance in Vietnam misled terribly—matériel destroyed, dogfight kill ratio, and the infamous body count—contributed not only to mission failure but to undue suffering and countless wasted lives on both sides of the conflict. Robert McNamara's heartbreaking book, *In Retrospect: The Tragedy and Lessons of Vietnam,* showed how massive sets of metrics fooled the U.S. government and how a lack of in-depth analysis and hard debate enabled them to be fooled.[2]

No, we cannot categorically say that what gets measured gets improved. What gets measured *may get discussed* or, more likely, *may get manipulated.* Best would be to say, *metrics are invaluable for seeing and understanding and we can only execute when we see and understand*—a slogan unfortunately too long to fit on a poster with a wolf or an eagle.

Three design pitfalls get in the way of useful metrics:

- Too many metrics. Instead, minimize the number of metrics. There is no such thing as getting all the data.
- Metrics overly focused on financial results, not causes. Instead, be more specific about leading indicators that measure adherence to and the diagnosis of your framework, that is, measure execution.
- Metrics focused on the subgoals from strategy themes or cascading goals down the organization (Chapter 4). Instead, put more focus on progress against the bottleneck.

The four-station dashboard helps you to avoid these pitfalls and get the most out of your metrics.

The Four Stations

The four stations are *foundation*, *adherence*, *progress*, and *bottom line* (Figure 18.1). Foundation metrics audit whether the framework is still valid. Adherence metrics audit whether everyone (including leaders) is adhering to the framework when implementing, that is, whether they are executing. Progress and bottom-line metrics are measurements of results. The term *audit* is used broadly to mean a systematic examination including less-quantitative measures.

Figure 18.2 shows examples of each station for Courier Inc. entering the Old City to New City transport market. This dashboard would be for the early days of the venture, where Courier is not yet concerned about

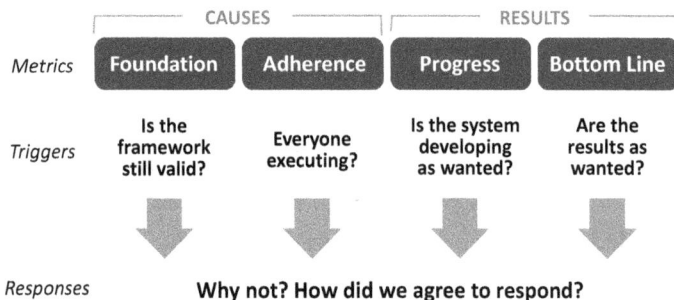

Figure 18.1 The four-station dashboard

Foundation	Adherence	Progress	Bottom Line
Public Opinion (Love Potion approval Index)	**Emergency fleet** (Plan updated quarterly?) 1st √ 2nd X 3rd √ 4th ☐	**New hire turnover** (% after 6 months)	**Growth** (transports/month)
100% 80% (6-month moving average) 2024	**12-week training** (% New-hires receiving) 100% 2024	100% 2024 **Transport quality** (incidents per month) (3-month moving average)	2024 Month →
Competitive Pricing Change? No ☐ Yes √ Describe: *Possible 5% increase on short-travel distance love potions deliveries.*	**Retention Issues?:** No ☐ Yes √ Describe: *Poor grasp of customer interaction policy.*	15 2024 Month →	**Transport quality** (Customer failures per mo.) (3-month moving average)
Drone Approval Scenario? Indicators changing? *The anti-drone public interest group was heard by the federal panel; impact yet unknown.*	**Marketing Strategy** Informal adherence audit by department heads. Result: *Acceptable; showing improvement*	**Drone Milestones** On-track for 1Q26 beta demonstration? No ☐ Yes √ Describe: *stability trial #3 successful.* **Customer feedback** (Net promoter score) *Begin next quarter when sufficient data; ask for feedback on couriers.*	3 2024 Month → **Marginal Earnings** ($/per transport) $80 $40 2024

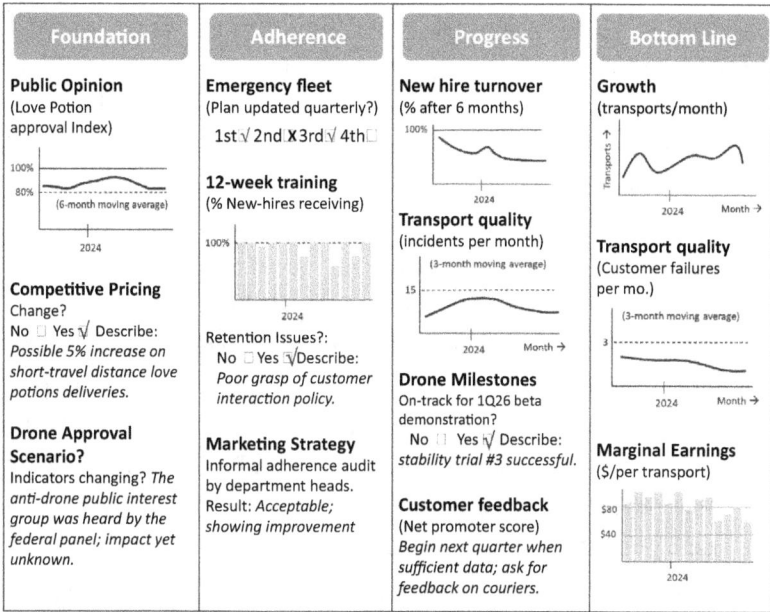

Figure 18.2 Example dashboard elements of Courier Inc. Old City to New City venture for the 3rd quarter, 2025

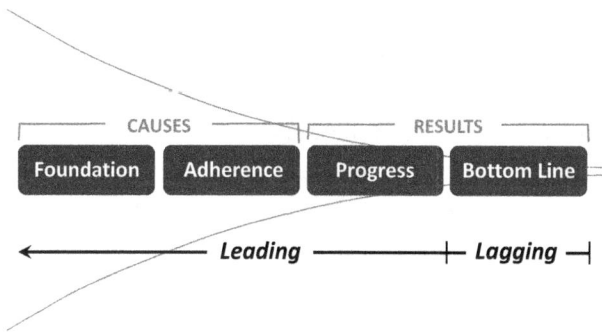

Figure 18.3 The four stations mapped onto influence diagram

overall profit. Instead, their focus is growth and marginal earnings, and also their ability to recruit and train personnel, which they have diagnosed the bottleneck to be at this point. After Courier becomes established in the new market, the bottom-line metrics may become more profit-focused. As a reminder from Chapter 1, for a measurement to be a metric, there must be a reference point.

They are called *stations* because each can be mapped onto a location on the influence diagram as in Figure 18.3. The right-hand side (RHS) is lagging, that is, the measurement of results. The further to the left-hand side (LHS) of the diagram the metric is, the more real-time feedback it supplies—that is, the more of a *leading indicator* it is. The goal is to capture fallacies and failures as early as possible and avoid the mediocrity that comes from managing by results. Here are more details:

Foundation metrics give feedback on whether your framework's diagnosis and assessments are still valid, including forecasts. Measurement of the foundation enables you to execute by indicating when the framework is no longer fit and requires modification. Schoemaker shows examples of foundation metrics described as a "checklist of assumptions."[3] Consultants from Boston Consulting point out, "Although companies put a great deal of energy into making predictions year after year, it's surprising how rarely they check to see if the predictions they made in the prior year actually panned out."[4] Keep your diagnosis in front of the organization during implementation including selected items from your scenarios such as: competitor actions, regulatory, geopolitical, economic environment, customer and public opinion, global technology trends, and even changes occurring elsewhere in the organization. A value of foundational metrics is many have an outside view, these metrics are a hedge against just talking to yourself.

It's tricky to turn the question "is my framework still valid" into a measurement you can put on a dashboard. Focus on low-level details, and never use high-level questions like "Is our strategy still good?" used the low-level questions from Figure 17.2 instead.

Adherence metrics audit the adherence to the framework aspect of execution. It is hard to judge a framework and its strategy if people are not adhering to it. It is a waste of precious time and money to find out the organization has failed to execute only after poor results become apparent. These metrics should measure adherence to strategy and tactical rules including policy tables such as Electro Ltd.'s marketing policy Figure 8.17 and Add-Co's product segmentation policy Figure 8.19.

Adherence is not easy to measure. You can consider *surveys* and *checklists*, such as the Oliver Wight series of planning methods and checklists.[5] You can use surveys for self-audit, though self-audit is difficult, better are third-party audits. Self-auditing is difficult because it's hard to be objective, and new frameworks require doing things differently, which is why good coaches are valuable. Another approach is simple observation, where auditors get out on the "front line," as suggested in the Electro Ltd. example. One challenge is that organizations tend to be on their best behavior when the boss arrives, so what they observe may be skewed.

Measuring adherence is not micromanagement. It is auditing whether the organization is staying within the agreed direction set by your framework. Greater freedom is easily enabled by relaxing the constraints of the framework.

Progress metrics are indicators of a good bottom line, because it is believed they will correlate with the bottom line. For Courier, new-hire turnover rate is believed to correlate with overall cost and capability of employees. Look for progress metrics in the categories:

- People (turnover, satisfaction surveys, training success)
- Milestones (sale funnels, product development and stage gate, projects in general)
- Financial (costs, prices, volume, taxes)
- Customer satisfaction (survey results, net promoter score, advertising performance)
- Production performance (asset utilization percent, asset turns, first quality rate, overtime)
- High-level financial measures (inventory days' supply, days sales outstanding, RONA, EBITDA, debt to equity ratio, margin)
- Ratios (results per person, or cost per sale),
- Benchmarks (any measure versus competition or some other target, including high level aggregate financial such as EVA (see Chapter 15)

These metrics give feedback on the direction of change earlier than bottom-line metrics and measure events of lesser severity.

Courier doesn't want transport incidences, but a close call that reveals problems with their training program is better than a customer failure. Progress metrics also give information on the success or failure of groups, functions, or policies influencing the bottom line, that is, feedback on the inner workings of an organization. If bottom-line customer service is degrading, a progress metric could tell you if it is product quality or delivery performance contributing to the problem. The value of progress metrics is well known. The challenge is to avoid piling on so many.

The **bottom-line** measures are what ultimately matters and aligns with the highest-level aspiration on the RHS. For a business overall, bottom line can include overall financials (e.g., earnings, free cash flow, perhaps stock price), growth, core values (e.g., safety, environmental, people treatment), customer acquisition, and benefit to society (e.g., enabling communities, improving lives). For a function, say manufacturing, it would include performance against the overall aspirations at that time (e.g., throughput at first quality, core value performance, capacity expansion completion).

Each metric station is insufficient on its own. Since everything and everyone in the company is supposed to be contributing to improvement in the bottom line, you learn nothing about causes by measuring it in isolation. On the other hand, measuring only foundational and adherence ignores whether the framework is creating good results. Think of the "how many meters in the sky" metaphor. Looking only at bottom-line results on the RHS of the influence diagram is like looking down from 10,000 meters, and progress metrics are like looking down from 1,000 meters. You can't see people or what they are doing from these heights. Looking at foundation and adherence gets down to under 10 meters, where people's actions and assumptions are visible, but at that height, you can't see results. We are back to the killer problems of change and Richard Rumult's Heisenberg analogy in Chapter 3. Results are everything, but they cannot be directly manipulated; actions and choices on the LHS can be seen and directly manipulated, but they don't mean anything without results. Breaking leading indicators into three categories—foundations, adherence, and progress—enables focus on each.

While foundation metrics are often suggested by strategists, measuring adherence to the framework is not because rules-based strategy and tactics are not common and because executing is conceived as getting results, not as adhering to the framework or fixing it if unfit. By isolating process metrics from the others, you can also be more cognizant of piling them on unnecessarily.

Metrics Design Principles

The following are general principles that apply to all four stations. (Task Set 5b includes further suggestions for metrics, and ideas for how to find them.)

Work Hard to Minimize the Number of Metrics

The opportunity to measure seems infinite. And the connectivity provided by the digital revolution may inspire measuring more: "Look how efficiently we can get data; we will learn so much." The KPI institute lists thousands of metrics possibilities, over 470 for the IT function alone.[6]

But how many numbers can people absorb and process? Twenty, thirty, or fifty at a time? When does a dashboard become a blur? After a relatively small number of metrics, the more you measure, the less you will see. The less you see, the more opportunity for cherry picking and seeing what you want to see. So, *measure less* and spend more time on choosing the right metrics and understanding what they are telling you.

Measure at the Bottleneck

The first page of *The Balanced Scorecard* asks the reader to "Imagine entering the cockpit of a modern jet airplane and seeing only a single instrument there,"[7] suggesting that business leaders shouldn't fly their "aircraft" with a single gauge either. Who would argue? But the pilot is not trying to improve anything: neither flying technique, nor the passenger experience, nor the plane itself. The pilot is using the gauges to keep the status quo, a successful flight from airport A to airport B.

Sure, it's hard to keep the status quo—improvement is needed just to stand still. But how many CEOs want metrics for maintaining the status quo? And while nearly all advice on metrics includes "measure what matters," if you want to measure improvement, you need to measure progress against the bottleneck. And this means a focus on only some of the gauges, or perhaps special-purpose gauges. Granularization of the foremost aspiration into strategy themes, as discussed in Chapter 4, leads to lists of subgoals and initiatives without determining the interactions between them or identifying the bottleneck needed to improve the entire system. Flowdowns from aspirations may also be called a *KPI tree*; trees that grow exponentially. In the absence of a strategy rule and tactics derived from the bottlenecks to progress to guide which matter, it is natural to measure progress against every subgoal and plan.

Question Process Metrics

You might ask, won't creating four stations exacerbate the dreaded piling on of metrics? No. Being specific allows you to target process metrics that can be dropped to achieve greater balance between stations, as in Figure 18.4. In their book *Six Simple Rules: How to Manage Complexity without Getting Complicated*, Morieux and Tollman show the fallacy of the proliferation of metrics and incentives, and cite the

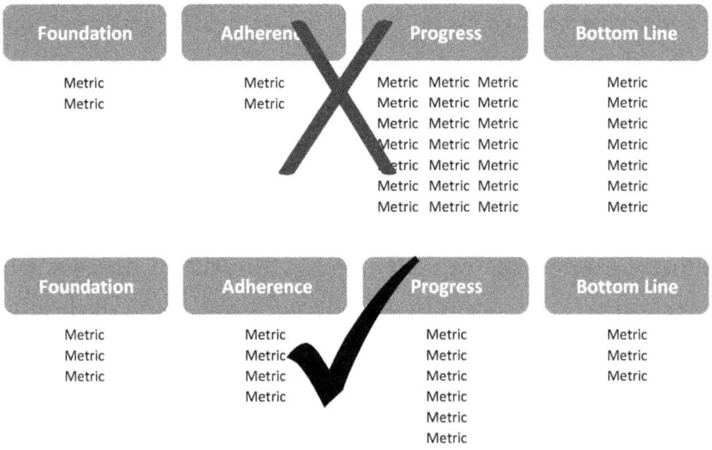

Figure 18.4 *Reduce number of metrics and find better balance over the four stations*

BCG Complexity Index: "In 1955, companies typically committed to between four and seven performance imperatives; today they commit to between twenty-five and forty. Between 15 percent and 50 percent of those performance requirements are contradictory. Around 1955, hardly any were."[8] These contradictory imperatives result from flow-downs and strategy themes without awareness of bottlenecks, and they are likely to be measured by progress metrics. Not only do such measurements mislead about profitability, but they encourage silo behavior in the organization.

In addition to measuring at the bottleneck, ways to reduce the number of progress metrics include:

- **Test for independence.** Use the same logic as applied to independence of fitness criteria (Chapter 16) to avoid having several metrics that measure roughly the same thing.
- **Beware of ratios.** Ratio of sales revenue and earnings to factory cost, fixed costs, working capital, earnings, and R&D spend might not give so much information.
- **Push back on the "usual suspects."** Every organization has its traditional measurements, be sure to question whether they are addressing the current situation and the current bottleneck.

One other option is to segregate your change metrics from maintenance metrics. While segregation doesn't reduce metrics, it illuminates progress against the bottleneck (see additional four-station examples {web:supplement}).

Getting "All" the Data

Information technology will be seen as the bottleneck to dashboard success if copious metrics are viewed as key to gaining insight, or in the worst case, if getting *all the data, and having it all automated* is viewed as the key. This may include discussion such as, "Can you imagine the benefit if leaders could know at a glance the price of products in, say, France, in real time?" Okay, what would the leader do with such information? If the price in France is important, then the price in every other country is important, as well as the price of every other product and every cost and every who knows what else. The amount of information from, say, a factory or a supply chain, might as well be infinite. As just discussed in Chapter 17, there's no such thing as making a decision with all the data.

Efficient data management is important, but IT challenges can't be faced until there is a proper framework and strategy. If what to measure is known, with conviction, then there will be a way to do it—approximately and somewhat manually at first, perhaps just taking samples, and only later refined and burned into the IT system. It requires effort over time to figure out what to measure, and what needs to be measured changes as the bottlenecks and the conditions change, and as you improve and adapt. For these reasons, there's no such thing as "future-proofing" IT systems with all the data.

Do Not Let Difficulty of Data Acquisition Be the Reason to Avoid a Metric

In another case of not letting IT be the barrier, as said about the data acquisition for making assessments in Chapter 16, if the difficulty of data acquisition sways you, it will drive you to look where the light is. Measure what you need to know, not what is readily available (though you may not need to measure as often as you think). Better a rough estimate at first, obtained in a clunky way, of a metric that matters (including qualitative ones) than an automated exact measurement of one that matters less or not at all.

Do Not Fear Using More Qualitative Metrics

Often qualitative information is needed to provide insight. In sports, it is easy to measure the scoring of runs, goals, and points. Century-long records of these are kept with fantastic precision. However, it's not so easy to capture how important the scoring was in a particular match without more qualitative information and judgment. Scoring a goal in a lopsided match in December is less important than scoring the equalizer with a minute to go in May that clinches Champion's League qualification, yet the two goals look the same in the record books. And while it is generally easy to determine the player who last touched the ball before it lands in the net, more qualitative information is needed to determine who truly created the scoring opportunity.

In more serious examples, how much harder is it to judge children's emotional- and learning-skills development than it is to judge their numerical test scores? (And what a travesty to wait until yearly "bottom line" standardized tests to determine if children were studying during the year, that is, "adhering" to what they need to do to learn.) In the Vietnam War, how much easier was it to measure body count (assuming it was correct) and *matériel* destroyed, than to measure the Viet Cong and North Vietnam's resolve, or whether the South Vietnamese people were being won over. Edwards Deming, a father of Six Sigma, said repeatedly that 97 percent of what matters cannot be put into numbers.[9]

Adherence and foundation metrics especially require interpretation, which belies their importance. Courier Inc. can easily measure the percent of new hires receiving the full 12-week training (Figure 18.2) but not so easily measure how much training is retained, yet retention is undoubtedly more important. Courier can easily capture if the Emergency Fleet plan has been updated, but not so easily judge the plan's quality. Completion of milestones can be difficult to judge, especially if they are loosely defined. In *Intrapreneuring in Action*, Pinchot and Perlman stress that checkpoints should not be just pass/fail; there must be a dialog about the outcome.[10]

Not all qualitative measures can be acquired through an IT system. Audits require people to actively seek out the situation, to go out to the front lines to discover whether people are following the framework, and whether the framework is still valid.

Consider the Style and IT Aspects of Dashboard Construction

Typical dialog with the IT function will include questions around dashboard implementation and maintenance cost; ease of data storage and retrieval for historical analysis (data warehouse); degree of automation;

and who will create, maintain, and own the dashboards for each nested system. Also consider,

The Need for Flexibility. If you put in a big costly metrics system, you will be loath to change it even if it does not meet your needs. It is better to start with fewer measurements at all four stations and at an approximate level, and then evolve and learn what you need and how to build in flexibility. Like protecting against scenario, flexibility may come at a cost, but it is worth it. Because bottlenecks change, there is no "future" proof system with all the data you could ever need as discussed earlier.

Incorporation of Less-Quantitative Metrics. IT functions have skills in the handling and visualization of enterprise data. Be sure there's also discussion about the less-quantitative information for the diverse types of dashboard metrics needed to convey foundational assumptions, adherence, and milestone completion. This data may not be on their radar in the same way as the more structured enterprise data.

Clarity Before Style. Highly stylized dashboards with wild colors, 3D graphics (usually these distort information), and skeuomorphs may be fun, but the novelty will quickly wear off if clarity is compromised. Airplane cockpit simulations, radar simulations, and speedometers may just add noise.

Approach to Data Accuracy. There are two fundamental approaches to data accuracy. One is to work from the point of view of the data—a *fix the data* program—where you task people to clean up the data and get it right. The other approach is based on the premise that data accuracy is driven by its proper use in management decisions. This approach is *fix the system*, and the data is part of the system. A fix the data approach has the overtones of "as soon as we get all the data, we will have insight." But because the amount of information from factories, supply chains, or markets is essentially infinite, you will have no idea which data is important. Only with awareness of its use can you fix the data and make it accurate. The fix the data approach is like designing products without thinking about customers or beginning laboratory research before asking, "what are we measuring, and why?"

Triggers and Reponses

Presumably, anyone who installs a metric intends to take action if the metric or a combination of metrics reaches some value during framework implementation. They will be *triggered* to respond as part of executing. Yet, while target values for metrics may be set, for instance, 95 percent success rate, usually unstated is how far from 95 percent the results must be before acting, and what the response will be. It may be tacitly assumed that lack of framework adherence or an unfit framework will be obvious from metrics, as will be what to do about it.

Consider instead spending some time articulating triggers and responses in the framework design phase. Like creating scenarios, these can sensitize leadership and enable quicker action. Triggers and responses are discussed in scenario literature more often than in the strategy literature.[11] Figure 18.5 shows an example of a few triggers and responses added to Courier's Figure 18.2 dashboard.

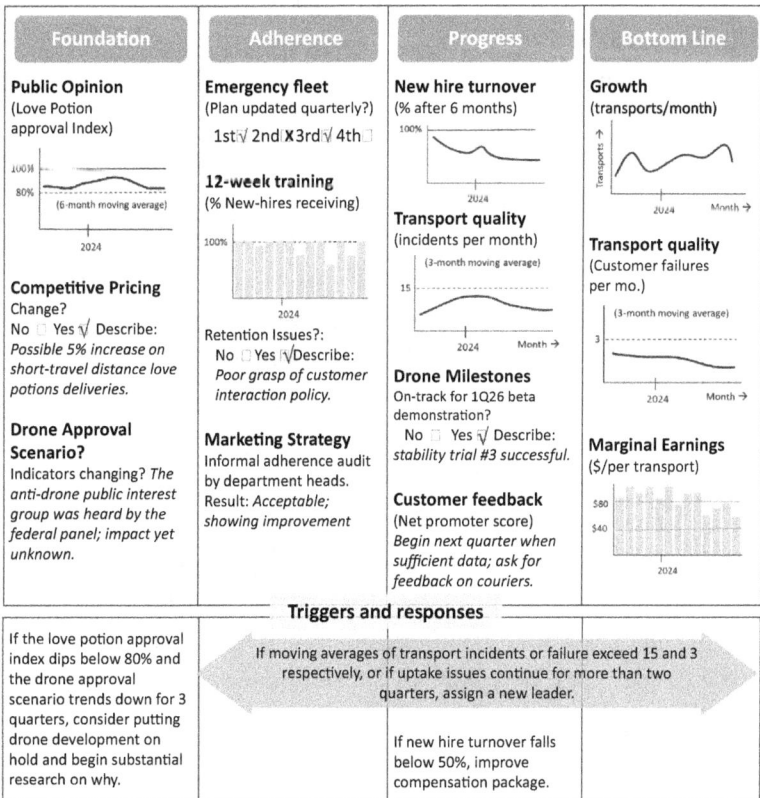

Figure 18.5 Adding triggers and responses to Courier's metrics

An argument against using triggers and responses is that it's impossible to know what future actions should be taken, so it is a waste of time to speculate. But sensitizing the organization to possibilities is valuable, and there's nothing that says the defined response needs to be followed. Another argument would be that revealing triggers and possible responses might distract or scare people (which could be good or bad). But leaders can articulate triggers and responses and not tell anyone.

Every metric doesn't need a trigger, but if a trigger isn't needed, maybe the metric is not needed—this is a good stressor for minimizing the number of metrics.

Design Guidelines for Triggers and Responses

Tuning triggers and figuring out the **expected time for change** are the keys to designing triggers. You don't want to react to noise. If you tune your triggers too sensitively, where any minor problem or deviation from target triggers an action, you will do nothing all day but react to the noise. If you do not tune them sensitively enough, it will be as though nothing can ever go wrong. To achieve a balance, you need to set a minimum threshold of deviation from target to trigger an action.

Say your organization averages a serious people-treatment or safety incident once every month or two. Each year, you will likely have several months with zero incidences and a few months with one, and occasionally a month with two or three. If you are triggered each month to praise the organization if no incidents have occurred, or to take disciplinary action in months when they do, the result will be praise one month and punishment the next. But the people's behavior and internalization of the core values are not likely changing month to month so such responses would be unrelated to people's behavior. Arbitrary praise and punishment will either paralyze an organization or teach people to ignore leadership. (Watch Deming's classic Red Beads demonstration.)[12] On a longer time scale, if bonuses are paid yearly based on financial performance, but business cycles don't line up with years, the incentives may have no relationship to what people do, and again, you reward and punish noise.

You have options for tuning sensitivity. In the example just given, a moving average, perhaps three-month trailing, would smooth out the noise in this case (ask your Six Sigma or design-of-experiment people for the appropriate design). You can still show the monthly numbers, but the moving average will tell you better whether there is a true change in behavior. Courier Inc. is triggered by the value of moving averages in several places on their dashboard in Figure 18.5. Other techniques for tuning include:

- *Telltale indicators,* sometimes nastily called *idiot lights* in automobile dashboards, flash if deviation of an operating parameter exceeds a threshold. There's little noise because there's just one piece of information. Use telltales if knowing details is unimportant, for instance for a measurement of the status quo.
- *Red-Yellow-Green traffic lights* that are similar to telltales but with a warning status.
- *Composite triggers,* where you are triggered to do something only after several events or conditions have occurred.
- *Escalating responses.* For example, if the marketing people are not adhering to the new strategy, the first action is discussion, then training, then leadership shakeup or reevaluation of the realism of the strategy.

The other key is to base your trigger reaction on the expected time for change. On the one hand, Winston Churchill said, "However beautiful the strategy, you should occasionally look at the results." And on the other hand, an adage says, "You can't keep pulling the sapling out of the ground to see if the roots are growing." These two truths need reconciliation. All change requires some minimum time as discussed in Chapter 4 (see The Shrinking the Time Problem), and the more systemic the desired change, the longer the time. Good leadership can reduce the time, but some minimum time is required. It was also discussed that in early stages of change results tend to get worse, and metrics may mislead you into believing the framework is a bad one. The flip side is true too. Not measuring intermediate outcomes can lead to the illusion that framework is a good one when in fact many of the changes and innovations it is supposed to be driving are not occurring. In general, focus on adherence at the beginning of endeavors, and as progress is made, migrate to add more measurement of results.

CHAPTER 19

Transitioning to Implementation

Once you have a "last standing" framework alternative, it is time to transition from the framework design phase into implementation. The better the framework is understood and internalized, the better the organization can execute by adhering to it and fixing it as flaws develop. In the nirvana case, this transition is no big deal because you modify your framework whenever needed (not the yearly budgets-and-goals process) and have solid practices for adopting and adhering to new and modified frameworks. The imperative is to get the framework internalized as part of the fabric of the organization at all levels, especially throughout the line organization.

Transitioning to implementation includes the following deliverables:

1. Complete your framework components:
   - Detailed plans: subgoals, budgets
   - Tactics; policy tables
   - Dashboard
2. Integrate the framework into your company's managing process, including:
   - Finalize organization change/staffing (if any)
   - Incentives (not recommended)
   - Charters, if needed
   - Connection to monthly/quarterly/yearly planning and reporting cadences
3. Decide on rollout approach, including:
   - Communication package
   - Training
   - What to publicize externally
   - Grand or modest rollout
4. Declare Good Enough to launch

You need these tasks (which are completed in Task Set 5) whether the new framework affects the whole business or a subset or function, such as manufacturing or R&D. If the new framework results in only a small modification to current practice, then the implementation package will be short and simple.

Complete Your Framework and Implementation Package

You may have created some plans, tactical policies, and metrics to simulate framework alternatives when evolving the SAM—now you complete them. Here's where detailed lists are useful. As discussed in Chapter 17, plans can include not only future actions assigned to people, but also budgets, organization structure changes, and roadmaps as needed and tactics can include policy tables. The four-station dashboard was presented in Chapter 18. Be sure plans, policies, and dashboards are completed for each nested organization as needed.

As you compile your final framework and package, aim to minimize the length of communication material and PowerPoint decks and spend more time getting people to understand and internalize what the material means. It's not what is on the paper that matters—it's what gets into people's heads and hearts. The amount you need to write is inversely proportional to how much you involved the people in the design process. Task 5e suggests needed and optional working documents and media.

Integrate the Framework Into Your Managing Process

Incorporate the dashboard and any charters unique to the framework into the company's managing process.[1] These processes will likely include monthly, quarterly, and yearly cadences for planning and reporting; integration of business and functional organizations in nested systems, personnel management, individual goal setting, and any impact on compensation; working techniques, such as Agile Scrums and Lean Six Sigma; training; and communication. Your dashboard must be central to the process. Be sure to act on triggers.

If the framework is for a smaller-scale endeavor within the company, it may need its own program management. If your company does not have a standard program management method, then you may need to create your own, including charters for individuals and groups. Methods can range from simple checklists and punch lists, Gantt-type approaches, or sophisticated software-based techniques of which there are many.

Hopefully, any major organization changes were considered as part of the framework design process; and hopefully, the people you need now for your "guiding coalition" were part of design (Chapter 11), especially those on the front lines. If not, you will need to create a coalition as best you can now.

Focus Less on Decision Rights and More on Clear Rules and Policy

Be cautious of establishing decision rights for all levels in the organization using techniques like RACI (responsible, accountable, consulted, and informed) or related approaches (PARIS, DACI, RAPID). These are meant to minimize micromanagement, speed decision making, and enable decisions to be made at the right level in the organization. However, the copious details of RACI-type methods are not easily remembered by the organization, and the methods are not very adaptable as conditions change. It is better to integrate decision rights into tactical policy, as done in Add-Co's and Electro Ltd.'s policy tables in Chapter 8. In general, focus more on a clear understanding of the framework and its policies and less on who makes decisions.

Rollout Options

If you have involved the organization in the strategy process, then 80 percent of your rollout may already be accomplished. If ongoing design modification is part of the company's habit, then rollout may more or less happen on its own. However, if you have a major change to explain to and teach the organization, then a rollout or launch of some kind is needed. Rollouts or launches are also necessary if some secrecy has been required throughout the SAM process, or if a new strategy and framework are likely to scare the organization.

No matter how much you have involved the organization, and no matter how many people have been involved with design, you still have options for officially rolling out the new framework to the broad organization. In Task Set 5, you make decisions on:

- Naming the program (be cautious of internal marketing; see *naming* technique in the introduction to the task sets {web/tasksets})
- Training approach (spread it out, avoid one-time introductions)
- What to publicize externally
- Grand or modest rollout

The first three are discussed in Task Sets but consider the following for the last.

Grand or Modest Rollout?

You can roll out your new framework in a grand way, in a modest way, or in some way in between. Grand rollouts may include large mandatory meetings with scripted presentations, audiovisual fanfare, and perhaps giveaways with a program logo. The grand rollout might be a big surprise or be preceded by precommunications or purposeful leaks that prepare the organization for the significance of what's to come. A modest "cook a frog" rollout would still involve corporatewide communication, but it would sound more "business like," with less fanfare and scripting.

A grand rollout would seem best for getting people's attention, creating excitement, and "shaking things up." But nothing is more damaging than a big rollout with a less-energetic follow-through. It is easier to be energetic at rollout than during the dog days of implementation, especially when difficulties occur or when problems elsewhere in the company are distracting. Leaders who feel that, except perhaps for monitoring the dashboard, their job is done after rollout, believing that the people "executing" is all that's left to do, may be deeply disappointed.

Consider using a modest kickoff and conserve the leadership energy for three, six, twelve, or more months out. The organization will notice the ramp up in energy and see that the new framework is for real. This may really get their attention, especially if grand rollouts have led to little real change in the past, or if the fanfare of such rollouts has exceeded the quality of the work.

Other cases for a modest kickoff may include if you believe major course corrections will be needed, perhaps because you are trying something truly new, or a case where the framework will scare and destabilize people in a way you would like to avoid. Destabilization and shaking up an organization are needed at times, but sometimes they can be counterproductive. If the framework is difficult to understand, people may be discouraged from learning it unless they have time. New ideas may invite cynicism in the wrong culture. And some people may be losing position, but you still need them on your side. If leadership has the power to lay down the law and make everyone toe the line—and fire anyone who gets off the line—then there is no issue. But if leaders still need to build power and understanding, they may need to bide their time, and a quiet rollout might help.

Last, if you are a lower-level leader rolling out a new framework, but you have limited support from higher-levels, you may want to start modestly and wait for a success to occur before any big announcements.

Related to grand or modest rollout is whether the line organization or corporate leadership should kick off the new framework. One could imagine that corporate leadership would be best. But if the line organization kicks it off, and then, perhaps even a month or two later, corporate leadership comes in with big support; it could raise the prestige of the line organization and demonstrate just how important the change is.

When Are You Ready to Launch?

You can create a simple checklist like Table 19.1 {web/templates} to audit for readiness. Make it as specific to your endeavor as you can. If you are used to modifying the framework you will have a checklist that you can start with. As you work through your final package, also ask if there is anything that can be removed—a metric, a plan, or an explanation. You want minimum essential materials and explanations.

Table 19.1 Checklist for auditing if ready to launch

Choice area	Elements	Status
Implementation team	• Use the line organization? • Special roles? • Charters?	
Plans and tactics	• Names and dates? Budgets, and roadmaps (if needed) • Policy tables (if needed)	
Dashboard	• Have metrics at all four stations? • Triggers and responses as needed? • Number of metrics minimized?	
Organization structure	• Changes needed that were not considered in the framework development?	
Communication package	• Completed communication materials including the final framework in a form that people will understand? • Short and simple as possible? • Program named?	
Managing processes	• Is framework integrated into corporate managing process? • Special program management required?	
Training	• Ongoing training instead of a one-time introduction?	
Rollout design	• Modest or grand, or in between? • Corporate leadership or line organization introduction? • Are secrecy requirements understood; internal and external?	
Nested systems	• Does an appropriate version of this table exist for each nested system?	

When you are satisfied with your checklist, declare good enough, start living it, and be ready to go back. You know that what you have ain't perfect, and that's good because there's no such thing as perfect. So long as the organization accepts that doing great things is an ongoing effort to adapt—reacting to the environment, understanding how the customers have been served, and honestly judging if what you are doing is making a difference—there's no need for perfection. Just be willing to go back at any time necessary to modify the framework to get it right. As in Figure 11.7, in Chapter 11, sometimes the changes will be minor, and sometimes major, but either way, execute by keeping your framework valid. The ability to take the pain of executing—the effort to adhere to the framework and the discipline to when change is needed, sometimes very quickly—is what makes many organizations great.

Outro

The Heroic Leader

There's an old joke that an orchestra conductor is someone who can follow 70 people at a time. The adaptive view of change and innovation might suggest this is no joke. Certainly, adaptation conflicts with the idea of leaders defining and planning the high-level future and then telling everyone top down how to do their job to achieve that future, or just telling them to achieve it. The adaptive model wouldn't look kindly on leaders who blame the people's lack of execution for bad results when they do not know the actual system cause. Or look kindly on leaders who manage by results and wait for failures before learning what's happening at low levels, and then take credit for fixing problems that never should have occurred. Adaptive systems rely on distributed knowledge and decision making, which certainly seems counter to top-down command. So maybe heroic leaders are not needed so much.

I disagree. The adaptive model shows just how important leaders are. Consider how difficult it is to stick with the discipline of execution, sticking to the strategy framework, especially with the boss or Wall Street wanting quick results, even though it's never clear what the emergent outcome of implementing the framework will be. Consider that the adaptive model brings ambiguity to the leadership role. An adaptive leader doesn't have a standard focus. Sure, there are fixed responsibilities, but adaptive leaders will focus wherever needed to enable the people to succeed. They will sense where the bottlenecks are. They will ensure the people in all nested systems have a valid strategy and framework and assist them when they struggle. They will not wait until problems arise to ask, "Do you have a plan?" Yet they will work top-down when the people need the guidance because sometimes top-down control is essential until a system stabilizes. Once stable, the leader can reduce constraints and enable people to lead themselves. In some situations, teaching may be the need. In others, it may be having the humility to allow the people, or a peer, to take charge. Still, in others, the leader's focus may be buying time for the organization to succeed by holding off Wall Street, a board, or their superiors in the organization. To do all these things is heroic. Much more heroic than simple top-down command. And especially heroic if the leaders hold themselves to the same rules and standards that they expect their people to follow, despite their position.

In some complex adaptive system writing, orchestral conductors are held up as examples of the old top-down view of leadership in contrast with self-organized systems. But it's silly to imagine that without a conductor telling the players what to do, all you would get from an orchestra is scratching noises from violins and honking from trombones in a cacophony of directionless noise. Compositions, players' skills, instruments, musical notation, and performance and conducting practice have coevolved over centuries. Pull 70 random people off the street and put instruments in their hands and you will get directionless scratches and honks. But for a good many pieces in the popular repertoire, the orchestra would do just fine without a conductor leading them in a performance. Some cues from the concertmaster violinist would suffice.

A conductor's job goes much deeper than leading a performance. They interpret composer's wishes and enable a given style of an orchestra to emerge—an artistic direction. They uphold the discipline of standards for playing, and they teach during rehearsals. They determine how much freedom to give players and must earn their respect. They determine programing. The majority of what conductors do occurs outside of the performance.

We fight the adaptive and emergent world in part because it's harder and more unsettling to work at low levels than managing by results or command and control. Certainly, just as every strategy method is meant to be adaptive in some ways, leaders naturally work in adaptive ways. Hopefully the principles and techniques of the emergent approach will be of help to further this mission.

Notes

Introduction

1. Rumelt (2011), Chapter 3.
2. Mintzberg (1994), p. 321.
3. Christensen, Raynor, and McDonald (2015).
4. For example: find at least 33 different uses in the textbook, *Strategic Management* by Wheelen and Hunger (2010); and at least 42 in Pentland, *Creating Defense Excellence: Defense Addendum to Road Map for National Security*, 2001.
5. Pinchot (1985), p. 17.
6. See *References for an Adaptive View of the World*, a collection of references from multiple fields of endeavor www.emergentapproach.com/supplement/
7. See web supplement "Planning Under Uncertainty—Is there any Other Kind?" in www.emergentapproach.com/supplement/
8. Raynor (2011), p. 171.
9. Bradley, Hirt and Smit (2018a).
10. Mintzberg (2007), p. 171.
11. Pinchot (1985), p. 16.

Part I

1. Gleason, J. H., 1952, CBS, New York

Chapter 1

1. See Porter (2006) and Porter (2009).
2. See for instance, Kaplan and Norton (2001), p. 1, where they distinguish "managing strategy" from "managing operations."
3. Jeffrey W. Meiser, "Ends + Ways + Means = (Bad) Strategy," *Parameters* 46(4) Winter 2016–17, 81–91. Available at SSRN: https://ssrn.com/abstract=3762221
4. McGinn, Treverton, Isaacson, Gompert and Bunn (2002); Chermack (2011); Dranove and Marciano (2005), call their book a framework for strategy evaluation.
5. Meyer and Coffey (2015); [Maybe he should have added, "and everybody has goals."].
6. Collis and Rukstad (2008).

Chapter 2

1. Horse figure adapted from MacFadden (2005), pp. 1728–30 with permission from AAAS; iPhone genealogy created by Sherlly Xie and Peter Compo.
2. Kocienda (2018).
3. Slywotzky (2011).
4. Taleb (2012), p. 3.
5. Womack, et al. (2007), Chapter 2.
6. See *Solutions to the paradox of freedom and discipline* {Web/Supplement}
7. Schacter (2012).
8. See for instance, Steven Johnson's writings in the references for an adaptive view {web/supplement}.
9. Grove (1997).
10. Nichol (2012).
11. OSHA. 2012. "Report 459. Typical Minimal Lockout Procedures." *International Association of Oil & Gas Producers*. Occupational Safety and Health Standards.
12. Charlie Rose interview 1989? (Taylor, born 1921, mentions that he is 68 years old) www.youtube.com/watch?v=UO4Ta2_Wv0w (accessed April 23, 2017).
13. Taleb (2012), p. 9.

Chapter 3

1. See, for instance, Oliver and Smith (1996).
2. Rumelt (1979).

Chapter 5

1. Goldratt (1990).
2. See discussion in *Continuum of Rules* from Chapter 6 supplement {web/supplement}, including the connection with Cynefin "best practices."
3. Catmull and Wallace (2014).

Chapter 6

1. For a short additional discussion on the scope-based view of rules, see *Continuum of Rules* {web/supplement}.
2. Tse-tung (1936).
3. For references and more details, see *More on Tactics Versus Strategy* {web/supplement}.
4. Handel (2001), p. 355.
5. Tse-tung (1936).

Chapter 7

1. Moltke, in Craig and Paret (1986), p.291; he also said battlefield command-ers can change an order if it gives tactical (battlefield) advantage, but he should have added, so long as it does not violate the parent framework.

Chapter 8

1. Malik, F. (2016), p. 73, Martin (2015a), also see https://rogermartin.medium.com/is-the-opposite-of-your-choice-stupid-on-its-face-5b247ffd7f94
2. Hughes (1997).
3. Pinchot (1985), p. 22.
4. www.nytimes.com/2017/05/31/books/review/john-grishams-tips-how-to-write-fiction.html
5. www.nobelprize.org/nobel_prizes/economic-sciences/laureates/2009/ostrom_lecture
6. Downloaded from www.whitehouse.gov/ on May 27, 2008; this 2005 docu-ment is the "upgraded" February 2003 Iraq strategy with "added updates and additional details".

Chapter 9

1. Deming (1990).
2. Sull, Homkes, and Sull (2015).
3. De Jong, Marston and Roth (2015), see also Chapter 1, note 1.
4. Unfortunately, I lost the name (2014–2015).
5. Dranove and Marciano (2005), p. 2.
6. www.fool.com/investing/2020/10/09/these-3-stocks-are-absurdly-overval-ued-right-now/
7. www.youtube.com/c/DemingInstitute/videos
8. Sull, Homkes, and Sull (2015).
9. Martin (2015b).
10. Hendricks (2009).
11. Gray (1999), p. 99.
12. See Peter Senge Video, *Systems Thinking and The Gap Between Aspirations and Performance* (at 46'55"). "culture is habit" and Gibbons (2015) p. 213.

Part II

1. Bradley, Hirt and Smit (2018b), p. 177.
2. Lafley and Martin (2013), Chapter 8.

Chapter 10

1. Sørensen and Carroll (2021).
2. See *Planning Under Uncertainty—Is there any Other Kind?* {web/supplement}.
3. Roxburgh (2009).
4. Kahn and Mann (1957).
5. der Heijden (2005 and 2000).
6. See the heading *scenario planning* for several scenario planning methods in *References for an Adaptive View of the World* {web/supplement}; Lindgren and Bandhold (2009) gives a short history on p. 37.
7. For instance, Lindgren and Bandhold (2009), p. 28; Davis, Bankes, and Egner (2007), p. 1; Holman et al., (2007), p. 342; Wade (2012); KL1042, says that "From a scenario planning point of view, the best strategy is the one that gives the organization the greatest degree of flexibility," but there is no such thing as a "non-scenario planning" point of view. There are *always* multiple futures that cannot be controlled.
8. Roxburgh (2009).

Chapter 11

1. Mintzberg and Ginter et al. (in Mintzberg (1994)), p. 52, show many stepwise framework design examples and label them as the *normative approach* to strategic planning.
2. See discussion in Continuum of Rules from Chapter 6 supplement {web/supplement}, including the connection to Cynefin framework domains.
3. Ken Kocienda (2018) p. 244, used the puzzle analogy in his book Creative Selection as described in Chapter 2.
4. Lafley and Martin (2013) KL 2652, p. 183.
5. Kotter (2012), Chapter 4.
6. Doshi et al., (2014). (Apparently no longer available online, document reproduced in {web/supplement})

Chapter 12

1. https://jobs.netflix.com/culture (Retrieved January 04, 2021).
2. Lagorio-Chafkin (2019).
3. wholefoodsmarket.com/mission-values/core-values(Retrieved August 23, 2021).
4. Neubauer (2020); Ulwick (2017). www.christenseninstitute.org/jobs-to-be-done

5. For instance, www.strategyzer.com/canvas/value-proposition-canvas; also, much of Blue Ocean Strategy (Mauborgne and Kim, 2015) is devoted to value proposition and business models. For a compendium of business models see Johnson (2010), p. 131.
6. See Figure 17.4 for additional techniques.
7. Collis and Rukstad (2008).
8. Rumelt (2011), p. 53.
9. Rumelt (2011), p. 54.
10. See Stretch Goals {Web/Supplement}; also see discussion against stretch goals in Blue Ocean Strategy (Kim and Mauborgne 2004), p. 160.

Chapter 13

1. Wendy Schultz and Nichola George, "Scenarios Compendium: Natural England Commissioned Report NECR031," 2011.
2. Schoemaker (2002), Chapter 1.
3. "House Bill 819," April 07, 2011 (www.nccoast.org/uploads/documents/CRO/2012-5/SLR-bill.pdf); See also North Carolina Lawmakers Pass 4 Year-Ban on Sea Level Policy Changes.html and Denying sea-level rise: How 100 centimeters divided the state of NC (https://sacguide.libguides.com/c.php?g=272318&p=1817399).

Chapter 15

1. See for instance, Kim and Mauborgne (2004, p. 164); Felin and Zenger (2018); and Bradley, Hirt, and Smitick (2018), pp. 87–88.
2. Koller et al. (2020).
3. Bradley, Hirt, and Smitick (2018c).
4. Schragenheim, Camp, and Surace (2019), Chapter 7.
5. Presentation by Annie Duke, (www.youtube.com/watch?v=Qvbm_flCZds), start at 6:10 for quote.
6. See a similar discussion in Raynor (2007), p. 51.

Chapter 16

1. See Porter (2006) and Porter (2009), also, for some history and suggestions on generic strategies and commentary on Porter see Raynor (2007), p. 51.
2. Hiltzik (1999).
3. Cutolo, Hargadon, and Kenney (2021).
4. Gandhi, Mandefield, and Stubbs (2021).
5. See his 7 *Baby Steps* in www.ramseysolutions.com

6. Olenick, M. n.d. "Why You Should Eliminate and Reduce To Find New Blue Oceans." *Blue Ocean Strategy*. (accessed August 23, 2021).

7. Hax and Majluf (1991). Chapter 15; Note that some textbooks may call these grand strategies, which is unrelated to the traditional concept of grand strategy as the highest-level military/security framework of a country.

8. Schoemaker (2002), Chapter 6.

9. www.pokernews.com/strategy/esfandari-and-the-folding-pocket-kings-preflop-puzzle-28765.htm

10. Ogilvy (2011), p. 168; Schoemaker (2002), also describes cases of successful contingency alternatives (Chapter 6).

Chapter 17

1. Some listed in Figure 17.4.

2. www.lean.org/the-lean-post/articles/how-to-go-to-the-gemba-go-see-ask-why-show-respect/; www.christenseninstitute.org/jobs-to-be-done/; www.strategyzer.com/

3. Klein (2007); see also interview with Gary Klein and Daniel Kahneman, Strategic decisions: When can you trust your gut?, McKinsey Quarterly, March 01, 2010; and https://fs.blog/2014/01/kahneman-better-decisions/

4. See staircase models tested using the five disqualifiers showing they are not strategies {web/disqualifiers}.

5. See story of Dell in *Planning Under Uncertainty—Is There Any Other Kind* {Web/Supplement}.

Chapter 18

1. fiscaldata.treasury.gov/datasets/daily-treasury-statement/operating-cash-balance

2. McNamara (1995).

3. Schoemaker (2002); See discussion of Rita Gunther McGrath and Ian MacMillan's study of Euro Disney. Kindle location 2075.

4. Reeves, Love, and Tillmanns (2012).

5. www.oliverwight-americas.com/

6. marketplace.kpiinstitute.org/the-kpi-dictionary-information-technology.html

7. Kaplan and Norton (1996), p. 1.

8. Morieux and Tollman (2014), p. 4.

9. See *Deming* in *References for an Adaptive View of the World* {web/supplement} for the many ways he expressed that 97% of what matters cannot be measured.

10. Pinchot and Pellman (1999), p. 76.
11. Wade calls them Signposts in his book, Wade, *Scenario Planning: A Field Guide to the Future.* See scenario planning heading in *References for an Adaptive View of the World* {web: supplement}.
12. www.youtube.com/c/DemingInstitute/videos

Chapter 19

1. Managing methods are widely available from consultants, including www.oliverwight-americas.com/

References

Bradley, C., M. Hirt, and S. Smit. March 23, 2018a. "How to Confront Uncertainty in Your Strategy." *McKinsey Quarterly*.

Bradley, C., M. Hirt, and S. Smit. 2018b. *Strategy Beyond the Hockey Stick: People, Probabilities, and Big Moves to Beat the Odds*. John Wiley & Sons.

Bradley, C., M. Hirt, and S. Smit. April 19, 2018c. "Eight Shifts That Will Take Your Strategy into High Gear." *McKinsey Quarterly* 2, pp. 89–89.

Catmull, E., and A. Wallace. 2014. *Creativity, Inc: Overcoming the Unseen Forces That Stand in the Way of True Inspiration*. Random House.

Chermack, T.J. 2011. *Scenario Planning in Organizations: How to Create, Use, and Assess Scenarios*. San Francisco, CA: Berrett-Koehler Publishers.

Christensen, C.M., M.E. Raynor, and R. McDonald. December 01, 2015. "What Is Disruptive Innovation?" *Harvard Business Review*.

Collis, D.J., and M.G. Rukstad. 2008. "Can You Say What Your Strategy Is?" *Harvard Business Review* 86, no. 4, pp. 82–90.

Cutolo, D., A. Hargadon, and M. Kenney. March 09, 2021. "Competing on Platforms." *MIT Sloan Management Review*. Spring 2021.

Davis, P.K., S.C. Bankes, and M. Egner. 2007. *Enhancing Strategic Planning with Massive Scenario Generation: Theory and Experiments*, Vol. 392, 1. Rand Corporation.

De Jong, M., N. Marston, and E. Roth. 2015. "The Eight Essentials of Innovation." *McKinsey Quarterly* 2, pp. 1–12.

Deming, W. *The W. Edwards Deming Institute® Podcast: Deming Speaks – Episode #3 – 1990*. http://podcast.deming.org/deming-speaks-episode-3-1990 (accessed September 03, 2018).

Doshi, V., et al. 2014. "From Compliance to Commitment." Strategy&. (Apparently no longer available online, document reproduced in {web/supplement})

Dranove, D., and S. Marciano. 2005. *Kellogg on Strategy: Concepts, Tools, and Frameworks for Practitioners*, 9. Wiley.

Felin, T., & Zenger, T. (2018). What sets breakthrough strategies apart. *MIT Sloan Management Review*, 59(2), 86–88. For a short additional discussion on the scope-based view of rules, see *Continuum of Rules* {web: supplement}.

Gandhi, R., T. Mandefield, and E. Stubbs. February 10, 2021. "Beethoven, Schubert, and Bank Technology Modernization." *BCG*.

Gibbons, P. 2015. *The Science of Successful Organizational Change: How Leaders Set Strategy, Change Behavior, and Create an Agile Culture*. FT Press.

Goldratt, E.M. 1990. "Theory of Constraints", North River, Croton-on-Hudson.

Gray, C.S. 1999. *Modern Strategy*, Vol. 1, 99. Oxford University Press Oxford.

Grove, A.S., Dr. 1997. "Navigating Strategic Inflection Points." *Business Strategy Review* 8, no. 3, pp. 11–18.

Handel, M.I. 2001. *Masters of War: Classical Military Thought*. London: Frank Cass.

Hax, A.C., and N.S. Majluf. 1991. "The Strategy Process and Concept: A Pragmatic Approach." Prentice Hall International Edition.

Hendricks, M. October 14, 2009. "An Unsung Hero." *Journal Sentinel*.

Hiltzik, M.A., and others. 1999. *Dealers of Lightning: Xerox PARC and the Dawn of the Computer Age*. HarperCollins Publishers.

Holman, P., T. Devane, and S. Cady. 2007. *The Change Handbook: Group Methods for Shaping the Future*, 342. 2nd ed. San Francisco: Berrett-Koehler Publishers.

"House Bill 819," April 07, 2011. (www.nccoast.org/uploads/documents/ CRO/2012-5/SLR-bill.pdf); See also North Carolina Lawmakers Pass 4 Year-Ban on Sea Level Policy Changes.html; and ("Denying sea-level rise: How 100 centimeters divided the state of NC" https://sacguide.libguides.com/c. php?g=272318&p=1817399).

Hughes, W.P. 1997. "Naval Maneuver Warfare." *Naval War College Review* 50, no. 3, pp. 25–49.

Iruthayasamy, L. 2021. *Understanding Business Strategy*, 178–179. Singapore: Springer.

Johnson, M. W., (2010). Seizing the white space: Business model innovation for growth and renewal. Harvard Business Press.

Kahn, H., and I. Mann. 1957. *Ten Common Pitfalls*. Santa Monica, CA: RAND Corp.

Kaplan, R.S., and D.P. Norton. 1996. *The Balanced Scorecard: Translating Strategy into Action*. Harvard Business Press.

Kaplan, R.S., and D.P. Norton. 2001. *The Strategy-Focused Organization: How Balanced Scorecard Companies Thrive in the New Business Environment*, 1. Harvard Business Press.

Kim, W. Chan and Mauborgne, Renée 2015. *Blue Ocean Strategy : How to Create Uncontested Market Space and Make the Competition Irrelevant*. Boston, Massachusetts: Harvard Business Review Press.

Klein, G. September 01, 2007. "Performing a Project Premortem." *Harvard Business Review*.

Klein, G., and D. Kahneman. March 01, 2010. "Strategic decisions: When can you Trust Your Gut?" *McKinsey Quarterly*.

Kocienda, K. 2018. *Creative Selection: Inside Apple's Design Process During the Golden Age of Steve Jobs*. Pan Macmillan.

Koller, T., et al. November 02, 2020. "Are Scenarios Limiting Your Pandemic Recovery Strategy?" *McKinsey Quarterly*.

Kotter, J.P. 2012. *Leading Change*. Harvard Business Press.

Lafley, A.G., and R.L. Martin. 2013. *Playing to Win: How Strategy Really Works*. Harvard Business Press.

Lagorio-Chafkin, C. May 28, 2019. "The Radical Self-Improvement Plan That Pushed Trek Bicycles to $1 Billion in Sales." *Inc.Com*.

Lindgren, M., and H. Bandhold. 2009. *Scenario Planning: The Link between Future and Strategy*, 37. 2nd ed. New York, NY: Palgrave Macmillan.

MacFadden, B.J. 2005. "Fossil Horses–Evidence for Evolution." *Science* 307, no. 5716, pp. 1728–1730.

Malik, F. (2016). Strategy: Navigating the complexity of the new world (Vol. 3). Campus Verlag.

Martin, R. (2015a). *The First Question to Ask of Any Strategy*, Harvard Business Review.

Martin, R. (2015b). *Stop Distinguishing Between Execution and Strategy*. Harvard Business Review.

McGinn, J.G., G.F. Treverton, J.A. Isaacson, D.C. Gompert, and M.E. Bunn . 2002. *A Framework for Strategy Development*. Santa Monica, CA: RAND Corp.

McNamara, R. 1995. *In Retrospect: The Tragedy and Lessons of Vietnam*. New York, NY: Times Books.

J Jeffrey W. Meiser, "Ends + Ways + Means = (Bad) Strategy," *Parameters* 46(4) Winter 2016–17, 81-91., Available at SSRN: HYPERLINK "https://ssrn.com/abstract=3762221" ssrn.com/abstract=3762221

Meyer, U., and W. Coffey. 2015. *Above the Line: Lessons in Leadership and Life from a Championship Season*, 19. New York, NY: Penguin.

Mintzberg, H. 1994. *The Rise and Fall of Strategic Planning: Reconceiving Roles for Planning, Plans, Planners*, 52. Free Press.

Mintzberg, H. 2007. *Tracking Strategies: Toward a General Theory*. Oxford University Press on Demand.

Moltke, in Craig, G.A., and P. Paret. 1986. "Makers of Modern Strategy." Princeton.

Morieux, Y., and P. Tollman. 2014. *Six Simple Rules: How to Manage Complexity without Getting Complicated*, 4. Harvard Business Review Press.

Neubauer, S. May 06, 2020. "7 Must-Read Books on Jobs To Be Done." *PM Library | Medium*.

Nichol, K. July 18, 2012. "Safety 101: The Safety Triangle Explained." https://crsp-safety101.blogspot.com/2012/07/the-safety-triangle-explained.html

Ogilvy, J.A. 2011. *Facing the Fold: Essays on Scenario Planning*, Triarchy Press Limited.

Oliver, R.M., and J.Q. Smith. 1996. *Influence Diagrams, Belief Nets and Decision Analysis*.

Pinchot, G. 1985. *Intrapreneuring. Why You Don't Have to Leave the Organization to Become an Entrepreneur*. New York, NY: Harper & Row.

Pinchot, G., and R. Pellman. 1999. *Intrapreneuring in Action: A Handbook for Business Innovation.* Berrett-Koehler Publishers.

Porter, M.E. 2006. "Strategy for Museums." In *American Association of Museums,* 28. Conference, Boston, Massachusetts.

Porter, M.E. October 17, 2009. "Strategic Thinking: Implications for Turkish Companies." Istanbul, Turkey. www.hbs.edu/faculty/Pages/item.aspx?num =46522

Raynor, M.E. 2007. *The Strategy Paradox: Why Committing to Success Leads to Failure (and What to Do about It).* Currency.

Raynor, M.E. 2011. *The Innovator's Manifesto: Deliberate Disruption for Transformational Growth.* Crown Pub.

Reeves, M., C. Love, and P. Tillmanns. September 2012. "Your Strategy Needs a Strategy." *Harvard Business Review.*

Roxburgh, C. November 01, 2009. "The Use and Abuse of Scenarios." *McKinsey Quarterly.*

Rumelt, R.P. 1979. "Evaluation of Strategy: Theory and Models." *Strategic Management: A New View of Business Policy and Planning,* pp. 196–212.

Rumelt, R.P. 2011. *Good Strategy/Bad Strategy.* Profile books.

Schacter, D.L. 2012. "Constructive Memory: Past and Future." *Dialogues Clin Neurosci.* 14, no. 1, pp. 7–18. doi:10.31887/DCNS.2012.14.1/dschacter

Schoemaker, P. 2002. *Profiting from Uncertainty: Strategies for Succeeding No Matter What the Future Brings.* Simon and Schuster.

Schragenheim, E., H. Camp, and R. Surace. 2019. *Throughput Economics: Making Good Management Decisions.* New York, NY: Productivity Press. https://doi.org/10.4324/9780429020124.

Schultz, W., and N. George. 2011. "Scenarios Compendium: Natural England Commissioned Report NECR031."

Slywotzky, A. August 29, 2011. "Steve Jobs and the Eureka Myth." *Harvard Business Review.*

Sørensen, J.B., and G.R. Carroll. June 03, 2021. "Why Good Arguments Make Better Strategy." *MIT Sloan Management Review.*

Sull, D., R. Homkes, and C. Sull. March 2015. "Why Strategy Execution Unravels—and What to Do about It." *Harvard Business Review.*

Taleb, N. 2012. *Antifragile: Things That Gain from Disorder.* Random House.

Tse-tung, M. 1936. Problems of Strategy in China's Revolutionary War (*December 1936*) *Selected Works of Mao Tse-Tung,* Vol. 1. Marxist.org. https://www.marxists.org/reference/archive/mao/selected-works/volume-1/mswv1_12.htm

Ulwick, T. January 05, 2017. "The History of Jobs-to-Be-Done and Outcome-Driven Innovation." *JTBD + ODI.*

Van der Heijden, K. 2000. "Scenarios, Strategy, and the Strategy Process." *Global Business Network*.

Van der Heijden, K. 2005. *Scenarios: The Art of the Strategic Conversation*, 2nd ed. John Wiley & Sons.

Wade, W. 2012. *Scenario Planning: A Field Guide to the Future*. John Wiley & Sons.

Womack, J.P., D.T. Jones, and Roos, D. 2007. *The Machine That Changed the World*. Simon & Schuster, 2007.

About the Author

After earning a doctorate in Chemical Engineering from City College New York and a background in music, **Peter Compo** spent 25 years at E.I. DuPont. Working in both commodity products and tech ventures, he held leadership positions in marketing, supply chain, product, and business management and was the corporate lead for integrated business planning. Seeing the same strategy challenges and the same adaptive patterns of innovation in all these areas of experience inspired him to create the emergent approach.

Index

Page numbers in italics refer to references in figures or tables.

OTHER TITLES IN THE SERVICE SYSTEMS AND INNOVATIONS IN BUSINESS AND SOCIETY COLLECTION

Jim Spohrer, IBM, and Haluk Demirkan, University of Washington, Tacoma, Editors

Concise and Applied Business Books

The Collection listed above is one of 30 business subject collections that Business Expert Press has grown to make BEP a premiere publisher of print and digital books. Our concise and applied books are for...

- Professionals and Practitioners
- Faculty who adopt our books for courses
- Librarians who know that BEP's Digital Libraries are a unique way to offer students ebooks to download, not restricted with any digital rights management
- Executive Training Course Leaders
- Business Seminar Organizers

Business Expert Press books are for anyone who needs to dig deeper on business ideas, goals, and solutions to everyday problems. Whether one print book, one ebook, or buying a digital library of 110 ebooks, we remain the affordable and smart way to be business smart. For more information, please visit www.businessexpertpress.com, or contact sales@businessexpertpress.com.